8A9 $ 5.00

WALTER LIPPMANN

Philosopher-Journalist

WALTER LIPPMANN

Philosopher-Journalist

Edward L. Schapsmeier

and

Frederick H. Schapsmeier

Public Affairs Press, Washington, D. C.

To Our Mother
whose self-sacrifice, self-discipline,
and love of learning serve as
monuments to her memory

Copyright 1969, by Public Affairs Press
419 New Jersey Avenue, S.E., Washington, D.C.

Printed in the United States of America
Library of Congress Catalog Card No. 70-96032

PREFACE

John Mason Brown once described Walter Lippmann as a "philosopher-journalist." Because that appellation is so appropriate, we have adopted it as the title for this book. In these pages we seek to present an overall analysis of Lippmann's contributions to both journalism and political philosophy.

In preparing this work we have benefited from the assistance of many persons who have known or worked with Mr. Lippmann, but we alone are responsible for all interpretations and conclusions. We especially thank Richard W. Van Alstyne, Huntington Library Research Fellow and Distinguished Professor of History at the University of the Pacific, and Eugene Trani of Southern Illinois University for their stimulating suggestions. Help from many archivists and librarians, particularly at the Sterling Memorial Library of Yale University, where the Walter Lippmann Collection is housed, is gratefully acknowledged. A research grant from Illinois State University facilitated a portion of our research and we are appreciative of that material aid.

EDWARD L. SCHAPSMEIER   FREDERICK H. SCHAPSMEIER
Normal, Illinois   *Oshkosh, Wisconsin*

Chapter I

STUDENT DAYS AT HARVARD

Every generation has a tendency to regard its own era as *the* pivotal period in history. Yet the same proportion of college students who seek change and commitment today probably existed at the turn of the century. When Walter Lippmann arrived at Harvard University in 1906, the academic world was seething with intellectual ferment. Rebellious thinkers like Thorstein Veblen, Louis Brandeis, William James, and John Dewey were instigating fundamental innovations in many avenues of American life. They were literally iconoclasts tearing down the traditional order of things so that they might be the architects of a new society.

New and bold ideas were challenging old ones. Institutional economics, which analyzed industrial activity statistically, replaced classical theories relying on natural laws. Sociological jurisprudence interpreted law according to society's needs instead of historical precedent. Pragmatism allowed philosophical values to be determined by human experience—not logic. Instrumentalism sought to reformulate educational standards by basing the curriculum on psychological needs of the learner rather than merely perpetuating traditional subject matter. This was the exciting milieu in which young Walter Lippmann received his higher education. It was bound to have a dramatic effect upon him.

Having come from a fairly wealthy but conventional middle class family, it was his original intention to become an art critic. His preference for some genteel profession was soon altered. Harvard's intellectual environment reoriented his interests. He had already rejected the ethnic heritage of his Jewish ancestry and refused to emulate his father by becoming a businessman. Now he was looking for a cause to give meaning and purpose to his life. This he found in campus activities aimed at furthering the movement for bold social reforms.

His entry into journalism came about because of his desire to be an activist. Campus leaders often gravitate to positions where they can influence student thought and so it was with Lippmann. He penned spirited articles for such Harvard student publications as *The Red and Blue*, the *Illustrated* (then edited by H. V. Kalten-

1

born), and the *Monthly* (of which he became editor during his junior year). His prose style was influenced by the muckrakers and the content of his writing reflected the liberals' demands for immediate reform. Championing everything from the need to alter the curriculum to women's suffrage, he sought to enthuse fellow students with his own zeal. "The spirit of advance is the inspiration at Harvard today," he wrote in one of his earliest articles. To him this venerable institution of higher learning was a "living bridge stretching into a splendid future."

Besides his studies and journalistic endeavors Lippmann helped found a local chapter of the Intercollegiate Socialist Society. His interest in socialism came about as a result of attending Graham Wallas' famous seminar "Government 31." Wallas, one of the original creators of the British Fabian Society, was an articulate and persuasive teacher. Lippmann, as the Socialist Club's first president, applied for and received an Intercollegiate Socialist Society charter from Upton Sinclair, its national president. Other members of the fledgling Harvard chapter included Heywood Broun, Arthur N. Holcombe, Nicholas Kelly, Lee Simonson, Kenneth Macgowan, and John Reed. The preamble to the club's constitution was in keeping with the atmosphere of reform so prevalent at the time. "Since," it declared, "there is widespread opinion that the present state of society is fundamentally imperfect and that a basis of reconstruction must be formed, the purpose of this club shall be the study of socialism and all other radical programs of social reform which aim to get a better economic development of society."

The "only evil we really fear," Lippmann told fellow would-be reformers, "is ignorance." He was thoroughly convinced that student opinion could be enlightened by a program of bold education. Accordingly, Harvard's Socialist Club set up a reference library, conducted informal seminars, sponsored public lectures, and petitioned the administration at Harvard for courses in socialist theory. Moreover, this action-minded group agitated for higher faculty salaries, organized a women's suffrage club at Radcliffe College, participated in a labor strike in nearby Lawrence, contributed volunteer services to settlement houses in Boston, and informed the state legislature of the need for reform measures. While such activities were hardly radical, they were considered almost revolutionary by most of the student body.

Lippmann's talents were soon utilized by the national office of the Intercollegiate Socialist Society. During the academic year 1910-1911 he was elected to its executive board. Other collegians on the board included Rene Hoguet (Harvard), Jessie Hughan (Barnard), Ellis Jones (Yale), and Mary Sanford (Vassar). The officers that year were J. G. Phelps of Yale, president; Upton Sinclair of the City College of New York, vice-president; Morris Hillquit of New York University, treasurer; and Leroy Scott of Indiana University, secretary. The membership rolls of the ISS contained the names of such liberal students as Paul Blanshard, Louis Budenz, Stuart Chase, John Dewey, Paul Douglas, Frieda Kirchwey, Broadus Mitchell, and Harry Overstreet.

"I wish I could adequately acknowledge the obligation I owe to my teachers," Lippmann wrote fifteen years after his graduation from Harvard. In addition to Wallas he singled out William James and George Santayana. All three were to have a profound and pervasive influence on his intellectual development. Wallas' blend of Fabian socialism and empiricism had an immediate impact. Although the pragmatism of James and the spiritual naturalism of Santayana were incorporated into his thinking in a less dramatic manner, they would eventually emerge as basic tenets of his evolving philosophy.

During his fourth year at Harvard (he had actually completed the requirements for graduation as a junior), Lippmann decided to pursue journalism as a career. He identified himself with the muckrakers and like them wanted to arouse the public by revealing society's ills. His frame of mind was revealed in a note in which he hailed Randolph Bourne, a recent Columbia graduate, for his "damnation of orthodoxy." To further associate himself with protest writers he wrote an adulatory letter to Lincoln Steffens for instilling "courage" and "confidence" in the younger generation. This well known muckraker, who had acquired a national reputation for his books (especially *The Shame of the Cities*), responded kindly to his youthful admirer. It was Steffens' suggestion that prompted Lippmann to take a position as a reporter with the *Boston Common*.

The trivial chores of a journalistic apprentice were boring. Instead of writing feature articles or ringing indictments against the status quo, Lippmann was encumbered with mundane chores. In desperation he complained that the "work is so mechanical . . . I am learning nothing." He pleaded: "What I have dreamed of doing is to work under you. Can you use me in your work? There is no position I should go at with more eagerness, because there is no kind of work that appeals to me as much as yours."

This direct request elicited a favorable response from Steffens, then

editor of *Everybody's Magazine*. He employed Lippmann as his secretary and was so impressed by his "keen, quiet, and industrious" traits
that he soon promoted him to assistant editor. Besides tutoring his
protege in the art of skillful writing, stressing in-depth analysis and
lucidity of expression, Steffens introduced the twenty-one year old
Harvard graduate into the exclusive circle of the "Liberal Club."

The "Dodge gatherings," so named because they were held in the
fashionable Fifth Avenue salon of Mabel Dodge, afforded Lippmann
opportunities to mingle with New York's leading intellectuals. Here
he met artists, poets, editors, labor leaders, and *avant-garde* radicals
of all types. He had the occasion to display his own virtuosity by
presenting some lectures about the new psychology of Sigmund Freud.
Ernest Jones, Freud's colleague and biographer, later was to single out
Lippmann as the first person to use Freudian concepts for the purposes of political analysis. This came about almost accidentally while
Lippmann was vacationing in Maine where he met Alfred Booth
Kuttner, a former classmate. Kuttner allowed him to read the translation of Freud's *Interpretation of Dreams* shortly before it was
published.

Lippmann did not emulate the bohemian life of the intelligentsia
but he enjoyed its stimulation. Mabel Dodge, a dilettante patroness
of the arts, characterized him aptly in her memoirs: "Walter was
thoroughly free intellectually. He was 'Harvardized,' well bred, and
in possession of himself. There was no incontinence there, a cool
understanding, and with all the high humor in the world shining in
his intelligent eyes."

In 1912 George R. Lunn, a Presbyterian clergyman ran as a Socialist and was elected mayor of Schnectady. He asked Morris Hillquit, then New York's Socialist leader, to find him an administrative
assistant. Hillquit recommended Lippmann, who accepted the post
with some misgivings because he considered himself more of a Fabian
than one suited for involvement in the details of politics. As a student
he had spent summers abroad and had attended Fabian discussions
conducted by George Bernard Shaw and the Webbs (Sidney and
Beatrice). Their gradualism and intellectualized socialism appealed
to him. He was an esthete, liked books better than bellicose agitation, and felt infinitely more comfortable with a pen than a placard.
New York was the cultural center of the nation and now he would
have to leave it for a job that did not look promising. Before depart-
ing from the surroundings he enjoyed, his appreciation for what
Lincoln Steffens had done prompted him to write: "You often asked

me whether the year has been worthwhile. Lord, if I could only tell you and make you believe it. You gave me yourself, — and then you ask me whether it has been worthwhile. For that I can't write down my thanks. I shall have to live them."

Schenectady proved to be not only a disappointing experience but a disillusioning one. Gone were the exhilarating contacts of Manhattan. Instead of scintillating conversation he found himself immersed in the mundane matters of municipal government. He could see no connections between the glamorous Socialist goal of remaking society and Mayor Lunn's routine administrative procedures. In an article addressed to the socialist community at large, the dejected reformer questioned the wisdom of his chief's entire program. The Mayor, who ultimately became Lieutenant Governor of New York as a Democrat, moved very cautiously and acted much like any conventional politician. Lippmann commented caustically that "nothing [unique] is being done . . . that twenty reform cities can't duplicate." He seemed to think Lunn's entire approach was fallacious. "Schenectady Socialism is a sharp object lesson in what always results when we turn from education to politics," he wrote in the *New York Call,* "when we seek to win votes rather than to make converts, when we look for immediate concrete return in political victory rather than the more distant intangible return in greater understanding."

Hillquit, from his vantage point in New York, was shocked at Lippmann's confusing attitude. Schnectady was a showcase as far as he was concerned; it proved that Socialists were not wild-eyed radicals but responsible public servants. Success there would "force other cities into the path of social progress," Hillquit argued. Lippmann disagreed. In a lengthy letter to Carl D. Thompson, the Socialist party's secretary, he again set forth his objections. Using the logic of a Fabian, he denounced the strategy of "playing the old game of the old political parties." This led only to "empty victories." Socialists, in his opinion, should refrain from dissipating their energies on the "external clap-trap" of crass politics and crude campaigns. Long-range reforms could best be effected by the establishment of a "standing committee of experts" as part of the Socialist "machinery" for educating the public. "Elections are the last goal of political action, and not the first," he protested, "they should come only when the social forces are organized and ready."

In effect Lippmann was urging the cessation of all direct political activity by the Socialist party. Its officials could hardly believe he was serious; they tried to convince him that winning elections and assuming power on the local level was a practical way of implementing reform.

Being temperamentally unsuited for precinct politics, Lippmann left Schenectady and soon quit the Socialist party altogether. He submitted his resignation on November 3, 1914, pointing out that he had voted "a split ticket in violation of the rules of the party." In a private communication to Upton Sinclair, he was more explicit: "I know that agitation is not my job . . . Each of us can do only a little, and he ought to try to do what he can do best."

Before Lippmann severed all connections with the Socialist party, he served briefly on the editorial board of *The New Review*. His associates in this venture were Max Eastman, W. E. B. DuBois, Floyd Dell, and Robert H. Lowie. Contributors ranged from moderate Socialists to extreme left-wingers. According to Theodore Draper, an historian who has traced the course of American Communism, Louis C. Fraina ultimately made this journal a "vehicle for his development from a disciple of DeLeon to a disciple of Lenin."

This type of political activism was far too strong for Lippmann. His college-inspired infatuation with Socialism waned perceptibly after he left Harvard's environs. Ideas intrigued him but not political details. The doctrinaire quality of Socialism bothered him considerably. His questioning mind would not submit to ideological limitations or party discipline. He wanted to be a persuader—not a propagandist. In retrospect, his brief association with Socialism was but a passing episode in his intellectual development. His idealism and youthful desire to share in the remaking of society found more gratifying outlets in writing. It was in this realm that he would make his first notable contribution to American reform.

Chapter II

THEMES FOR A POLITICAL PHILOSOPHY

While on the staff of *Everybody's Magazine* and as a free lance writer during his unhappy interlude in Schnectady, Lippmann struggled to construct a meaningful political philosophy for himself. His earliest articles displayed little of the quality that later became characteristic of his commentaries on public affairs.

With some insight into the problems that were plaguing the nation, but possessing no workable solutions, he strove to make himself knowledgeable in many fields. He studied the theories of Freud, read the works of Henri Bergson, delved into the writings of Friedrich Nietzsche, and examined the ideas of Georges Sorel. His quest for knowledge was insatiable and made him receptive to the new and the bold. James Mackay's *Americanized Socialism: A Yankee View of Capitalism* caught his eye, as did the speeches and articles of Theodore Roosevelt. In eclectic fashion he absorbed a wide range of ideas and then set about to integrate them into a systematic philosophy for political action.

At this stage the pluralism and pragmatism of William James seemed attractive. In *Everybody's Magazine* (1912), young Lippmann saluted the Harvard philosopher for giving "all men and all creeds, any idea, any theory, any superstition, a respectful hearing . . ." Ideas had power if only men could harnass them for their own ends. His own optimism for the future burst to the surface with brash words: "The world was never so young as it is today, so impatient of old and crusty things. Men feel that they can make their own fate instead of letting fate make them . . ." What was still needed was some unifying theme or rationale for reform.

Weaving together many divergent concepts in an effort to synthesize current thought, Lippmann produced *A Preface to Politics* in 1914. He modestly claimed that this book was but a "preliminary sketch for a theory of politics." This disclaimer belied its intent. It was written to supply a "philosophic basis," as one reviewer noted, for Progressivism. The keynote of his work was set forth with these words: "We need a new sense of political values . . . We cannot expect to meet our problems with a few inherited ideas, uncritical assumptions, a foggy vocabulary, and a machine philosophy. Our political thinking needs the infusion of contemporary insights."

A Preface to Politics was a handbook for intellectuals—not party workers. The latter would not have understood it. It reflected erudition but little experience in political matters. Lippmann wove together such varied concepts as Bergson's creative evolution, Sorel's creative myth, Nietzche's will to power, and tenets of Freudian psychology to establish the proposition that man could determine his own destiny. Instinct, intuition, and innate impulses were the drives that would propel mankind to new heights of attainment. Dynamic leaders, unfettered by tradition, could channel the vitalistic impulses of the masses into constructive avenues of reform. Old routines, inhibitions, and mechanical attitudes had to be jettisoned; time-encrusted taboos and archaic systems of authority had to be destroyed. While such rebellious ideas aroused the enthusiasm of the younger generation, they ran counter to those of the old.

The estabilshed social order of the nineteenth century was sustained by the inherited Protestant ethic with its emphasis on work and thrift and general acceptance of a laissez faire type capitalism which prevented governmental regulation of business. An English sociologist, Herbert Spencer, reinforced the apparent veracity of these precepts by linking them to the theory of evolution. Thus the struggle for survival in nature was transferred to society and given scientific validity. Yale's William Graham Sumner codified this set of beliefs into a system called Social Darwinism, but Lippmann rejected the rigid determinism inherent in such a philosophy because it made reform virtually impossible. He preferred the flexibility of relativism. "Nietzsche and James were the best watchers over the citadel of truth," he maintained, since "there is nothing disastrous in the temporary nature of our ideas." The old modes of thought with their false claims of infallibility were mental prisons. Originality and social invention were stymied by insuperable barriers to reform. His prescription for progress was simple: "The dynamics for a splendid human civilization are all about us. They need to be used. For that, there must be a culture practiced in seeking the inwardness of impulses, competent to ward off the idols of its own thought, hospitable to novelty, and sufficiently inventive to harness power."

Once men were liberated they could be masters of their world. But how was this to take place? A massive revision of the political system was needed. The task of "statecraft," Lippmann insisted, was to instigate the "invention of forms and institutions which satisfy the inner needs of mankind." Creativity, especially among leaders,

was the vital ingredient for success. "It is this power of being aggressively active toward the world," he stressed, "which gives man
a miraculous assurance that the world is something he can make."

Who on the contemporary political scene qualified as a creative
leader? It was certainly not Williams Jennings Bryan or William
Howard Taft. The Great Commoner was "too simple" and Taft's
placid progressivism typified the unimaginative approach of the
"routineers." Nor did "tinkering reformers" qualify as potential
leaders. His highest praise was bestowed upon former President
Theodore Roosevelt; he admired T. R. for his "new social vision" and
acclaimed him the "most complete" statesman of the era.

Judging Woodrow Wilson by his speeches in the 1912 presidential
campaign, Lippmann considered him "less complete than Roosevelt."
Wilson occupied the White House but a short time when it became
evident that he intended to utilize fully the powers of his office. His
strong executive leadership was responsible for obtaining passage of
the Underwood Tariff, which lowered import duties significantly, and
establishment of the Federal Reserve System as an instrument to
strengthen the nation's monetary system. Because these legislative
achievements furthered the Progressive cause of reform, Lippmann
altered his estimate of Wilson. He told the readers of the *New
Republic* that President Wilson was "worthy of our deepest interest."

Many adherents of today's New Left are likely to find *A Preface
to Politics* quite contemporary in outlook. Their favorite themes are
all elaborated upon—freedom from inhibitions, destruction of old
institutions, and reliance on the inherent goodness of human nature
for the attainment of happiness. Challenged were moral codes, rules
laid down by the Establishment, and authoritarian roadblocks to
personal fulfillment and universal bliss. But what if, perchance, man
was not innately good? That important question, which never seemed
to arise in the minds of most liberals, did occur to Lippmann. To raze
the old order assured a pile of rubble but in no way insured intelligent rebuilding. Perhaps there were irrational drives within the breast
of man that, once unleashed, might well lead to anarchy instead of
progress. Relativism or the lack of established norms might be a
danger to that new society reformers were intent upon creating. If
no absolutes existed would not man flounder amid temporary truths?
Was it wise to advocate nihilism as the first step toward reform?
These were questions that needed answering.

A year later, after serious reflection, Lippmann wrote *Drift and*

Mastery. This book reaffirmed the assumption that reality consisted of a "world full of variety and spontaneous creation," but it also acknowledged the existence of a "disorderly" universe. The tone of this work was more cautious in outlook. "In liberal thought there is chaos," he conceded, "it lacks the foundation of certainty." Attacking the libertarians for their excesses, he wrote: "We have lost authority. We are 'emancipated' from an ordered world. We drift." His *caveat* was clear: "We inherit a rebel tradition. . . . Our times, of course, believe in change. The adjective progressive, is what we like, and the word new, be it the New Nationalism of Roosevelt, the New Freedom of Wilson, or the Socialism of the syndicalists . . . The battle for us, in short, does not lie against encrusted prejudice, but against the chaos of new freedom."

Elaborating upon this theme, Lippmann emphasized that the reformer must "substitute purpose for tradition." Leaders had to formulate "conscious intention for unconscious striving." It was "scientific discipline" that could replace the older bonds of authority. Such orderliness would channel "mere emotions of futurity" into salutary activity without the danger of either stifling initiative or settling for random innovation. "The scientific spirit is the discipline of democracy, the escape from drift, the outlook of a free man," Lippmann contended. "Its direction is to distinguish fact from fancy; its 'enthusiasm is for the possible,' its promise is the shaping of fact to a chastened and honest dream." Under these circumstances the reformer had to become a social scientist in order to remold society and his technique would be the use of rational planning to give order and meaning to life.

Utilizing the analysis presented by Graham Wallas in *The Great Society: A Psychological Analysis* (this 1916 publication was dedicated to him), Lippmann came to the conclusion that the most significant aspect of modern society was the factor of scale. Since science and technology had given birth to the industrial revolution, the trend of economic growth moved from the simple to the complex. Small companies had given way to giant corporations; competition had yielded to monopoly; and the new social practice was inimical to individualism, since it was corporate and collective. This new dimension of industrialism had provoked two responses, both of which he rejected. They involved either state ownership or an indiscriminate policy of trust-busting. "As bad as big business is today," he countered, "it has a wide promise within it, and the real task of our generation is to realize it." Modern capitalism could be reformed by the "infusion of scientific method, the careful application of administrative technique, the organization and education of the customer for control, the discipline of labor for an increasing share of management."

With much less precocity than before, Lippmann conceded, "Our vision is murky, fragmentary, and distorted." For this reason he advised reform minded liberals to adequately inform themselves. Problems needed systematic analysis. He called for a comprehensive "survey of national resources" to be followed by a "national plan for their development." Research was equal in importance to the very desire for change. Expertise was needed to resolve the complex matters stemming from the transition from a rural-agrarian society to one dominated by an industrial-urban mode of life.

Lippmann's admiration of Theodore Roosevelt was based on the skill displayed by the former President in meeting this issue. It was T.R. who appointed a Country Life Commission to examine the needs of the rural sector, who stopped the ruthless exploitation of the nation's national resources by implementing a broad program of conservation, and who initiated the investigation of big business by the newly established Bureau of Corporations. In addition, legislation like the Pure Food and Drug Act dealt concretely with problems resulting from lack of government regulation. In Lippmann's view this was reform at its best.

Drift and Mastery signified a shift from extreme radicalism toward orthodox Progressivism. Lippmann liked the New Nationalism of Theodore Roosevelt, but Woodrow Wilson had just won the presidency. The division of Progressive ranks into Rooseveltian and Wilsonian camps caused him concern lest it weaken the impetus for reform. He and other liberals had to decide which party, the Democarts or Republicans, would be the best vehicle for change. The choice came after much soul searching.

CHAPTER III

THE NEW REPUBLIC AND NEW HORIZONS

In 1914 Willard Straight, a wealthy financier, took the initiative in starting a liberal journal to be called the *New Republic*. This public spirited businessman and his wife Dorothy, a vivacious woman active in the Consumer's League, chose Herbert Croly as its editor. Croly's book, *The Promise of American Life* (1909), made quite an impression on Theodore Roosevelt and other Bull Moosers who supported his third party venture. The Straights admired T.R. both for his domestic and foreign policy views, and they very much wanted to propagate his New Nationalism type of Progressivism. To them this meant the positive use of government to implement reform without needless destruction of the nation's industrial complex. They met with Croly and decided on a weekly publication "which, without speaking to a large audience, would seek to liberalize and leaven American political and social opinion." The Straights intended to promote T.R.'s future candidacy, as Willard confided to the ex-President: "The country needs more than anything else Construction — Nationalism — Americanism — hopeful, effective, and above all sane. You can sound the note and enunciate the broad policy that is required and I believe the people would respond."

Croly was given great latitude in determining editorial policy. He would select the staff of the *New Republic* and determine its policies. The Straights reserved only one vote for themselves with no power of veto. Croly as editor-in-chief asked Walter Lippmann and Walter E. Weyl to join the editorial board. Lippmann's reputation had been established by the two works, *A Preface to Politics* and *Drift and Mastery*, and Weyl for his book, *The New Democracy*. Francis Hackett, Philip Littel, and Charlotte Rudyand were engaged as staff specialists. Later, after the publication gained prominence such outstanding writers as Alvin Johnson and George Soule were brought in. The magazine addressed itself to liberal intellectuals, not the mass public. The format and content represented a singularly high quality in journalism. Johnson described the venture in his memoirs as an endeavor that "came into existence when liberalism, often called progressivism, was emerging in scattered nuclei through America . . . the *New Republic* was set up to draw these nuclei together into a co-ordinated liberal movement . . . In its early years the *New Republic* operated like a Committee of Correspondence at the time of the American Revolution."

The newly established journal made no effort to broaden its appeal to make contact with the public at large. Its offices served as a meeting place primarily for intellectual leaders of the academic and literary world. Seldom did it entertain labor leaders, heads of farm organizations, or local politicians.

Present at some of the private gatherings over the years, including frequent visitors from England, were such famous names as Gifford Pinchot, Albert J. Beveridge, Thomas L. Lamont, Louis D. Brandeis, Benjamin Cardozo, Learned Hand, Felix Frankfurter, Newton D. Baker, Dean Acheson, Adolf Berle, Dorothy Thompson, Edna Ferber, Sinclair Lewis, Gilbert Murray, Lord Robert Cecil, Sidney and Beatrice Webb, John Maynard Keynes, H. N. Brailsford, Norman Angell, H. G. Wells, and Harold Laski.

The original purpose of the *New Republic*, Lippmann later reaffirmed, was to "explore and develop and apply the ideas which had been advertised by Theodore Roosevelt when he was leader of the Progressive Party." It was T.R. whom he credited with "turning the American mind in the direction it had to go in the Twentieth Century." He took advantage of the ex-President's invitations to join him at Sagamore Hill for discussions. T.R. regarded his youthful guest as a gifted thinker and writer of great potential. In a letter to a foreign diplomat he described Lippmann as a "personal friend of mine . . . [who] is, I think, on the whole the most brilliant man of his age in all the United States. He is a great writer and . . . has a real international sense."

The former Bull Moose leader, as a member of the editorial board of *The Outlook*, often utilized that magazine as a forum for his own views. On one occasion, he wrote a dual review of Lippmann's *Drift and Mastery* and Croly's *Progressive Democracy* in which he lavishly praised the two men. "Both of them — and Mr. Lippmann especially — are believers in a great increase in the application of the principles of collective action," wrote Roosevelt. "Nowhere," he added, "is Mr. Lippmann's clear sight and courage better shown than in his treatment of the trusts." He then singled out *Drift and Mastery* for this special comment: "The dominant note of Mr. Lippmann's book is the insistence that in the present unrest there is altogether too much aimless drift, aimless beating of the waves to and fro, and what is needed is a mastery of the movement; which can come in a democracy only if the people, or at least the leaders of the people, have the courage to face the facts and the wisdom and vision to think rationally about them . . ."

Unanimity of opinion did not always exist on the editorial board of the *New Republic*. While Lippmann was being increasingly influenced by Roosevelt, Croly appeared to be veering toward Wilson. This cleavage was particularly apparent when the war in Europe broke out. Willard Straight was disturbed both by Croly's editorial shortcomings and his pro-Wilson attitude. The financial backer of the magazine complained to his wife about the editor's "talky-talky" prose which lacked the "kick" so evident in Lippmann's writing. He also thought Croly was becoming too idealistic and impractical. Harsh criticisms of business were being made as if capitalism were evil *per se*. Straight's displeasure grew to the extent that he wrote Croly: "Capital must have a certain return . . . As you know I am entirely at one with you in hoping that the *New Republic* can do something to better labour as well as other human conditions, but to do really constructive work, to really build and have something of the satisfaction of accomplishment as well as the job of utterances, we've got to keep our heads clear as well as having our hearts warm. Is it not so?"

The advent of World War I caught Lippmann by surprise. He had been in Europe during the summer of 1914, but saw nothing serious enough to warrant fear of future hostilities. Like many liberals, he presumed man had evolved beyond the stage where massive bloodlettings were necessary to settle disputes between nations. In his discussions with Roosevelt at Oyster Bay, he sought new insights into the realm of international diplomacy. T.R. enlightened him and also guided his reading by introducing him to the works of such international realists as Admiral T. Mahan. While Croly was supporting Wilson's policy of neutrality, Lippmann thought a wiser course was one of preparedness, aid to Great Britain, and, if need be, U.S. intervention to guarantee Allied victory. The *New Republic* staunchly defended the position of strict neutrality.

The Stakes of Diplomacy (1915) was Lippmann's third book, but the first one to deal with international relations. The work was unusual in many ways. It read like a Rooseveltian primer in realistic diplomacy. A brilliant piece of analysis in an area where the author had just educated himself, it advocated a practical balance of power method for maintaining peace. After it appeared he joined the Wilson

administration and proceeded to promote war aims quite contrary
to what he had just stated.

Like Lippmann's previous book, *The State of Diplomacy* constituted
a further movement away from the utopian liberalism of his post-col-
lege days. Although he was to fall prey to the errors against which
he warned, he challenged some of the popular liberal assumptions
regarding the relationships between nations. The twin canons of foreign policy, he asserted, were securement of national "vital interests"
and readiness to engage into meaningful negotiations to attain these
ends. It was liberal dogma to presume the "people" did not want
war and if they were not constantly led into conflicts by their leaders
the world would be at peace perpetually. This myth was countered
by his explanation that issues of "national prestige" often inflamed
the populace of a nation to such an extent its leaders were bound to
take inflexible positions. National honor often took precedence over
national self interest. Because of the emotional character of nationalism, which evoked a patriotic response within populations of nation
states, he counseled against allowing the public at large to determine
matters of diplomacy. Heads of governments could compromise, adjust their positions, and even retreat rather than resort to war if
they could but avoid the pressure of mass hysteria.

Another *bête noire* of Progressives, since it allegedly violated the
standards of international morality, was the balance of power system.
It was assumed that self-determination and equality among nations
were noble ideals, but that colonies, spheres of influence, and power
blocs were evil. Lippmann assessed the world community realistically
and not as a wishful thinker might view it. Powerful nations did
carve out "orbits." It was an international fact of life that major
powers controlled certain geographic areas. They exploited so-called
underdeveloped countries, because, he averred, "commercial development of the world will not wait until each territory has created for
itself a stable and fairly modern political system." Big powers also
performed a service. They maintained stability in their respective
spheres. Thus the real question was not whether large nations should
dominate smaller countries, they already did that, but "who should
intervene in backward states, what the intervention should mean,
how the protectorates shall be conducted — this is the bone and sinew
of modern diplomacy."

Disequilibrium and power vacuums were as much a cause of war
as national rivalries. The "weak spots of the world are the areas of
friction," he reasoned; that was why "diplomacy has appealed to

arms because no satisfactory international solution has been found for the Balkans, Turkish, African, and Chinese problems." The "anarchy of Europe," insisted Lippmann, was due to "the anarchy of the Balkans, Africa, and Asia." Some practical peace-keeping machinery was needed to prevent confrontations of big nations over problems arising from regional instability. An institutional device was needed to make negotiations automatic in case of a collision between major powers. Many liberals dreamed of the day when world government would end forever the system of nation states. International strife and discord would then cease, went the argument in favor of such a course. Lippmann regarded this goal nothing but a "valiant dream," since it was impossible of attainment. Without the prior existence of "world patriotism," no supergovernment was possible. Nations would not surrender their sovereignty nor would inhabitants yield up their mystical identity with ethnic groups residing within recognizable territorial areas.

"Internationalism will not rise much higher than its source" and in a more realistic vein he proposed setting up "permanent international commissions to deal with those spots of the earth where world crises originate." Lippmann thought of the means whereby T.R. had taken the initiative to call for an international conference at Algeciras (Spain) in 1906. Here the explosive colonial question regarding the control of Morroco was settled through negotiations, thus avoiding a military confrontation between Germany and France (with England backing the French). This settlement came about because an American president initiated diplomatic steps for such a meeting. Why not establish permanent international machinery for that specific purpose? The Balkans mixup might have been resolved in August of 1914 had an institutional device existed to get the various parties in the dispute around a conference table. "What makes it especially plausible is that it grasp [ed] the real problems of diplomacy, that it provide [d] not a panacea but a method and the beginning of a technique." This was Lippmann's alternative to world government, since it was "internationalism, not spread thin as a Parliament of Man, but sharply limited to those areas of friction where internationalism is most obviously needed."

What bothered Lippmann at the time was the failure of President Wilson to serve as a mediator in the European war. Theodore Roosevelt set an excellent precedent when he brought about the end of the Russo-Japanese War by inviting the participants to Portsmouth, New Hampshire for a peace conference in 1905. Negotiations were successful and a treaty of peace was signed. Wilson, in contrast, avoided any involvement with the warring nations of Europe. His interest had been diverted to Mexico where he was determined to bring down the government of the revolutionary leader, Victoriano Huerta. No sooner had he extricated himself from that affair when he ordered General John J. Pershing to hunt down the insurgent Francisco "Pancho" Villa. The presence of U.S. troops on Mexican soil in 1916 almost triggered off a war.

T.R., through his mediation role, tried to preserve the balance of power both in Europe and Asia. Wilson's interventionist policy was aimed at teaching the Latins democracy by force. Roosevelt's actions contributed to world peace whereas Wilson's moral imperialism did not even serve the vital interests of the United States.

After 1914 leadership of the Progressive movement began to move from T.R. to Wilson because of the latter's domestic policies. The New Freedom program of the Democratic administration initiated a concerted action to break up monopolies with the passage of the Clayton Anti-trust Act. Significantly it utilized the regulatory features of T.R.'s New Nationalism. The Federal Trade Commission was set up to police the business community. The reform agenda was carried forward to an even greater degree by 1916 when Wilson threw his support behind measures designed to provide financial aid to farmers, improvement of employment conditions for maritime workers, discouragement of child labor, construction of roads, etc.

Revealing its partiality in explicit language, the *New Republic* took editorial note of Wilson's "increasing initiative in legislative policy" aimed at achieving reforms. When Roosevelt reacted strongly, leveling sharp criticism at Wilson for allegedly watering down of New Nationalist measures, the magazine editorialized that these unfair charges were an "example of the kind of fighting which has turned so many of his natural admirers into bitter enemies." As leader of the loyal opposition, T.R. felt it was his duty to attack the administration. Even Lippmann, whose respect for the former President was great, now characterized Roosevelt's bombast as "brutally unfair."

During 1916 Wilson granted Lippmann several interviews. The Chief Executive, who had been president of Princeton University before entering politics, made an extremely favorable impression upon the young editorial writer. The persuasive rhetoric of the President aroused within him intense idealistic aspirations. Whereas he had previously entertained doubts about Wilson's Progressivism, these were now completely dissipated. Actually this feeling was not altogether warranted. The Democratic President had fallen far short of what Lippmann expected in the way of legislative reforms. In a series of articles for the *New Republic,* he had called for bold action to overcome the "evil of localism" by intensifying the "nationalization of America." By implication it meant decisive intervention by the federal government so as to "integrate America." That inferred central direction of the economy, regulation of trusts, and a well thought out procedure for implementing social justice for the masses. The only way to avoid the "thoughtlessness and drift of . . . national life," in his judgment, was to recognize the superior "interests of the national government." Only then, he claimed, would the people's representatives be able to "nationalize education" and instigate a "comprehensive, nation-wide system of health, accident, maternity, old age, and unemployment insurance." Despite the shift of the New Freedom away from its Jeffersonian insistence on individualism and small business, Wilson still regarded welfare measures as being tantamount to socialism.

The proof that centralization and voluntary collectivism were superior to laissez faire and decentralization came to the forefront as war mobilization took place. Industrial production rose dramatically in Europe after governments supervised production. The exigencies of war made it necessary for all types of economic controls. Efficiency increased and effective distribution was assured. The so-called immutable laws of classical economics were more than ever recognizable as transparent myths invented to serve special interests. "If this welter of [pre-war] inefficiency . . . [was] the product of natural law," Lippmann was quick to point out, "every civilized person will cry out for the interference of human law." He did not think the urgency of war should be the only reason for government guidance of the nation's productive capacity.

The Progressive philosophy Lippmann was espousing considered it proper for the federal government to intervene in the economy. The foundation of this belief was the concept of positive government initially enunciated by Alexander Hamilton. As the nation's first Secretary of the Treasury, Hamilton had borrowed freely from British mercantilistic policies to formulate a series of proposals whereby the government took the initiative to undertake an ambitious economic program to promote the general welfare. This concept was further Americanized by Henry Clay in the pre-Civil War era. His "American System," a well-rounded plan for internal improvements, was in turn modified by Abraham Lincoln. Land grants for railroad construction and federal aid to education were a part of that program. The Progressives of the early twentieth century were the political heirs of Hamilton, Clay, and Lincoln — not of Thomas Jefferson or Andrew Jackson, who emphasized individualism, laissez faire, and small government.

In Lippmann's views it was this tradition, codified by Theodore Roosevelt in the New Nationalism and adopted by Wilson as part of the New Freedom, that provided the means to modify the institutional structure of the nation. It could be accomplished within the framework of the existing political structure and without causing economic chaos. This prompted him to be less tolerant of "dilettante rebels" who talked foolishly about demolishing the old order. They had neither a political program nor plans for reconstruction. Utopianism was not the same as Progressivism. Caustically he claimed that radicals were too prone to "mistake a discussion in a cafe for an artistic movement, or a committee meeting for a social revolution." His castigation of those still to the left of the mainstream of Progressive reform was worded strongly because he believed them blind to realities. Counseling moderation, he penned the following axiom: "They see the world most effectively who see reality luminous in a cold light dissolving into a warm aura of possibilities."

A corollary to the Hamiltonian concept of positive government was the necessity for strong presidential leadership. Without any doubt it was clear to Lippmann that the "executive impulse" of which Hamilton spoke was a necessary ingredient of the democratic process. It had been exercised brilliantly by Theodore Roosevelt for the good of the public weal. Woodrow Wilson also demonstrated the efficacy of strong leadership. The social service state would come to fruition through the efforts of talented leaders.

Because the Wilson administration seemed to be moving in the right direction, the *New Republic* felt reassured: "The Democracy has both a leader and a policy, while the Republicans have neither a leader nor a policy." Another article in 1915 conceded that "during Mr. Roosevelt's second administration the Republican party was bursting with new ideas," but pointed out that the Democrats had taken over some of these ideas, modified them "with an infusion of traditional Democracy," and served them to the public as old ideas. Who should the journal support for president in the election of 1916? It decided to go with Wilson.

Theodore Roosevelt was not one to take political defection lightly.

Word got back to the editorial staff, as Alvin Johnson remembered, that T.R. told friends he "cared no more for the *New Republic* which was run by three anemic Christians and three circumcised Jews." This type of ranting did not enamor the editors to T.R. Lippmann defended his position to Willard Straight by upholding his right to editorial freedom and by reminding his friend, "I started with an immense prejudice in his favor." Any articles discussing either Roosevelt or Wilson, written by him, he insisted, had been both candid and fair. He tried to explain that by backing Wilson they had not meant to detract from Roosevelt's past record. It was simply a matter of a party with a program and a President who had displayed energy as a leader.

T.R. complained directly to Straight about the political stance of the *New Republic*. Straight too had become a bit irked by Roosevelt's rancorous criticism of the Wilson administration. While he admired the former President immensely, he felt the success of the Progressive movement had to have priority over personal loyalty. With mixed emotions he informed Roosevelt: "Neither Dorothy nor myself is responsible for the utterances of the *New Republic*. The editorial conduct of the paper has been entirely in the hands of the editors. I have not approved of all that has been said . . . , but I am, nevertheless, in hearty agreement with most of the editorial policies. I am sorry we disagree. I feel sure, however, that you will respect my motives, even though you disapprove of my views."

The President regarded the support of the *New Republic* as the key to the Progressive vote in 1916. Wilson kept abreast of liberal thought by reading the journal regularly. His policies were undoubtedly influenced by its editorial position. Colonel Edward M. House, Wilson's closest adviser, was also cognizant of the value of its endorsement. He made personal contact with Croly and Lippmann in order to court them and cultivate their friendship and he went to considerable pains to keep them informed on administration policy.

On domestic issues, Lippmann was quite satisfied with Wilson's performance, but he harbored serious doubts about the President's handling of foreign affairs. In 1915 he wrote a strong editorial prodding the President to alter his neutrality policy. After the *Sussex* crisis in March, 1916, which seemed to indicate Wilson was weakening on his stand against unrestricted submarine warfare by Germany, Lippmann advised outright a course leading to Anglo-American control of the seas. That was the only means to insure the survival of Great Britain. His plea for intervention concluded with the argument: "The supreme question of foreign policy is our relation to the British Empire; the supreme danger lies in ignoring it or challenging it; and the greatest hope, I believe, for western civilization lies in agreement with it."

Despite the President's call for all Americans to be neutral in word and deed, he was not adhering to this policy himself. The fact of the matter was that neither Wilson nor the majority of the American people was ever actually neutral in the true sense of the word. The President had never really placed British violations of international law or its arbirtrary restrictions on free use of the seas in the same category as German submarine warfare. It was truly ironical that when William Jennings Bryan, the Secretary of State, tried to steer a course consistent with the President's declared intentions, he was forced to resign from the cabinet in protest over the seemingly pro-British behavior of the President. Wilson's actions were motivated by antithetic aims — namely, to stop submarine warfare and to keep the United States out of war. His hatred for the practice of sinking ships without warning was matched in intensity by his aversion to war itself. But by holding Germany accountable, he was allowing himself to be drawn into a position where intervention was inevitable without clearly discerning the danger involved. Lippmann, and other balance of power realists, were applauding Wilson's gradual movement toward open intervention against Germany without fully understanding the President's basic attitude. They would have been surprised if they had known how little the President considered national self interest and how much he valued moral righteousness in international conduct.

The same struggle that went on in Wilson's heart and soul caused a crisis of conscience for Croly. His idealism made him regard war as a monstrous evil, but his moral instincts were offended by the alleged barbarism of submarine warfare. This dichotomy of feeling manifested itself in Croly's editorials. On one occasion they would herald the President as a peacemaker; then on another, they would chastise him for not taking a firmer stand against Germany. At no time did the *New Republic* editor consider such facets of the problem as preserving the balance of power in Europe or preventing German domination of the Atlantic Ocean. Croly's support of the war effort came only after Wilson made participation acceptable on moral grounds.

The nominating conventions of the two parties prepared to meet in 1916 for the purpose of selecting their respective presidential candidates. Wilson's renomination was certain, but the choice of the Republicans was not so predictable. Theodore Roosevelt very much wanted to be the standard bearer for the G.O.P. His chances were slim. The scars left by his third party venture in 1912 had not yet healed. A more likely prospect was the Governor of New York, Charles Evans Hughes. Having acquired a fine record of reform in the Empire State, he presented himself as a candidate who could appeal to Progressives. Little was known of his foreign policy views except that he was for preparedness, but that was an asset. In all ways Hughes fulfilled the qualifications for his party's nomination. He possessed the attributes of a winner.

The Democrats nominated Wilson and came up with a potent slogan, "He kept us out of war." While the Republicans deliberated over their choice, the German High Command was also debating whether to gamble on the submarine as a decisive weapon for victory. Little did Lippmann know what the next four years had in store for him or his country. The wheels of fate were turning and where they would stop no one knew.

CHAPTER IV

CRUSADING WITH WILSON

"Love blinds," so the saying goes, but so does political loyalty. The *New Republic's* outlook became myopic when it dealt with Wilson, but it seemed to see things with magnified clarity in dealing with his critics. The journal censured Theodore Roosevelt for his "unnecessary opposition" to the Wilson administration, proving, an editorial claimed, his "inability to be fair to opponents." William Jennings Bryan was made the target for Wilson's foreign policy failures. The Secretary of State was castigated for his "do-nothingism" although the charge should have been leveled at the President. No condemnation was forthcoming relative to Wilson's actions in Mexico. His misguided zeal was merely labeled an excessive display of "moral enthusiasm," but the inanity of the entire affair with Mexico was not attacked.

Walter Lippmann also seemed to be afflicted with the same malady which caused the *New Republic* to be so shortsighted. The closer he came into contact with the Wilson administration the less objective was his outlook. He went to the Republican National Convention to observe its proceedings and saw what he wanted to see. The G.O.P., he complained, totally "ignored the Progressives." Under the circumstances one could hardly have expected the regular Republicans to embrace those who had bolted its ranks just four years earlier. His bias got the better of him when he dismissed Governor Hughes of New York, the party's nominee for the presidency, as a "drag-net for all possible anti-Wilson votes." It would have been highly unusual for a party out of power not to have chosen such a candidate. Lippmann also insisted, basing his judgment on some strange prescience, that Hughes possessed neither the "genius for brilliant intuition" displayed by Theodore Roosevelt nor Woodrow Wilson's "extraordinary power to learn quickly." Certainly no one could have predicted with certainty how Hughes would perform had he been elected president.

It was a far different story when Lippmann appraised the incumbent. The best construction was put on events so as to minimize failures and magnify achievements. Yes, he acknowledged that Wilson had entered office as a "laissez faire Democrat." But because of

the Chief Executive's "extraordinary growth," so went the explanation, Wilson was transformed into a "constructive nationalist." The
President was given exclusive credit for remolding the "reactionary,
parochial fragments of the Democracy" into the "only party which
at this moment is national in scope, liberal in purpose, and effective in
action." That attributed far more to Wilson than he deserved. Many
of the liberal measures of his administration represented the ideas of
others. A considerable portion of the momentum for reform after
the mid-term election of 1914 came from Progressive Congressmen —
not the White House.

The Lippmann-Wilson relationship grew closer after the President
won reelection in 1916. When writing for the *New Republic,* Lippmann couched his words in such a manner to catch Wilson's eye and
not to arouse his ire. This persuasive approach worked. Ray Stannard Baker, many years later, while compiling the Wilson papers,
informed him the President did indeed take note of his articles. "I
find," Baker wrote in 1928, "that Wilson kept quite a number of your
editorials in the file which we have come to know he used when he
was working out his decisions." As a specific example of this influence, he thought the presidential decision in favor of establishing
a Belgium Relief Organization was the direct result of an editorial
entitled "Uneasy America." That particular item decried the invasion of this small country and suggested some act must be forthcoming to tell the world of American displeasure. Circumventing his
neutrality policy, President Wilson responded with the humanitarian
gesture of supplying the victims of Germany's aggression with food
and clothing.

Lippmann found himself very much in presidential favor. He was
asked to accompany Wilson on a post-election tour designed to
increase public support for preparedness measures. The President
solicited his counsel. On one occasion Lippmann's suggestion to alter
the wording of a speech was accepted most graciously by a man
known to be headstrong and exceedingly proud of his prose. The
milder phrase the "most adequate navy in the world" was substituted
for Wilson's more blatant call, in a St. Louis speech, for the "greatest
navy in the world."

Because of his wide range of contacts with prominent Englishmen,
Lippmann made an excellent middleman. In one instance he received
a communication from H. G. Wells which he passed on to Colonel
Edward M. House. In his letter Wells proposed an "American Peace
Idea" in which he urged the U.S. government to become a mediator

by notifying all belligerents of the "peace the American mind would like." His ideas gave birth to the so-called House-Grey Memorandum. This secret document of February 22, 1916, signed by Colonel House and Sir Edward Grey, the British Foreign Secretary, involved the United States in a plan to terminate the war. President Wilson was to issue a call for a peace conference. Simultaneously he was to warn Germany that a refusal to attend would force U.S. intervention on behalf of the Allies. Because of his hesitation to make such a bold commitment, Wilson inserted the qualifying word "probably" before the sentence about American entry into the war. British officials dropped the proposal immediately. Without conclusive assurances relative to U.S. participation, they did not want to proceed any further. Their fear was that Germany would then interpret it as a sign of weakness.

Lippmann's associates on the *New Republic* began to regard him as sort of a liaison man for the Wilson administration. They were correct. Colonel House, Wilson's closest confidant, gave Lippmann confidential information so that he "might write intelligently and not conflict with the purposes of the government." Harold Laski, a British contributor to the journal, made the following observation: "One can see, indeed, from its pages that, after 1917, it was as natural for Mr. Lippmann to become the *eminence grise* of Colonel House as it was fo rthe latter to become the same role to Woodrow Wilson. It was in the light of his first years on the *New Republic* that Mr. Lippmann became one of the vital authors of the President's famous Fourteen Points."

There was no doubt in the minds of readers where the *New Republic* stood with regard to the administration. It was an undisguised Wilson organ. There was, however, no clear cut consensus in favor of American participation in the war. Discussions among the editorial board over foreign policy provoked sharp disagreements. Willard Straight worked on Croly to break down his antipathy to U.S. intervention. He wrote the senior editor, "Dorothy tells me that both you and Walter think me pro-English." His admission, "So, I am," was followed by the argument, "Looking at it purely from a selfish American standpoint, it is going to be better for us if the Allies win than it will be if Germany is successful." Later he pressed the point that American security had traditionally relied upon British sea power. The preservation of Britain's prowess on the oceans was a vital ingredient of U.S. safety. So much so, he vowed, it was a compelling reason to conclude an "alliance with the British."

It was only after acrimonious debate that the majority of the editorial staff agreed to come out publicly in favor of military intervention. This decision, made only a few months before Wilson asked Congress for a declaration of war, was approved by Croly, Lippmann, and Alvin Johnson. Opposition came from the pacifistically inclined Walter Weyl and the "militant Irish patriot," Francis Hackett. The task fell to Lippmann to explain why the *New Republic* took the stand it did.

This was done in an article entitled "The Defense of the Atlantic World." He set forth cogent reasons why national self interest made it mandatory for the United States to guarantee an Allied victory. America's security and economic welfare were linked to the "Atlantic community" in an interrelated "web of interests." In his view it was a "crime" for Germany to use submarines to threaten the "safety of the Atlantic highway." Continued neutrality was out of the question. Wisdom dictated military intervention now to prevent German control of the Atlantic sea lanes. "Britain, France, even Spain, Belgium, Holland, the Scandinavian nations, and Pan America are in the main one community in their deepest purposes," ran his argument, therefore "they have a common interest in the ocean which unites them . . ." The welfare of the communities bordering the Atlantic Ocean made it imperative for them to cooperate in defeating the Central Powers.

The concept of an Atlantic community was the matrix from which Lippmann developed his ideas on international relations. He regarded Western Europe and those countries linked to it by history and heritage as the nucleus of Western civilization. United by culture, commerce and common customs, the destiny of these nations were inextricably intertwined. Although his reasoning seemed quite tangible and concrete, there was an abstract quality about it that was not so apparent. The Atlantic community was in many respects an idealized projection. Would not the contours of this fictive community still have remained intact despite Germany's ascendency in Europe? The power he wanted preserved was that of Anglo-American hegemony. He was an anglophile at heart. Implicit in his thought was a belief in the superiority of British institutions over those of the Germanic nations. In purely realistic terms the rise of Germany to a world power would have boded ill for the United States. Theodore Roosevelt and Admiral Mahan had always watched the Kaiser's growing empire with a wary eye. The Atlantic community was but a mental configuration, but future fear of Germany was a valid cause for maintaining the balance of power on the European continent. Only then would the United States not have to worry about German conquest of the Atlantic or Pacific oceans.

The year 1917 was a turning point for Lippmann both in terms of his private life and public career. First, it was the year in which he married Faye Albertson. Her father, Ralph, was an old-line social-ist and a member of the editorial board of the *Boston Common*. Lippmann worked for this journal immediately after his graduation from Harvard. It had afforded him the opportunity to meet his future wife. The second important event was his decision to leave the *New Republic* on June 9, 1917 to become a special assistant to New-ton D. Baker, the Secretary of War. Now directly involved in the war effort in an official capacity, his first assignment was to serve as an adviser to the Industrial Relations branch of the War Depart-mnet. One of his duties was to represent his department on the War Labor Board. Other members of this group, which ultimately evolved into the War Mediation Board with ex-President William Howard Taft as chairman, included General Carlington, John Alpine, and Franklin D. Roosevelt, then Assistant Secretary of Navy. Serving periodically as legal counsels or mediators were Felix Frankfurter and the president of Dartmouth College, Ernest M. Hopkins.

The new environment in which Lippmann found himself had a direct bearing on his immediate outlook. He mingled almost exclu-sively with Wilson admirers and absorbed their point of view on many issues. At informal gatherings, held at the apartment of Robert G. Valentine, the Commissioner of Indian Affairs, he met other members of the Wilson administration. Many of their discussions re-volved around the topic of how future wars could be prevented. The idealistic tone of these sessions had its effect on Lippmann. He too began to think one of the aims of the war should be the creation of a world society based on precepts of international cooperation. Justice Oliver Wendell Holmes, Jr. frequented these meetings at the Valentine residence, which the participants dubbed the "House of Truth," but he evinced skepticism about their Edenic visions of a new world. He once quipped, in a sardonic vein, "You young men seem to think that if you sit on the world long enough you will hatch something out."

A fundamental change in Lippmann's attitude on international re-lations revealed itself in an article written for *The Annals*, the journal of the American Academy of Political and Social Sciences. The man who wrote *The Stakes of Diplomacy*, which was so thoroughly realistic in outlook, now took an entirely different view. Where he had formerly advocated the pursuing of national self interest as the basic function of foreign policy, his major concern at this time was how to find ways to curb "unlimited national sovereignty." What Germany did, he claimed, was to demonstrate "*ad nauseum*" the extreme dangers inherent in the "doctrine of competitive nationalism." This explained his turn about. Nations could not be "free," he wrote, unless they learn to "co-operate." Heretofore, he admitted, only a "handful of visionaries dared to hope for some kind of federation." His present feeling was that "nothing less" than such an institution could prevent future conflicts. Thinking almost exclusively in Wilsonian terms, he concluded: "We can win nothing from this war unless it culminates in a union of liberal peoples pledged to co-operate in the settlement of all outstanding questions, sworn to turn against the aggressors, determined to erect a larger and more modern system of international law upon a federation of the world."

The reform impulse of the Progressive movement was being transferred from the domestic to the international scene. A great deal remained to be done to reconstruct the institutional patterns of the United States; yet the liberals were determined to set their sights on reforming the world. The war was looked upon as the golden opportunity to build a new international society from the rubble of war. A world organization, guided by international law, was to replace nationalism and control rampant militarism. Wilson's lofty utterances about making the world safe for democracy and of waging a war to end all wars enthralled many — including Lippmann. Aspirations quickened as the President elevated American participation in the war to the level of a glorious crusade for mankind.

While serving as Secretary Baker's assistant, Lippmann also worked for Colonel House. He ultimately became a trusted member of House's staff. In addition to these duties, he was appointed Secretary of the Inquiry. This group, of which more will be said later, was established to examine problems relative to postwar setltements. At still another time, he accepted a commission in the Army as a Captain of Military Intelligence. His final service for the Wilson administration was his involvement in staff work at the Paris Peace Conference. In all of these endeavors, Lippmann's intellectual ability, writing talent, and contacts with the intellectual community were fully utilized. He was well liked by Baker and House. Even President Wilson, who usually saw only the final product of his labors, wrote to his Secretary of War that "Lippmann is always not only thoughtful but just and suggestive."

The dissemination of information under wartime conditions involved complicated matters of security as well as the need for bolstering morale. The temptation was to manufacture propaganda and pawn it off as news. When discussions within the administration arose over the necessity for a "press bureau," Lippmann took a keen interest in it. He told House that such an agency should involve itself more with the preparation of public opinion for America's postwar role than the issuing of mere news bulletins. "Peculiar psychological problems" existed, he explained, because "objects for which we are at war are delicate and difficult." Taking Wilson's words literally, he reminded the Colonel, "We are fighting not so much to beat an enemy as to make the world safe for democracy."

To further this project, Professor Henry S. Canby of Yale University was asked by Lippmann to "draw up a memorandum . . . of the kind of work you think ought to be done and suggestions for the proper organization for it." When these recommendations were channeled to Wilson the result was the establishment of the Committee on Public Information. It was headed by the newspaperman George Creel. The Creel Committee subsequently publicized the war as a glorious crusade. It helped arouse expectations to such a degree complete fulfillment was impossible of attainment. Germany was painted so villainous as to incite crude violence in the name of patriotism. Lippmann complained to House about this wartime hysteria. It was manifesting itself in obnoxious censorship; indiscriminate and illegal campaigns against alleged "seditious newspapers"; excessive "jingoism"; and "fierce heresy hunting" that trampled underfoot basic rights of free speech. These frenzied acts of flag waving were "breaking down the liberal support of the war," he warned. Once unleashed this type of super-patriotism could not be contained. It constituted the most unsavory aspect of home front mobilization during World War I.

One of the most significant roles Lippmann was to play in the Wilson administration was his participation in the work of the Inquiry. Acting on a suggestion from Robert Lansing, who succeeded Bryan as Secretary of State, that initial "preparation of data for the peace conference" should begin, Wilson acted promptly. The President transmitted the Secretary's suggestion to Colonel House with the notation: "Lansing is not only content that you should undertake the preparation of data for the peace conference but volunteered the opinion that you were the very one to do it."

House quickly enlisted the aid of Lippmann. The Colonel asked him to form a committee of experts as a study group. He was to serve as the group's secretary. Scholars representing all areas of the academic community were summoned for help. Those approached included President Mezes of the City College of New York, as Director; James T. Shotwell for geography; David Hunter Miller to head the legal staff; George Louis Beer on colonial questions; Charles H. Haskins for problems dealing with Western Europe; Clive Day on Balkan affairs; and Allan Young for issues involving economics. Since many of the Inquiry's meetings took place in the office of the American Geographic Society, its president, Dr. Isaiah Bowman, became closely affiliated with the work of the group. Professor Charles Seymour of Yale University also served as a consultant.

Colonel House instructed Lippmann to see that "studies" were made on ways to achieve war aims, territorial settlements, and preservation of peace in the postwar era. He also extended the scope of such investigations to include: "Discussions and interviews with various Government officials and leaders of thought, some of whom were mentioned in our conferences, but also such other examinations of the problems included in the present and future readjustments as may seem appropriate or necessary."

As the Inquiry proceeded with its preliminary survey, Lippmann solicited ideas from all sources. He sought to utilize the brainpower of academicians in all specialized areas. "We are skimming the cream of the younger and more imaginative scholars," he informed Newton Baker. "I am confident that no important center of scholarship will be able to say that it has not been allowed to contribute." One suggestion from Thorstein Veblen, a major economist, was a proposal with the title "Suggestions Touching the Working Program of an Inquiry into the Terms of Peace." This document attacked the balance of power diplomacy of prewar times and called for the establishment of a "League of Pacifistic Peoples." His plan resembled the League of Nations. Another of Veblen's recommendations was contained in a memorandum designated "An outline of a Policy for the Control of 'Economic Penetration' of Backward Countries and of Foreign Investment." It criticized the imperialistic exploitation of colonies and underdeveloped nations by the major powers. Anticipating the "mandate system," he proposed such regions be placed under the "guardianship of the Pacifistic League."

These germinal ideas paralleled the thinking of others and collectively provided the constructs for Wilson's postwar program.

Research progressed and reports were sent to Lippmann. All too many of them displeased him. Finding that numerous recommendations deviated from Wilson's stated objectives, he returned them for revisions. Members of the Inquiry found it extremely difficult to reconcile the President's avowed war aims, which were imprecise, with the specific problems at hand. To remake the world was a rather large order even for expert scholars. The agony of applying grand principles to concrete issues prompted him to confide to Baker:

"We have been compelled practically to train and create our own experts. This is especially true of problems connected with Russia, the Balkans, Turkey and Africa. Those are lands intellectually practically unexplored.

"What we are on the lookout for is genius — sheer, startling genius and nothing less will do because the real application of the President's ideas to those countries requires inventiveness and resourcefulness which is scarcer than anything.

"It isn't difficult to win a war and lose a peace. England did it over and over again in the nineteenth century in regard to Turkey."

The war effort suffered a serious blow in the fall of 1917 when the Bolshevik Revolution caused withdrawal of Russia from the Eastern Front. Once Lenin signed the Treaty of Brest-Litovsk in March, 1918 he initiated a peace offensive aimed at the liberal elements in all countries. The proclamation of the Petrograd formula contained the principles of a new diplomacy to be based on self-determination and justice for all nations. Colonel House tried to persuade the Inter-Allied Council, meeting in Paris on October, 1917, of the importance of using a specific set of liberal war aims to bolster anti-Bolshevik forces in Russia. This was not done. No Allied nation wanted to renounce the postwar claims contained in a series of secret treaties among themselves. House then alerted the Inquiry to prepare a document spelling out just what type of peace settlement the United States desired.

The Inquiry completed its work on this assignment within a few months. The final draft of a report, entitled "War Aims and Peace Terms," was completed by S. E. Mezes, David Hunter Miller, and Walter Lippmann. Early in January of 1918 the recommendations were sent to the President. Wilson formulated six of the famous Fourteen Points immediately after an initial reading (points eight to thirteen respectively). Section IX yielded further inspiration when it castigated the "bankrupt" features of the "old diplomacy," while reaffirming the idea that the "great hope" of the world lay in the establishment of a "league of nations." The Fourteen Points were announced formally by the President in an address to Congress on January 8, 1918. His speech achieved a threefold purpose. As a major policy statement, it laid down the framework for a new world order; it undermined German morale by holding out the promise of an equitable peace; and it regained for the President his position as the chief spokesman for a new diplomacy of international morality and world cooperation. Wilson now regarded himself as the undisputed leader of all the Progressive forces in the world.

After examining the substance of the Fourteen Points, one wonders how Lippmann could have helped prepare them even in their embryonic form. They run so counter to his earlier views on foreign policy. Having once criticized Wilson for expressing too many noble sentiments, he now helped put words in the President's mouth expressing grandiose objectives which by their very nature were impossible to achieve. Wilson should have been warned against making such vast commitments. Many of them were not plausible and most unacceptable to the Allies. The Fourteen Points, as the very embodiment of Wilsonian idealism, laid down the following foundations for peace:

"1. Open covenants of peace, openly arrived at . . .

"2. Absolute freedom of navigation upon the seas . . .

"3. The removal, so far as possible, of all economic barriers . . .

"4. Adequate guarantees given and taken that national armaments will be reduced . . .

"5. A free, open-minded, and absolutely impartial adjustment of all colonial claims . . .

"6. The evacuation of all Russian territory and such a settlement of all questions affecting Russia as will secure the best and freest co-operation of the other nations of the world in obtaining for her an unhampered and unembarrassed opportunity for the independent determination of her own political development and national policy and assure her of a sincere welcome into the society of free nations under institutions of her own choosing . . .

"7. Belgium . . . must be evacuated and restored . . .

"8. All French territory should be freed and the invaded portions restored, and the wrong done to France by Prussia in 1871 in the matter of Alsace-Lorraine . . . should be righted . . .

"9. A readjustment of the frontiers for Italy should be effected along clearly recognizable lines of nationality.

"10. The people of Austria-Hungary . . . should be accorded the freest opportunity of autonomous development.

"11. Rumania, Serbia, and Montenegro should be evacuated . . . and international guarantees of the political and economic independence and territorial integrity of the several Balkan states should be entered into.

"12. The Turkish portions of the present Ottoman Empire should be assured a secure sovereignty, but the other nationalities . . . should be assured an undoubted security of life and an absolutely unmolested opportunity of autonomous development, and the Dardanelles should be permanently opened as a free passage to the ships and commerce of all nations under international guarantees.

"13. An independent Polish state should be erected . . .

"14. A general association of nations must be formed under specific covenants for the purpose of affording mutual guarantees of political independence and territorial integrity to great and small states alike."

To undermine German morale high ranking American officials decided to engage in psychological warfare. Lippmann accepted a commission as a Captain in Military Intelligence primarily to assist in this work. He was assigned to Propaganda Section D of Army G-2. The immediate activities of this unit were under the nominal direction of Captain Heber Blankenhorn, but the overall program of breaking Germany's will to wage war was within the jurisdiction of General Dennis E. Nolan.

Captain Lippmann arrived in France with credentials of the highest classification. He presented his orders directly to General John J. Pershing, the Commander of the American Expeditionary Force, who was also informed by the Secretary of War that Lippmann's mission involved the "aggressive spreading of carefully prepared propaganda." In an offical communique Baker told Pershing the newly arrived Captain was to conduct his operation "under the supervision of Colonel House." This virtual autonomy from Army control was reinforced when further instructions came from the Secretary of State. Robert Lansing notified Lippmann it was "entirely" up to his own "discretion" on how to proceed with these "political matters" in carrying out the "confidential instructions of the Secretary of War."

Plans for undermining the enemy's morale were relatively simple.

Lippmann revealed to House the best approach was a "frank campaign of education . . . simply addressed to German and Austrian troops explaining as persuasively as possible the unselfish character of the war, the generosity of our aims and the great hope for mankind we are trying to realize."

The technique employed to accomplish this task was through the use of "balloon propaganda" and the dropping of leaflets by airplane. Copies of the Fourteen Points and transcripts of Wilson's speeches were scattered among front line trenches and in accessible civilian areas. Subsequent intelligence reports indicated "the pamphlets dropped by Allied aviators are having a decided effect upon the morale of the civilian population." Further information was processed and relayed to Washington, D.C. indictating the Fourteen Points were creating a "favorable impression on the German people." From sources inside Germany it was revealed that certain newspapers were calling for an end to the war on the basis of "guarantees that the Allies accept President Wilson's peace terms." The war weary Germans embraced the Fourteen Points as terms they could live with even in defeat, but their armies fought on.

To hasten the end of the war, Lippmann sought to implement a scheme whereby Russia would be brought back into the conflict on the side of the Allies. His plan was the outgrowth of a visit to Moscow by Lincoln Steffens. His former mentor in journalism tried to convince Leon Trotsky, then Commissar for Foreign Affairs, of the "sincerity of the President's diplomacy." Lippmann proposed that he be allowed to contact his former Harvard classmate, John Reed, who in turn would act as an intermediary between the Bolshevik leaders and the U.S. government. Reed, an American rebel turned Communist, had been in Russia during the 1917 revolution and reported it in *Ten Days That Shook the World.* He was to be authorized to offer "assurances" of American good will and to convince the Soviet hierarchy they could place their "confidence" in the American President. The scheme was never carried out. It was doubtful whether Reed would have been receptive to any overture from Lippmann. The latter had criticized his onetime friend, when writing for the *New Republic,* for his "befuddled" ideas and juvenile habit of "rushing" to take part in one of Mexico's numerous insurrections. The mission undertaken by Steffens also failed and all U.S. efforts to establish normal relationships with the Bolshevik government ceased after Wilson condoned Allied intervention on Soviet territory. The peripatetic revolutionary John Reed, by the way, was given the dubious honor of being the only American to be buried within the Kremlin walls.

When Pope Benedict XV, who was acting as a mediator for Austria, asked for a negotiated peace, Newton Baker hastily requested Lippmann to draft a reply to the Vatican proposal. He responded with a "Memorandum for the Secretary of War," which disclosed the depth of his personal commitment to the principles of the new Wilsonian diplomacy. The document embraced all of the President's hopes for a reformed Europe that was to emerge chastened by the war and transformed by adversity into a new order. It justified the American war aims on these grounds:

"1. We are conducting a war on the assumption that there is a difference between the German government and the German people . . .

"2. If the German people are to be weaned from their governing class they must be made to believe that they can be safe . . .

"3. We are not interested in particular territorial settlements; we are interested in the method of settlement . . . The world made safe for democracy [offers] . . . assurance that the future method of settlement between the powers shall be by a civil procedure.

"4. Germany can be a future member of the League of Nations when ready to be a 'fit partner.'

"5. Democracy should replace militarism as a condition.

"6. Changes should occur in Germany as they did in Russia.

"7. With such 'guarantees,' Germany can be accepted as 'a partner in the League.'

"8. America was not to 'specify terms of territorial settlements since they wanted to focus on the method of peace rather than on the terms of peace.' This keeps us 'clear of entanglements' and if it is 'rejected' the President 'cannot be accused either by Germany or by the American people of prolonging the war.' "

After Germany's last great military offensive failed to gain a victory for them on the Western Front, the Imperial government had no alternative but to issue peace feelers. German officials knew the Allied demands exceeded those of the United States because the Bolsheviks had published the text of all their secret treaties. As could be expected from a nation skilled in the art of realpolitik, the German High Command and civilian government were not only interested in the method of peace but in the exact terms that would follow their capitulation. Since they lacked the resources to continue the war, they simply had to take their chances. An Armistice was successfully negotiated on the basis of the generous Fourteen Points; but they mistakenly assumed that the peace treaty would also be based entirely upon its principles.

Part of the difficulty in translating the American peace formula into specific terms revolved around the very vagueness of many of Wilson's phrases. The British were particularly apprehensive about the precise meaning of the second of the Fourteen Points which dealt with the "absolute freedom of navigation upon the seas." Colonel House assigned to Lippmann the task of defining what it meant when applied to actual international usage. He succeeded in tracing the phrase back to Hugo Grotius a seventeenth century Dutch jurist who first endeavored to establish the principle of *"mare liberum."* The War of 1812 was allegedly fought over this issue when British men of war stopped American vessels on the high seas to search for deserters. Lippmann's historical research failed to uncover very much and prompted the conclusion that the term was "rarely used if at all" after the nineteenth century.

Historically maritime nations controlled the seas just as major land powers dominated the territory adjacent to them. The Romans, the British, and even the Americans utilized their fleets to exert control over bodies of water vital to their security or commercial interests. Wilson himself approved the mining of the North Seas once the United States had entered the war. Neutrals were deprived of their rights with blacklists and blockades simply because the combined navies of Great Britain and the United States possessed the power to enforce such decrees. This was quite consistent with the nature of warfare, since major powers had always utilized their superiority in weapons to insure victory. A novel aspect of the American stand was its contradictory position of advocating one thing in theory and doing another in practice.

Lippmann failed to come up with a meaningful definition of the nebulous term "freedom of the seas." He could only make the bold-faced claim, "But at least this much is certain, . . . the idea has long been championed by the United States and . . . the phrase appeared as long ago as 1798." The difficulty encountered in explaining this point prompted him to advise Colonel House that a thorough analysis of all the generalizations used by the President was in order or they would again encounter trouble. Stating the case rather bluntly, Lippmann insisted upon a "rigorous examination" of Wilson's "abstract ideas." He was unaware of it at the time, but that was to be his next assignment.

The Armistice became a reality on November 11, 1918. A high level conference was required to arrive at a consensus of all the Allied and Associated powers as to the exact terms of the truce. The confab took place at the Quai d'Orsay in Paris. Present were such dignitaries as Georges Clemenceau, the French Premier; Stephan Pichon, French Foreign Minister; David Lloyd George, the British Prime Minister; Arthur Balfour, British Foreign Minister; Sidney Sonninio, the Italian Foreign Minister; and Colonel House representing the United States. Walter Lippmann and Frank Cobb, the editor of the *New York World*, were members of the Colonel's staff. Since the discussions were to revolve around the use of the Fourteen Points as a basis for the armistice, the Allied leaders wanted a clear understanding of what they meant. In response to House's request, Lippmann and Cobb prepared a memorandum entitled the 'Official American Commentary of the Fourteen Points."

They labored hard to render beautiful phrases into concrete definitions. The initial point, "open covenants of peace, openly arrived at," seemed to preclude all secret negotiations. This was an untenable position since the very discussions going on were private. The Lippmann-Cobb explanation was ingenious. They said Wilson's dictum did "not mean to exclude confidential diplomatic negotiations," but it related only to the "final covenant made public to the world." It was made clear, however, that no treaty was "binding" upon the signatories if there were concealed provisions not known to others. This was a direct criticsim of the secret treaties then binding the Allies together.

The second point — "absolute freedom of navigation upon the seas" — had already perplexed Lippmann when he sought to trace its historical origin. The interpretation they gave at this time demanded the "rights of neutrals shall be maintained against the belligerents, the rights of both to be clearly and precisely defined in the laws of nations." These were words without substance, since neutral rights were being violated the moment the explanation was being written. The Atlantic Ocean was, so to speak, an Allied lake and anything of value to the Central Powers had been declared contraband. Total war had made it impossible to protect the rights of neutrals.

The third of the Fourteen Points called for the "removal . . . of all economic barriers." Here Wilson committed himself to something he could not deliver. With all the difficulty he had getting the American tariff lowered during his first term of office, it should have been evident to him a program of free trade was an impossible goal. Even though the United States was traditionally a protectionist nation, Lippmann and Cobb rendered the following definition: "It means the destruction of all special commercial agreements, each nation putting the trade of every other nation in the League on the same basis, the most favored nation clause applying automatically to all members of the League of Nations."

Concerning the fourth point, which stated that "national armaments will be reduced to the lowest point consistent with domestic safety," they suggested, "It will be necessary to adopt some kind of international commission of investigation to prepare detailed projects for its execution." This avoided any commitment for unilateral disarmament on the part of the United States and it sidestepped the necessity for spelling out a specific formula for carrying out the provision. Experienced diplomats would have anticipated the extreme reluctance of any country, especially France, to jeopardize its national security by self-imposed limitations on military power. Collective security sounded fine in theory but afforded no real guarantees. Too many features of the Fourteen Points were being left for the proposed League to resolve. This delaying procedure did not remove the problems involved, it just postponed coming to grips with them.

Lippmann and his colleagues construed the fifth point, which dealt with "impartial adjustments of all colonial claims," to mean "that a colonial power acts not as owner of its colonies, but as trustees for the natives and for the interests of the society of nations." They made no recommendations as to the disposition of Germany's colonies and that was the focal point of interest. Concerning points six through thirteen, which treated of territorial settlements, they elaborated upon them in terms of information supplied by the Inquiry. The principle of self-determination was not easy to apply. For instance, how large should an ethnic group be before it was considered worthy of a homeland? What happened when it became impossible to draw neat boundaries because of mixed and confused populations? Furthermore nothing was said about the wisdom of transforming Europe into a checkerboard of small nations which might actually increase international tensions instead of lessening them.

On the final point, the fourteenth, no further elucidation was considered necessary because of the President's pronouncements on the League of Nations. It seemed evident to them that this proposed institution was to be the "foundation of the whole diplomatic structure of a permanent peace." Actually Wilson had not really explained precisely what was implied by U.S. membership in the international organization. His vagueness may have been the result of his own lack of understanding of exactly what was involved. The President acted too often as if this project were his private property, to be accepted on faith because it represented what he thought was the best means for maintaining peace. The tragedy of the years ahead, when the Senate refused to approve U.S. participation in the League, were in large measure caused by his refusal to consult with Congressional leaders, especially Republicans, on the detailed mechanics of the world organization. Prior to the publication of the final peace treaty, it was doubtful whether many Americans really knew what the League was all about.

The President accepted the Lippmann-Cobb memorandum as a "satisfactory" interpretation of the Fourteen Points subject only to minor alterations in "detail." Since Wilson had decreed the United States an Associate but not an Allied power, it was imperative that unanimity of opinion be achieved. His oft repeated war aims were actually litanies of hope. They were inadequate for the momentous negotiations to follow despite the explanations offered by Lippmann and Cobb. The Allies never were in agreement about their meaning or on the amount of commitment involved.

Not only did German leaders misapprehend what they had done, many American liberals were erroneously convinced the Fourteen Points were to be the basis of an equitable peace settlement. Their hopes had been aroused to such an extent they presumed the New World was dramatically about to reform the Old. This buoyant optimism also affected Lippmann. He wrote to Colonel House, just before the Peace Conference convened, "This is a climax of a course taken that has been as wise as it is brilliant . . . The President and you have more than justified the faith of those who insisted that your leadership was a turning point in modern history."

The Allied leaders, however, went to Paris as victors to divide the spoils and to reestablish the balance of power. President Wilson, on the other hand, made his triumphant appearance in Europe on December 13, 1918 as the representative of all humanity. Like a veritable god descending from Olympus, he received the plaudits of huge throngs of people in every country visited. The masses hailed him as the savior of Europe. It was a far different story when he attended the first plenary session of the Paris Peace Conference. Now he had to deal with his peers.

At first the main business of the conference was conducted by the Council of Ten. Then it was reduced to the Big Four; and finally after Italy's Orlando left in a rage, only the Big Three remained to make the important decisions. Wilson, Lloyd George, and Clemenceau debated endlessly over the fate of Germany. The "Tiger" from France and the British Prime Minister were tough adversaries and blunt bargainers. As the days and weeks passed it became apparent to insiders that the American President was not going to emerge as the architect of a new world order.

Two fears haunted Lippmann while observing the proceedings at close hand. He was apprehensive lest the President "demand too little" and was frankly puzzled why Wilson insisted upon doing all the negotiating himself. It was his belief the President could have wielded more power by returning to Washington, D.C. and from that distant point remain aloof from the cruder aspects of the bargaining. Since Wilson insisted on remaining, Lippmann did his best to help the beleagured President. He was, as S. E. Mezes and James T. Shotwell later attested, in the "thick of things" supplying needed information and "interpreting and phrasing policy." Sir William Wiseman, head of the British Intelligence in the United States, also believed his contributions were of considerable importance. "It is my impression," Sir William observed, "that Lippmann furnished the abstract ideas which found their way into a good many of the memoranda of the American delegation and ultimately into some of President Wilson's speeches."

The protracted parleys and rancorous debate gnawed at Lippmann's patience. He got the impression Wilson was faltering and yielding far too much. When the President was forced to compromise, it appeared to him that principles were being abandoned. Giving vent to his pent up frustration in a letter to Dorothy Straight, he complained the American delegation was "wandering in the labyrinth of indecision." He confessed, "I am very anxious to get back into the fresh air."

Idealism and impatience no doubt made too many well intentioned liberals view the conference as a travesty of justice. Negotiations by their very nature involved give and take, above all, generalities had to be hammered into concrete agreements. It was one thing to speak fondly of self-determination or impartial adjustment of colonial claims, but is was something else when the time came for determining specific boundaries or what country got control of a former German colony. As substantial portions of the treaty were completed Lippmann viewed the results as a "deplorable breach of faith" on the part of the victors. On could find little trace of the Fourteen Points amid the voluminous pages of the treaty. He warned Colonel House that "resentment" was building up because of the "President's failure to explain what he is doing." Disclosing his feeling of disillusionment, he advised House: "I don't need to tell you how disappointed I am at the outcome at Paris. I hoped up to the very last for a Treaty which would in a measure redeem our promises to the world, for a Treaty that would not open the suspicion that the Covenant is a new Holy Alliance . . . My only hope now is that the President will not pretend that he has realized his vision and his promise."

After his return to the United States, Lippmann resigned his Army commission, severed his relationship with the Wilson administration, and rejoined the editorial staff of the *New Republic*. His first major journalistic endeavor in 1919 was a book-length study called *The Political Scene: An Essay on the Victory of 1918*. "A new Europe will emerge from this war, he asserted, "that much is certain, and the only question is whether it will be organized at Paris or disorganized at Moscow." His central theme was that "three great influences" were striving for the hearts and minds of Europeans. They were the forces of "Reaction . . . Revolution . . ., and Reconstruction." France was identified with reaction, the Soviet Union with revolution, and the United States and Great Britain with "liberal reconstruction."

It was his contention that the "old diplomacy" of Clemenceau was reactionary in that it wanted to restore the old order of things. The Soviet Union, in contrast, was seeking a "new order" through violence. Both were condemned by Lippmann. He maintained Europe's reconstruction and the reestablishment of its stability could be achieved only through the process of international cooperation. The League of Nations was the instrument for this, since it alone provided a "new framework for human society" to move forward. The world organization was not to be considered merely as a "useful annex to the structure of peace," but the primary means for warding off revolution or a return to unbridled nationalism.

In this work Lippmann focused on the manner in which the League could keep the peace. A group of nations might send representatives to Geneva, where the League headquarters was to be built, but that in itself guaranteed little. If small countries voted one way and even one major nation objected, the decision would finally be determined by sheer power — not ballots. How was the League to enforce its dictums if disagreement occurred among big nations? His solution to this dilemma was the consumation of an Anglo-American power bloc within the confines of the League. Such an "entente means the substitution of a pool for a balance," he wrote, "and in that pool will be found the ultimate force upon which rests the League of Nations."

Despite his clever use of semantics, substituting pool for balance, his proposal sounded much like a power arrangement of the old diplomacy. An unofficial alliance between the United States and Great Britain would, in effect, constitute a voting combination with military strength. A dual leadership of that type would insure success, he claimed, "For if the united power of Britain and America — potential or actual — is wielded for the ends they now both officially profess, they are assured of the active assistance of the smaller nations everywhere." This assessment seemed much more realistic than his view of the League while serving as Wilson's adviser.

When the final text of the Treaty of Versailles was released, it came as a bombshell. Most American liberals were stunned by the harsh terms imposed on Germany. Liberal opinion turned against Wilson with the fury of a betrayed lover. On the insistence of Herbert Croly, the *New Republic* came out against Senate ratification of the treaty. It seemed incredible that Lippmann did not publicly disassociate himself from this stand. Defeat of the treaty also meant eliminating all opportunity for American participation in the League. And the consequences of that action involved the efficacy of the League itself. Without an Anglo-American coalition, the inner strength of the new organization would be missing even before it began to function. The only explanation he gave for his unusual behavior was a rather remorseful statement some ten years later: "The decision to oppose ratification was Croly's. I followed him, though I was not then, and am not now, convinced that it was the wise thing to do . . . If I had to do it all over again I would take the other side; we supplied the Battalion of Death with too much ammunition."

It was indeed a strange twist of fate that liberal internationalists would join with isolationists to defeat the treaty, thus insuring non-involvement in the League. The "irreconcilables," or Battalion of Death, were led by Senator William E. Borah of Idaho. This confirmed isolationist took advantage of the liberal's defection in his battle against ratification. Such an unholy alliance prompted Walter Weyl to observe that the "idealists" of the war years became "half-reactionary, half cynical." The *New Republic* bolstered anti-treaty sentiment by both serializing and then publishing an inexpensive edition of John Maynard Keynes' *The Economic Consequences of the Peace*. This type of opposition and Wilson's illness turned the tide decisively against the treaty. Public interest waned while the vocal minority sustained their efforts to kill the treaty. As an invalid in the White House, seclusive and uncompromising to the end, the President finally snuffed out any remaining hope himself. He regarded a vote for the treaty as disloyalty if any reservations were attached. None were to be approved, whether they were those of Senator Henry Cabot Lodge or anyone else. Ratification failed. By 1920 Wilson's tragedy was complete. He was a broken and bitter man.

The wartime cheers for Woodrow Wilson turned to jeers not only because the American people were tired of idealistic crusades, but because of domestic turmoil in the United States. The President had tried to remake the world but forgot to prepare plans for reconversion at home. "The war," Lippmann noted in one of his articles, "resulted in domestic reaction at home and a defeat of the official war aims abroad." To him the "Red scare," namely the postwar hysteria against all forms of radicalism, was a "grotesque performance." The violation of civil liberties by the Attorney General of the United States, A. Mitchell Palmer, and the extent of government controls in general, made him ponder the dangers involved in over-centralization of power. He, and many other Progressives, had been ardent nationalists. For years he had continually advocated more authority for the federal government. The postwar experience made him question the wisdom of this. Some safeguard was needed, he wrote, to "prevent the coagulation of power." Justification for his reversal of opinion was rationalized by calling attention to the fact that liberalism was not a rigid doctrine but a viable philosophy. Had not the "Progressives of 1912" become the "Wilson Democrats from 1916 to 1918"? Once again, he counseled, an adjustment in outlook was necessary to realign political thought with domestic realities.

While Lippmann worried about too much centralization, farmers and workers suffered economically because of a paucity of federal planning. Inflation plus wage cuts placed labor in a position where it resorted to the strike weapon in order to hold its wartime gains. The farmers lost government price supports without any program for reduction of acreage. Price levels fell and mortgages came due. Lippmann had no solution for agriculture, but he did draw upon his wartime experience with the War Labor Board to propose remedies for management-labor disputes. His plan was quite prophetic of things to come. One aspect of it involved the use of a "cost of living index" to determine wage levels automatically. The second innovation called for the establishment of a "grievance tribunal" for handling strike situations. Other novel suggestions included measures for profit sharing, merit promotions, and a voice in management for labor leaders. These were imaginative and practical recommendations, but the anti-union sentiment of the postwar era made adoption of them impossible.

As the election of 1920 approached, Lippmann sensed the public's resentful attitude. The American people were "tired of greatness," he felt, because the years in which Roosevelt and Wilson drove the nation forward "combined to create a nausea at strong men, moral heroes, and supermen." In anticipation of the reaction of the electorate, when it took refuge in "normalcy," he made the astute observation: "At the time when the world needs above all other things, the activity of generous imagination and the creative leadership of planning and inventive minds, our thinking is shriveled with panic." And so it was.

CHAPTER V

THE TURBULENT TWENTIES

The 1920's constituted a period of sudden and dramatic change in social mores. As moral values underwent deflation, the restraints of religion were cast off. Antics of flappers with their bobbed hair and short skirts prefigured the cult of emancipated youth. Automobiles gave the younger generation mobility and movies educated them in the sophisticated ways of city life. Interests of the man in the street also altered dramatically. He frequented the speak-easy, liked jazz, and whooped it up for everything one hundred per cent American. Sports heroes, screen idols, and daring gangsters captivated him to an extraordinary degree. Truly United States was in the process of devising a new popular culture unrelated to past ideals.

Many intellectuals found it difficult to adjust to this newly evolved set of values. Impetus for reform dwindled away and many serious cultural endeavors seemed on the verge of dying out. Some artists took refuge in foreign lands as expatriates while others became bitter critics of their own country. It was during the onset of this transitional era that Walter Lippmann decided to leave the *New Republic*. Frank J. Cobb, his co-worker in Paris, persuaded him to take a position as an assistant editor of the *New York World*. Commencing in 1921, he began to write editorials for this large metropolitan daily. In a period when mass communication was coming into its own, this move provided him with a forum much more suitable for the times.

A last project undertaken for the *New Republic,* important because of its effect on Lippmann's thinking, was a perceptive study of American news coverage regarding the Soviet Union. Working with Charles Merz, a former member of his propaganda unit in military intelligence (and later in life an editor of the newspaper about to be scrutinized), he carefully examined close to a thousand issues of the *New York Times*. Analysis of this paper's reporting from 1917 to 1920 indicated that the personal prejudices of its writers "profoundly and crassly influenced their news columns." Conclusions of the Lippmann-Merz study, printed as a special supplement of the *New Republic,* claimed that the "net effect" of biased *New York Times* coverage created a distinctly misleading picture of what was happening inside Russia. Precisely when the American people needed accurate and impartial reporting, Lippman and Merz asserted, they were unable to "secure the minimum of necessary information of a supremely important event." This investigation motivated Lippmann to explore further the shortcomings of the American press.

In *Liberty and the News* (1920), Lippman focused attention on the failure of the press to live up to its responsibilities. The newspaper was supposed to be the "bible of democracy," Lippmann pointed out, yet the reading public received "practically nothing that . . . [was] not propaganda." Was it not ludicrous to profess that government must react to the "will of the people" without making a "serious effort to guarantee the news without which a governing opinion cannot exist"? His indictment of the Fourth Estate was far-reaching. Publishers, he claimed, were subject to no standards of objectivity nor did they display a genuine concern for the public's right to know the truth. Most newspaper owners, it seemed to him, were self-appointed "Defenders of the Faith" who printed the news in procrustean fashion to serve their economic and ideological interests and, to a large degree, those of their advertisers. Condemning this, Lippmann contended that "government by consent" could not survive when the "manufacture of consent is an unregulated private enterprise." True liberty was dependent upon free choice. If mass decisions were not made on the basis of reliable information, then the democratic process itself was in jeopardy.

To rectify this situation, Lippmann recommended the training of journalists in order to make them genuine professionals. In addition he urged establishment of research institutes for the "development of expert records and analysis."

In an article he wrote for *Century Magazine,* Lippmann pinpointed various obstacles which interfered with accurate news dissemination. The first of two barriers, as he discerned them, was the distortion that took place in the process of transmission. A second involved "preconceived notions" of both journalists and their readers. Thus a chain of misinformation originated when the reporter witnessing an event altered what he saw and the reader perverted the facts again while extracting meaning from the news. A persistent tendency on the part of the public to interpret everything in terms of "stereotypes" made matters even worse.

Accurate information was primary, Lippmann reasserted, but equally important was making the news intelligible. To do this it was necessary to explain events within the context of their historical setting. A journalist had to do more than just observe and record the facts. It was important that he know the meaning or significance of what had transpired. Only then could he report, in the fullest sense, what had actually happened. Since many facets of this problem remained unclear, Lippmann decided to pursue the subject further in a book length study.

Public Opinion (1922), the end product of considerable research and reflection, remains an outstanding work to this day. Sociologist C. Wright Mills described it in 1960 as the "definitive statement" in terms of "conception and theory." Viewing man in relation to his total environment, Lippmann interpreted individual response patterns psychologically. The "real environment" did exist, but it was "altogether too big, complex, and too fleeting for direct acquaintance" by the average citizen. When distorted news or "pseudo-facts" reached the ordinary person he responded to this stimuli by interpreting it within the context of his own narrow range of experience. Descriptive words could at best only symbolically approximate the larger world of reality. Individuals generally ignored the "real" world in favor of their own "pseudo-environment." The average person thus attached biased meaning to what he read. "Looking back we can see how indirectly we know the environment in which nevertheless we live," he explained. "We can see that the news of it comes to us now fast, now slowly; but that whatever we believe to be the true picture, we treat as if it were the environment itself." Resembling Plato's famous example of people in a cave, the newspaper reader's only contact with external reality came via inadequate word pictures of the outside world.

What conclusions could be drawn from this dilemma? If the common citizenry perceived reality so dimly, many liberals placed entirely too much confidence in the ability of a mass electorate to render competent judgments. Lippmann called this the myth of the "omnicompetent citizen," who barely understood what was happening in the world around him. "What reached him of public affairs, a few lines of print, some photographs, anecdotes, and some casual experiences of his own, he conceives through set patterns and recreates with his own emotions. He does not take his personal problems as partial samples of the greater environment but as a mimic enlargement of his private view." Certainly an uncritical faith in the collective wisdom of an amorphous public opinion was unwise. Hence, Lippmann reasoned, it was "no longer possible to believe in the original dogma of democracy; that the knowledge needed for the management of human affairs comes up spontaneously from the human heart."

Democratic decisions based on ignorance were pure folly. Likewise, it was distinctly improper to manipulate the electorate by providing it with propaganda. Instead people had to be moved to act wisely through "cultivated symbols" devised for them by their leaders. Complex issues thus simplified (but not twisted) could be understood. Although democracy meant popular sovereignty, the people were helpless without adequate leadership. "By mass action," Lippmann declared, "nothing can be constructed, devised, negotiated, or administered." While the American people could indeed ratify decisions or render mandates, they simply were not qualified to be the "prime mover" in a democracy. Good government depended upon imaginative leaders, effective communication, and an enlightened body of public opinion.

"Men have to go forth and study the world in order to govern it," Lippmann insisted. Empirical evidence—not outmoded theories and superficial reporting—was needed. The entire decision-making process was hampered by a paucity of reliable information. No news media filled this void. To correct this situation—i.e., the dearth of knowledge that prevented intelligent program planning—he suggested the establishment of centralized "intelligence bureaus." Through them data could be collected, analyzed, and distributed to policy makers and administrators. Such an innovation, Lippmann believed, would do much to adapt democracy to the exigencies of an industrial-urban society. The machinery of government had been devised during the simpler days of the republic, but now the agrarian-rural way of life had yielded to the complexities of a "Great Society." Contemporary problems could not be handled unless they could be understood and they could not be understood until they were analyzed. His prognosis was optimistic: "The social scientists will acquire his dignity and strength when he has worked out his method. He will do that by turning into opportunity the need among the men of the Great Society for instruments of analysis by which an invisible and most stupendous environment can be made intelligible."

Public Opinion was widely acclaimed as a brilliant work. Governor Frank Lowden of Illinois read it and reacted enthusiastically. He agreed with Lippmann that public officials themselves could not govern adequately without accurate knowledge. To make representative government more effective in his own state, Lowden had started a "Legislative Reference Bureau." It provided authoritative information to legislators quickly and conveniently. Writing to Lippmann, the Governor offered one criticism: "It might well be urged that an independent organization such as you propose would still further circumscribe the power of the head of the department. I am wondering if, in the first instance at any rate, it would not be sufficient to establish the permanent intelligence section that you propose in the several departments . . ." Lippmann's original proposal envisaged the creation of a "central agency," subsidized but not controlled by the government, to serve many departments. He responded to Lowden, "There is no one whose judgments on problems of administration I value so much as yours, and I think the criticism you make of my suggestions are fully justified."

When Frank Cobb died in 1923, Lippmann gained a greater measure of control over the editorial policy of the *New York World*. Using his power to alter the overall tone of the paper, excellence of style and accuracy in reporting were stressed. According to James W. Barrett, last managing editor of the *World* before Joseph Pulitzer sold it to Roy Howard in 1931 (when it became the *New York World Telegram*), Lippmann placed far more emphasis on solid news and "fine writing" than did his predecessor. Sans its previous tradition of sensationalism, the *World* was transformed into a newspaper of exceedingly high quality.

Lippmann certainly did not resemble most big city editors. Placing little stock in the fable that newspapermen should revel in the smell of printer's ink or enjoy the thunderous sound of presses, he conducted himself like a scholarly journalist. While many editors were hail-fellows-well-met, he was not. By temperament he was an introvert. He preferred solitude. With his detached demeanor and distaste for clamor or clatter, Lippmann worked quietly to elevate journalistic standards, mainly by setting an example with the excellence of his editorial writing. Poor reporting or sloppy writing irritated him. A newspaper to him was an instrument of enlightenment—not a toy or tool for publishers and advertisers. Each evening at his home on Long Island he reflected upon events of the day, then he wrote incisive editorials. Under his tutelage the *World* spoke authoritatively and with the voice of reason. Barrett, who was of the old slam-bang school, characterized his colleague as a "thinker, not a fighter." When he pushed for editorials with more punch in them, Lippmann told him, "Damn it—I can't be sounding bugle calls!"

The *World* continued to take up causes but it did not shriek its message in the vocabulary of a fourth grader nor did it rely upon emotional appeal. It was a partisan paper, openly supporting the Democrats, but it deftly combined wide news coverage with well reasoned editorials. Its staff was the best in the business. On the roster at one time or another were such notables as Ralph and Herbert Pulitzer, Herbert Bayard Swope, Allan Nevins, Arthur Krock, Charles Merz, Franklin P. Adams, Heywood Broun, Maxwell Anderson, and Ernest K. Lindley. The *World* still conjures up fond memories for those who remember the era when this great newspaper was in its heyday.

The arrest of Nicola Sacco and Bartolomeo Vanzetti in 1920 for murdering a paymaster while trying to pull off a holdup developed into a *cause célèbre* for liberals. General animosity toward immigrants and hysteria associated with the "Red scare" created an atmosphere where a fair trial was all but impossible. Found guilty and despite prolonged attempts to free them, the two were ultimately executed in 1927. The *World* and other liberal papers initiated a crusade to save the lives of these Italian-born anarchists. It appeared to many observers that presiding Judge Webster Thayer had prejudiced the outcome of their trial by his hostile attitude toward them. Lippmann wrote editorials on their behalf but cautioned against indiscriminate attacks on the legal system. He did not believe there was an appeal outside of the law. When the Lowell Commission reaffirmed the verdict, he wanted to drop the issue. The most flamboyant reporter on the *World* was Heywood Broun. Regarding Sacco and Vanzetti as martyrs, he wanted to keep their cause alive. At this point Lippmann used his influence to have Broun dropped from the staff. Although criticized for this disciplinary action he regarded Broun's attitude irresponsible. He thought there was a point where a continued assault of the courts would only serve to undermine the institutional stability of the nation.

Before coming to the *World*, Lippmann's political heroes had been Theodore Roosevelt and Woodrow Wilson. Each had left a distinct imprint upon his thinking. Now Alfred E. Smith became his new model for ideal political leadership. When Smith ran for the governorship of New York in 1922, he labeled this big city Democrat a "true reformer" and one who understood the urban masses. He praised Al Smith as the "real tested apostle of efficiency, economy, and scientific administration." The *World* aided materially in assisting the Governor to secure desirable legislation. It gave him constant editorial support and once in an open letter asked him to respond to the question: "What in his opinion are the reasons for refusal of the Republican Assembly to accept his governmental reorganization program, executive budget, and four year term for Governor?" His answer contained a sharp attack on the state G.O.P. for its obstruction and refusal to approve "consolidation and reorganization of all state activity." The purpose of these reforms, according to Smith, was to eliminate duplication, corruption, and bossism. This reply was printed up as a pamphlet and given wide circulation. It helped to build a groundswell of public support for the Governor's program.

Why was Lippmann attracted to Al Smith? He considered him a "great governor" who lived in "terms of today." The state of New York was, in a way, a microcosm of the nation. The upstate region was still rural and agrarian, and voted Republican; while New York City, on the other hand, represented the growing metropolis where a large polyglot population was centered. Al Smith, although inarticulate and uneducated in a cultural sense, understood the city. He grappled with problems that would later confront other states, particularly those stemming from the burgeoning growth of urban areas. Since state constitutions were more than often obsolete and legislatures disproportionately represented in favor of rural sectors, it was difficult for any governor to cope with the problems peculiar to cities. The New York Governor was already encountering difficulties borne of such outmoded state practices.

Because Smith was practical, non-doctrinaire, and knew politics, he sought workable solutions. His method of operation was to seek expert advice, insist on honesty, remain flexible in administration, and expedite reforms as effectively as possible. Lippmann saw in him the prototype of a new national leader for the Great Society. For this reason the *World* conducted a vigorous campaign for Al Smith in 1924 trying to secure for him the Democratic presidential nomination. His chances were enhanced materially when Madison Square Garden was chosen as the convention site. Lippmann urged the selection of Smith to be the party's nominee so that the "ideals for which he stands" may become "established in the nation." Outwardly circumstances seemed to favor the New York Governor, but a battle of unimagined proportions was in the making.

One might have assumed that Lippmann would have expressed sympathy for the candidacy of William G. McAdoo. Wilson's son-in-law and wartime cabinet member symbolized the link of Democrats with Progressivism. This Californian had amassed a fine record and gave every indication that he possessed eminent qualifications for the presidency. He was Director General of the nation's railroads during World War I; demonstrated expertise in fiscal matters while serving as Secretary of the Treasury; and headed the company which built the subway system in New York City. McAdoo was also well acquainted with agricultural problems, something which Smith knew very little about. To preserve party unity in 1920, he had withdrawn from the race; but this time he was convinced the nomination rightfully belonged to him.

McAdoo and Smith confronted one another not only as top contenders for the presidential nomination, but they represented rival factions within the Democratic party. McAdoo drew his heaviest delegate strength from the South, Midwest, and far West. Al Smith's power resided in the heavily populated East. But for the fact that the Californian had, as a lawyer, defended Edward L. Doheny in the Teapot Dome affair (which tarnished his reputation in the eyes of Progressives) and was endorsed by the Ku Klux Klan (which he repudiated), McAdoo might have won an early ballot victory. The two-thirds rule made it impossibel to obtain a nomination without a clear-cut preference on the part of the convention.

Neither combatant wanted to capitulate. Session after session passed and the deadlock continued. The convention which met from June 24 to July 10, polarized permanently into a Southern-agrarian-rural-dry bloc versus the Northern-industrial-urban-wet segment of the party. In view of this Lippmann editorialized, "As long as Mr. McAdoo remains a candidate, it is the duty of Governor Smith to resist him with all the power at his command." Insisting it was McAdoo and his followers who were "determined to rule the party or ruin it," he counseled the Smith forces to "stand firm if it takes all summer."

Lippmann's partisanship blinded him to such an extent he could not accurately assess McAdoo's qualifications. The floor fight, it was true, had brought into the open the bigotry that was present from the outset; but McAdoo was certainly victimized by his supporters. Lippmann hastily characterized the Californian to be a "gambler" and a politician with no "depth." He all but labeled him an opportunist with no talent whatsoever. "By experience as well as temperament he is an outsider who knows the inside wires," he contended, arguing: "He would win many skirmishes . . . but for the long strategic campaigning of democracy, it is hard to tell about him." The man he wrote off so quickly was later elected U.S. Senator from California.

On the ninety-third ballot Franklin D. Roosevelt, speaking for Al Smith, offered to withdraw the New York Governor's name if the Californian also retired from the contest. McAdoo felt this was his last opportunity and refused to budge. The roll calls continued amid the sweltering heat and inflamed passions. Aware by now that the deadlock was destroying the party's chances for victory, Lippmann switched from his own rigid position to propose Newton Baker, his wartime chief, as a compromise candidate. His editorial was ignored. With monotonous regularity the delegations continued on each call of the roll to reaffirm their support for Smith and McAdoo. Out of sheer desperation the convention, on the one hundred third ballot, bestowed the battered prize to John W. Davis. This relatively unknown corporation lawyer had for his running mate Charles W. Bryan, the Governor of Nebraska and a poor carbon copy of his renowned brother the three time nominee of the Democratic party.

After the disastrous convention adjourned, Lippmann wrote to Colonel House: "Davis was the only man to pull the whole thing out of the mud." That was wishful thinking since the Democratic nominee was mired down in the quicksand of party disunity. He could neither rally the party nor mount an effective campaign. When Robert M. LaFollette, the Progressive-minded Senator from Wisconsin, started a third party, it allowed Calvin Coolidge to win easy reelection. Lippmann confided to Senator Carter Glass, "John Davis has done as well as any man could do, but he hasn't had the kind of aggressive support which he deserves." That was, of course, the obvious outcome from the convulsive conflict experienced at Madison Square Garden. Why then did he aid and abet the schism by counseling against compromise until it was too late to salvage the election fortunes of the Democratic party?

A series of post-election articles, later collected with other essays and published as *Men of Destiny* in 1927, offered an explanation for his conduct. Lippmann claimed the "tragic conflict" that took place in New York City was more than a personal duel between Smith and McAdoo. Two totally different outlooks on life were contesting each other for supremacy. Al Smith, with his cigar and derby hat, personified the big city. The Southern-Midwest support for prohibition, with Klan backing, typified the virtues of the "village life." In a larger sense, he thought, the clash within the Democratic party symbolized the same struggle going on throughout the land. The "older American civilization of town and country" struggled to preserve itself from the inroads of the "new urban civilization." Representatives of rural sectors deeply believed the "clamorous life of the city should not be acknowledged as the American ideal." Lippmann felt this issue had to be settled. Problems of the Great Society were predominantly urban and political parties had to face that fact. The Democratic party's future lay in metropolitan areas, he reasoned, and urban leaders had to chart its course of action. The road of progress, as it were, existed on main thoroughfares of the East and not on Southern byways which led nowhere.

It was Al Smith whom Lippmann saw as the "new leader of democracy." The Governor of New York was truly a "man of destiny," because his career paralleled the rise of the city. Capturing the imagination of urban dwellers, the "Happy Warrior," as Franklin D. Roosevelt dubbed him, seemed to them the "incarnation of their own hope and pride." Popularity had been achieved "without the promise of the millennium, without a radical program, without appeal to their hatreds, without bribes and doles and circuses." Although a liberal, Smith was the "most powerful conservative in urban America." Why? "He believe[d] in the soundness of the established order and in the honesty of its ideals." His administrative abilities were well known. Lippmann attested:

"He has made his Republican opponents at Albany look silly, not because he was so progressive and they were so reactionary, but because he knew what he was doing and they did not . . .

"He is what a conservative ought to be always if he knew his business. He can operate with extraordinary skill, with fine deference to expert opinion, and with a sure instinct for realities . . ."

In sharp contrast to Governor Smith's model performance, Lippmann was incensed over the "corruption, complacency, paralysis, bunk and bigotry" of the Harding administration. His assessment of the man from Marion was totally negative. The Ohioan was portrayed as a small-town politician who simply could not cope with complex national problems. Scandals so tarnished Harding's image it was often overlooked that Progressivism persisted in his administration. Henry C. Wallace, a former Bull Mooser, was the Secretary of Agriculture. He enlisted the aid of both the President and the Farm Bloc to secure federal assistance for farmers. It would be Harding's successor who would enforce totally the Republican doctrine of negative government.

Calvin Coolidge was an intelligent man with high principles. His admirable traits carried to the extreme actually became vices. The Vermont-born Pressident possessed the village virtues of self-reliance, faith in God, and a stern belief that government should stay out of people's affairs. His Republicanism fancied a perfect fusion of laissez faire economics, Social Darwinism, and the Protestant ethic. That meant, in short, every individual was on his own without any expectation of help from anyone, least of all Uncle Sam. During Coolidge's tenure as President neither regulatory nor social welfare legislation had a ghost of a chance for passage. The taciturn man in the White House, when he did speak, uttered little moral sermonettes about the sanctity of work. He considered it a triumph to kill bills involving either expenditures or federal involvement. Lippmann evaluated the President in words that have become something of a classic in political literature:

"Mr. Coolidge's genius for inactivity is developed to a very high point. It is far from being an indolent inactivity. It is a grim, determined, alert inactivity which keeps Mr. Coolidge occupied constantly.

"Inactivity is a political philosophy and a party program with Mr. Coolidge, and nobody should mistake his unflinching adherence to it for a soft and easy desire to let things slide. . . .

"At a time when Puritanism as a way of life is at its lowest ebb among the people, the people are delighted with a Puritan as their national symbol."

Again in 1928 the *World* promoted Al Smith's candidacy for the presidency. Managing editor James Barrett simply put it this way: the paper "committed itself hook, line, and sinker" for him. Barrett added: "Swope, Ralph Pulitzer, Walter Lippmann, and Claude Bowers . . . [were] part of the brain trust affiliated with the Smith campaign." All were connected with the *World*. Herbert Bayard Swope, the executive editor, knew Al Smith personally and Walter Lippmann maintained close contacts with the Governor's aides, especially Judge Proskauer and Belle Moskowitz. The New Yorker won the Democratic nomination easily, but the campaign was an ordeal of bitterness he had not expected.

The boy from the Fulton Fish Market who made good could not overcome certain handicaps. Smith's Roman Catholicism and former affiliation with Tammany Hall made him suspect to those outside of the city. He could not defeat Herbert Hoover, the hero of Main Street, U.S.A. The Great Engineer was an Horatio Alger in politics; for he claimed truthfully to be an orphan who rose from rags to riches by his own efforts. Protestants accepted him (he was a Quaker) as did those favoring prohibition. Some Southerners who had never before voted Republican cast their ballot for him in the belief it would prevent the Pope's emissary from occupying the White House. Even though farmers were disgruntled, they could not bring themselves to support a man so alien to them. In the end the enmity of the 1924 Democratic convention was restaged on a national scale in 1928. Al Smith appealed to city people, but he simply could not win the confidence of those who dwelled in towns and hamlets across the nation.

The ugliness of the campaign appalled Lippmann. He had seen too much of it during the decade of the twenties. The uncertain intellectual climate of the times added to his genuine fear that the future course of America was to be one of trial and tribulation. Lippmann's own political thinking had traversed the "arc of liberalism," to use Arthur M. Schlesinger's phrase, and he found the stolid democracy of Al Smith to his liking. He neither resided, politically speaking, with rebels or reactionaries. His aim had been to create a liberal synthesis with a rationale that blended cultural conservatism with progressive liberalism. That dialogue with destiny proved to be an endeavor of supreme importance in an era where traditions were being dissolved with increased rapidity.

CHAPTER VI

TRADITION AND TRANSITION

Political triumph of conservatism obscured to some extent the underlying intellectual ferment of the twenties. Consecutive administrations by Harding, Coolidge, and Hoover evidenced a common acceptance by the average citizen of beliefs embodied in the work-thrift principle of Protestantism, individualism, adherence to a traditional moral code, and limited government. Generally speaking this religio-economic philosophy found expression in fundamentalism, anti-intellectualism, provincial localism, and even bigotry; but rival ideas that contradicted beliefs of the common people were gaining ascendency in urban centers of learning. The doctrine of evolution, for instance, had infiltrated into virtually every avenue of academic thought. Spawned by the Progressive movement, the intellectual revolution was now coming to fruition on college campuses. Liberal thinkers had devised a reformer's version of Darwinism and they were teaching it to the younger generation. But in the process of doing so, they were undermining the absolutes of the old order of things.

In many instances new ideas ran counter to dogmas of the past. The pragmatism of William James provided a utilitarian philosophy; the instrumentalism of John Dewey gave education a scientific methodology; sociological jurisprudence as projected by Louis Brandeis made law more responsive to social needs; Walter Rauschenbusch's Social Gospel theology sought to make religion relevant to contemporary life; and Thorstein Veblen's institutionalist economics encouraged detailed analyses of business practices. This philosophical rationale for liberalism held forth the possibility of remaking society. Hence the flux of evolutionary change received emphasis rather than the immutability of natural law. Relativism and reform were to be partners. Implicit in this new approach was the assumption that the social sciences would supply knowledge and techniques for remolding the social order. If human nature and institutions were malleable, and it was assumed they were, then the stage was set for drastic changes. Obviously the initial goal would be to liberate men from the bonds of ignorance, tradition, and ingrained habits of social behavior.

There was a profound paradox in all of this, historian David Noble has pointed out, since by undermining the authority of the old order

Progressives also subverted the ideals of the new. Shifting sands of relativism provided a precarious foundation for any type of orderly reform. The New Left of the 1960's carried the philosophical doctrines of this period to their ultimate extreme. Contemporary radicals have advocated drastic changes in the name of democracy while trampling many democratic traditions to attain them. By inviting anarchy, they doom their own values since they, by the same token, cannot exist without some stable foundation. These fundamental ideas that gave birth to this revolutionary activism had already pervaded the colleges during the 1920's.

Popular with the collegiate crowd were social critics such as the cynical H. L. Mencken, who savagely attacked boobs of the back woods and Sinclair Lewis, who ridiculed small town Babbitts. Mencken, whose magazine *Smart Set* captivated the rebel mentality, informed a friend in 1920: "As soon as I get rid of my editorial work I shall begin 'On Democracy' the damndest book ever written. Hitherto I have been polite, and even suave. Now for meat axe, blood on the moon, and three cheers for Pontius Pilate."

When this work came out as *Notes on Democracy*, it was reviewed by Walter Lippmann. Typically Mencken, the book was clever and dripping with vitriol. Despite its literary merit, Lippmann adjudged it to be the "subrational" bombast of an irresponsible critic. Its message did not relate "from mind to mind," he noted, but was a caustic outpouring from "viscera to viscera." Mencken's sophisticated cant did not impress him even though it did enthrall collegians. The rebel generation devoured Mencken's pungent prose, but Lippmann did not classify their idol as a first-rate thinker.

Only a few perceptive critics saw that unless precautions were taken the revolt against formal restraints might invite moral disintegration and social instability. Noteworthy among them were George Santayana, Irving Babbitt, and Paul E. More. Other works as *America and the Young Intellectual* (1921) by Harold Stearn and *The Modern Temper* (1929) by Joseph Wood Krutch likewise questioned the wisdom of indiscriminately destroying those values upon which moral authority rested. Paul More once complained to his friend, Professor Stuart P. Sherman of the University of Illinois, that after he had denounced "unrestrained democracy," liberal colleagues unfairly linked him with political reactionaries. Also when criticising pragmatism on philosophical grounds, he was "simply not understood" within the Liberal Establishment. Santayana, under whom Lippmann studied at Harvard, expressed disdain in 1913 over the "good-natured comedy" of liberalism. This cavil became deep concern by 1934 when he wrote in more somber tones: "But once the tradition-al order has been thoroughly destroyed . . . [by liberal thought] even the abundance of their independent sciences, without an ultimate authority to synthesize or interpret them, may become a source of bewilderment. Nothing may remain except a mechanical hurly-burly, moral disintegration, and intellectual chaos."

Lippmann fit in with this latter group. His evaluation of Sinclair Lewis, and the younger generation he represented, was based on his belief the novelist represented the "revolted Puritan" who remained "arrested in his adolescent rebellion." His characters were "free to be free," but were without any purpose in life. Their "taproots have been cut" depriving them of all spiritual nourishment. Lewis had not replaced the outmoded faiths of his characters with anything en-during, except in the case of Arrowsmith. For him the solace of pure science became a means of personal salvation. The "main question" in modern life, Lippmann asserted somberly, was to find for the masses an acceptable equivalent of those beliefs which were being destroyed. The satiric novels of Lewis offered no solution for that profound problem.

A widening dichotomy between the intelligentsia and the common man was the main topic of Lippmann's *American Inquisitors: A Com-mentary on Dayton and Chicago* (1928). He dealt specifically with the Scopes trial and the furor caused by William McAndrews' new interpretation of the American Revolution. In one case science con-tradicted religious beliefs and in the other history challenged naive patriotism. Abstaining from ridicule, Lippmann considered it a major responsibility of society's "civilized minority" not to treat the "whole world as a vaudeville stage." He did not intend to lampoon or lash out at human foibles. Employing the Socratic dialogue similar to the style used by Santayana in his *Dialogues in Limbo* (1920), he per-mitted the arguments of Williams Jennings Bryan and Clarence Dar-row to appear juxtaposed with writings of Thomas Jefferson and excerpts from the ancient wisdom of Socrates. The so-called "Monkey" Trial" and the principles involved were thereby placed in true his-torical perspective.

John T. Scopes, a high school teacher, stood accused in 1925 of teaching the theory of evolution in violation of a Tennessee statute. Converging on Dayton to take part in the trial were William Jennings Bryan, to help the prosecution, and the famous trial lawyer Clarence Darrow, to aid the defendant. Deeper issues existed than whether

Scopes had violated the law or not—neither Bryan or Darrow was capable of dealing with them. The Great Commoner did not qualify as a theologian and Darrow was no scientist. To be resolved were questions of great importance. Could scientific knowledge be reconciled with revealed religion? If the people were sovereign in a democracy, could they not protect their faith and morals by controlling what was taught in the schools? The trial was in many ways a test to see if reconciliation was possible. Yet it was treated by many as an *opera bouffe*. H. L. Mencken, reporting for the *Baltimore Sun,* had a field day casting his sarcastic barbs at what he called the simpletons of the South. Bryan was no doubt a senile has-been at this stage in his life, but Lippmann refused to poke fun at him or his ardent supporters.

He had observed William Jennings Bryan before at the 1924 Democratic Convention. The old political warrior fought against the wet plank and opposed all attempts to condemn the Ku Klux Klan. No one could deny that the old war horse from Nebraska battled valiantly for those causes which rural America believed in and he made no apologies for his stand. He was a courageous and sincere man who simply accepted the dogma of democracy literally, namely, that the people were sovereign. He meant it when he once wrote: "History teaches us that as a general rule, truth is found among the masses, emanates from them; a fact so potent that it has given rise to the old saying: 'vox populi vox Dei.' "

Lippmann blamed Bryan for turning the 1924 Democratic Convention into a fiasco. He called him the "most unsuccessful leader and the worst advisor the party has known in this generation." The former Populist was simply a political fundamentalist who as a "worldly democrat" (i.e. politician) took the teaching of Thomas Jefferson, the "mystical democrat," (i.e. theorist) too literally. What Jefferson wrote and what he did as President were two different things. In other words theoretical panegyrics about "the people" did not constitute a working program for democracy. "Owing to a confusion between the two," Lippmann deduced, "the mystical doctrine has been brutalized and made absurd, and the principle of majority rule has acquired an unction that protects it from criticism."

At Dayton Bryan again stoutly maintained the "people are sovereign" and when "speaking through their legislature" had a perfect right to prohibit the teaching of evolution in the public schools. Lippmann did not accept this argument, since ignorance compounded and given legal sanction still remained ignorance. He strove to raise the level of debate by treating Bryan's position rationally. Addressing himself to an educated audience he indicated his approach:

"But I have no advantage in winning a cheap victory just because the opposition has a poor lawyer. I propose, therefore, to ignore as irrelevant all the superficial absurdities of the attacks on learning, to ignore the discreditable motives which sometimes confuse the issue, to ignore above all the squalid ignorance which surrounds these controversies, and instead to examine them sympathetically, not in their weakness and folly, but in their strength."

"I propose, if you please, to be the Devil's Advocate. Need I remind you that the real title of that official is 'Promoter of the Faith.'"

The courtroom battle in Tennessee was basically, he reasoned, a "conflict between scholarship and popular faith." God-fearing folk of this Southern region, and it typified the feeling in other rural areas, did not want the religious beliefs of their children destroyed. Basically the exegetical methods used by their clergy, which was by and large unlearned, involved a literal interpretation of the sacred Scriptures. It never occurred to them their system of hermaneutics might be erroneous or that science had anything to teach them. They advised their parishioners to protect themselves from heretical ideas by securing passage of laws prohibiting the teaching of evolution. Sophisticated urbanites overlooked the real agony of rural folk which was the imposition of alien thought upon them when they were not prepared for it. From their point of view they were to be pitied not pilloried.

Because the nation was no longer a small "homogeneous community," Lippmann acknowledged that no general body of commonly held beliefs could endure as before. Uncritical acceptance of cherished convictions, whether they were true or not, was not possible in a land comprised of a polyglot population extending from ocean to ocean. Cultural advances made it inevitable for the intellectual and common man to part ways. The "redneck" farmer of the South vented his frustration by attacking all learning while the man of letters often reacted with disdain toward the "great unwashed public." Yet, anti-intellectualism versus intellectual snobbery resolved nothing.

The "relationship between faith and reason and authority," Lippmann warned, constituted an area of inquiry in which the enlightened minority had to "strike a prudent balance" when challenging commonly held notions. Simple people could not be treated as plebian trash nor was it proper to ridicule what they held sacred. Responsibility devolved upon intellectual leaders to help make new knowledge compatible with the old. Societal stability depended upon continuity and this was possible when change was made palatable to the broad masses. Socrates had also contested the religious beliefs of his generation, but he yielded to custom and drank the hemlock. He died rather than to subvert the laws of Athens. Contemporary critics could learn from this example. They too should be tolerant of the less informed.

The leadership principle which Lippmann had come to accept in the political arena was now applied to the intellectual realm. The "enduring work of the world" was done only by the enlightened few. Their "excellence is quiet" compared to the clamor of the many, he contended, "but it persists." Lest brilliant minds forget, he reminded them of the necessity for empathy with the uninformed populace. Very few men could strip away all myths and still find meaning in life. Only the "utterly self-sufficient and disinterested men" of any era could "endure complete freedom of thought." This creative minority uncovered truth by destroying cherished myths. Allowing Socrates to speak for him, he explained why scholars aroused fear and resentment:

"The point is that a man can only begin to be disinterested when he has ceased to be hungry and uncomfortable and frightened.

"I was free because I wanted so little . . . but people are never free who want more than they can have.

"Their wants create worries, then worries create prejudices, their prejudices demand guarantees, and under freedom of thought nothing is guaranteed."

The biblical injunction "Ye shall know the truth and the truth shall make you free" was a supplication to attain spiritual maturity. This meant neither the retention of a kindergartner's faith nor total rejection of all values which transcended the material. Lippmann thought too many Americans were already "living without any sense of the whole." Pushed off their religious rock of ages they drifted aimlessly amid a sea of spiritual uncertainty. Thus they, he observed, were forced to rely upon fads, ersatz religion, and "improvised ideas." What was needed was a grand synthesis. "Men of genius," imbued with a sense of noblesse oblige, should rise to the occasion and devise a rationale for modernity. Spiritual security was as necessary as social security, and during the twenties both were being undermined.

The *Phantom Public* (1927) was an in-depth examination of some consequences of unrestrained democracy. Critics condemned it as a denigration of democracy, but it was part of Lippmann's overall investigation of the transilient character of the twenties. As one who had modified his philosophical liberalism, he became more cognizant of recondite pitfalls inherent in "one grand system of evolution and progress." Scholars of the liberal persuasion seemed oblivious to the lack of historical evidence that any systematized version of man's ultimate perfectibility possessed validity. Certainly the moral transformation of the 1920's offered no consolation of human betterment. He told liberals outright that they were equally credulous with William Jennings Bryan in relying on the innate goodness of *the people*. Their fidelity to the progress theme, believing that man was ever evolving toward perfection, contradicted history. In point of fact, the collective wisdom of the masses contained no mystical element of truth and no utopia awaited mankind. Lippmann jolted liberals with the assertion:

"These various remedies, eugenic, educational, ethical, populist and socialist, all assume that either the voters are inherently competent to direct the course of affairs or that they are making progress toward such an ideal.

"I think it is a false ideal . . . An ideal should express the true responsibilities of its subject. When it does not it perverts the true possibilities.

"The ideal of the omnicompetent, sovereign citizen is, in my opinion, such a false ideal. It is unattainable. The pursuit of it is misleading. The failure to achieve it has produced the current disenchantment."

Liberals were prone to embrace the doctrine of popular sovereignty wholeheartedly when their ideas coincided with those of the electorate, but they frequently reacted to unfavorable decisions at the ballot box with anger and dismay. It was, after all, the will of the people that placed Harding and Coolidge in the White House. Citizens of Tennessee by and large favored the anti-evolutionary law. What Lippmann discerned was the existence of much confusion as to just what constituted public opinion. Who were "the people" and what made up "the public"? It was self-defeating for Woodrow Wilson when he made his appeal to "all mankind." That would presume a "single soul" for an abstract body that had no concrete existence. Such an approach, he avowed, was the "equivalent to an appeal to nobody." The public, in reality, was a nebulous, fictive *corpus* that served neither as an instrument for divine will nor as a dispenser of worldly wisdom. He elaborated: "I hold that this public is a mere phantom. It is an abstraction . . . The public is not, as I see it, a fixed body of individuals. It is merely those persons who are interested in an affair and can affect it only by supporting or opposing the actors."

The actors who dominated the political stage were the "ruling insiders" or leadership group; while the "whole public," so called, were the "outsiders" or "spectators of action." The voters could, when all was said and done, only choose between the "few alternatives" placed before them. For whatever reason ballots were cast the electorate could not "create, administer, . . . [or] perform the act they . . . [had] in mind." From previous studies on public opinion, which were confirmed by events of the twenties, Lippmann was convinced basic responsibility for moving any nation ahead rested with dynamic leaders. "The burden of carrying on the work of the world, of inventing, creating, [and] executing," he argued, "lies not upon public opinion but upon those who are responsibly concerned as agents in the affair."

There was a strong Hamiltonian flavor to his words when he insisted, "The public must be put in its place, so that it may exercise its own powers, . . . so that each of us may live free of the trampling and the roar of a bewildered herd." It was not from some spontaneous will of the people that concrete plans could be made or carried out; and his conclusion was decisive: "We cannot, then, think of public opinion as a conserving or creating force directing society to clearly conceived ends, making deliberately toward socialism or away from it, towards nationalism, an empire, a league of nations or any other doctrinal goal. . . ."

Voters affirmed or rejected, but could not originate policy. Leaders like Al Smith formulated plans and sought public support. Once elected, the New York Governor excelled in administration. He came to grips with concrete issues in a practical, down-to-earth manner. No one reveled in Smith's rhetoric. It contained no manifestos or promises of an impending paradise. He gave the people clear-cut choices. Lippmann admired Smith's practical approach in solving varied and complex problems of the day. There were no solutions hidden in grand formulas. Perhaps with Wilson's mistakes in mind, he declared the "liberal philosophy has an air of unworldliness" since it too often sought "to escape from particular purposes into some universal purpose."

When Lippmann declared "I set no store on what can be done by public opinion and the action of the masses," it appeared as if he was advocating some type of elitest rule. Was the electorate irrelevant or the desires of the people so undiscernible as to be impotent? For him to even suggest it seemed undemocratic. No doubt he overstated his case to make a point. His criticism was leveled at liberals for their doctrinaire creed and their subsequent failure in deeds. If, on the one hand, liberal thinkers were destroying the basis for uniform beliefs, then a corollary action involved the formulation of new values. Without a public consensus the politics of government would falter and ultimately fail. His concern focused on the inability of intellectuals to furnish positive leadership not only in the realm of politics but in the field of adjusting social mores to the exigencies of an age of science. Since man cannot live without moral guides, which involved governing oneself, he decided to make this the topic of his next book.

A Preface to Morals (1929), as Mary L. Coolidge wrote in *The Journal of Philosophy*, rendered a "vivid description of the dilemma of contemporary man." Succored by science and technology the denizens of crowded cities surrounded by marvels of man's inventive genius were slowly being dispossessed of spiritual certainty and meaningful moral codes. An alienation process was already discernible in the twenties. Lippmann observed a flood of fads, flowering of bohemian life in Greenwich Village, the self-imposed exile of expatriates, and general insecurity manifested by excesses of all kinds. Mad pursuit for prosperity did not seem to satiate the desire for material things but definitely created a spiritual void. The "acids of modernity" had dissolved the bonds of tradition; but, unfortunately, had substituted nothing but "trivial illusions" for the "majestic faiths" destroyed. Addressing his readers as a cultural conservative, he penned this lament:

"But the promises of liberalism have not been fulfilled. We are living in the midst of that vast dissolution of ancient habits which the emancipators believed would restore our birthright of happiness.

"It is evident to us that their prophecies were pleasant phantasies which concealed the greater difficulties that confront them, when having won their freedom to do what they wish . . . they are full of contrary moods and do not know what they wish to do."

Lippmann placed a goodly portion of the blame for the change in morality on the relativism of liberal thought. Man was liberated only to flounder in his new freedom. Could science be substituted for religion? It was the "most reliable method of knowledge" yes, but its temporary truths did "not pretend to justify the ways of God to man." The eternal verities derived from the Judaic-Christian tradition had once provided a "single destiny" and a "point of reference" for judging the "relative value of competing ideals." That comfort and criteria was being destroyed. Was he advocating a revival of orthodoxy? Not at all. His appraisal of revealed religion was incisive:

"Its dogma, as Mr. Santayana once said, is insensibly understood to be nothing but myth, its miracles nothing but legend, its sacraments mere symbols, its bible pure literature, its liturgy just poetry, its hierarchy an administrative convenience, its ethics an historical accident, and its whole function simply to lend a warm mystical aureole to human culture and ignorance.

"The modern man does not take his religion as a real account of the constitution, the government, the history, and the actual destiny of the universe. With rare exceptions his ancestors did."

If God were dead, philosophically speaking, then the spiritual foundation of moral authority had vanished. Purely supernatural aspects of the old orthodoxy had been annihilated, Lippmann would agree, but this did not negate the need for a true "religion of the spirit." History, not science or revelation, held out hope for mankind. The "wisdom of the past" supplied guidelines for a harmonious life. Had not both sage and saint spoken of self restraint? Aristotle had proclaimed the virtue of the golden mean and St. Paul had enjoined men to discipline carnal desires. Lippmann agreed that "Renunciation of appetites as a condition of happiness" was a truism borne of long experience. "When men can no longer be theists," he asserted, "they must, if they are civilized, become humanists."

Humanism offered, so thought Lippmann, the essentials for the restoration of moral restraints. What specific code of conduct could guide the behavior of men? To answer this, he drew on the teachings of Santayana and the philosophy of classical antiquity to propound the principle of "disinterestedness." This was to be the basic tenet of a high religion based on reason. Socrates, Lucretius, the Sophists, and many wise men of the past perceived that "to become detached from one's passions and to understand them consciously is to render them disinterested." That thought was implicit in Plato's dictum "know thyself" and among contemporary philosophers the concept was revived by George Santayana.

In his multi-volume work, *The Life of Reason or Phases of Human Progress,* Santayana developed the theme that true evolutionary progress involved the transition from a primitive reliance on sense data and impulse to the higher stage of rationalism; and, finally, a progressional leap to the highest realm of all—that of the imagination or life of the spirit. This spiritual naturalism, or "metaphysics of detachment," would allow men to attain inner harmony by controlling their desires. Here was a humanistic philosophy that took cognizance of evolution while recognizing the necessity for a life of the spirit.

Drawing heavily upon the teachings of his former mentor in philosophy, Lippmann formulated his own version of a rationally disciplined humanism. The concept of disinterestedness was a sublime ideal and it afforded the man of reason a profound moral precept beyond mere pragmatism. It was the type of high religion, he declared, that announced the "discovery . . . men can enter into the realm of the spirit when they have outgrown all childishness." Lippmann advocated a rational religion for those who could no longer accept the older and outmoded dogmas. It was, obviously, too abstruse for any but a few; and even then the redemptive quality inherent in orthodox beliefs was missing. He also overlooked what neo-orthodox theologians had not. And that was the natural perversity or recalcitrance of natural man (original sin), which corrupted even the best of human intentions. Lippmann nevertheless concluded his presentation in *A Preface to Morals* by stating: "We can begin to see, I think, that the evidence upon the theory that the sages have prophesied as high religion, what psychologists delineate as mature personality, and the disinterestedness which the Great Society requires for its practical fulfillment, are all of a piece, and are the basic elements of a modern morality. I think the truth lies in this theory."

George W. Howgate, Santayana's biographer, claimed Walter Lippmann and the poet T. S. Eliot (also of the Harvard class of 1910) were both true intellectual disciples of the Latin philosopher. "I can see more of Santayana in Lippmann than in Eliot," he contended, since: "He echoes certain principles of his former teacher, in general, . . . the need for a reconstructed morality which will be true to nature and yet find ample room for the ideal aspiration of man. Lippmann's 'high religion' or 'religion of the spirit' is very close to Santayana's 'religion of disillusion,' with some of the overtones of his 'spiritual life.' "

Because of the significant nature of Lippmann's work, Henry S. Canby, the editor of *The Saturday Review of Literature*, asked Santayana to review *A Preface to Morals*. The aged philosopher, then residing in Rome, assented readily. The "natural basis and rational principle of morals" as devised by Lippmann, he wrote, were "perfectly clear." He agreed wholeheartedly with that premise. What was not clear to him was how this ethical system could be applied to the

Great Society. It was not a religion for a materialistically oriented society. An urban environment and increased technology created a host of wants. His praise was tempered with some skepticism: "I can't help distrusting the apparent alliance of his 'high religion' with the material pressure of these undirected powers."

In rebuttal, Lippmann defended his attempt to devise a synthesis whereby traditional values and modern knowledge were reconciled. His former tutor was, seemingly, more intent on preserving the purity of an abstract system than in rendering it useful for contemporary man. His point was well taken in that Santayana's philosophy was known only to a very few. He had never made any attempt to popularize his ideas. "All I say is that if the present type of civilization is to fulfill itself," Lippmann wrote in *The Saturday Review of Literature*, "it will have to recognize as its ideal pattern of conduct the disinterestedness of the mature self-disciplined leader."

Santayana was perturbed by the reaction of his onetime teaching assistant. "I was a little surprised at the tone of Lippmann's reply to my article," he indicated to Canby in confidence, "I thought he would be pleased, and certainly I had liked his book very much; but apparently he requires us all to share his vague hopes of 'high religious' worldly organizations, and is angry if we are attached to some different political ideal." Whatever irritation he harbored was quickly forgotten when Lippmann visited him in 1929. They talked philosophy for hours and, according to Santayana's long-time secretary, Daniel Cory, the two men remained lifelong friends.

When the *World* was sold in 1931, Lippmann accepted an offer from Ogden and Helen Reid to write a regular column for the *New York Herald Tribune*, then a distinctly conservative but well edited newspaper that generally supported Republican party candidates at election time. Friends advised him not to join its staff. He did so with the understanding that complete editorial freedom would be accorded him; thus was born his famous "Today and Tomorrow" column. The name was one he used back in 1915 in a series of articles for the defunct *Metropolitan Magazine*. "T & T," as it was known in the trade, became a syndicated column that appeared in more than a hundred newspapers with a reading audience of some six million. In 1938, when Lippmann changed his residence from New York to the nation's capital, "T & T" helped usher into existence what has been called the "Golden Age" of newspaper columnists.

The move to the *Herald Tribune* was symbolic of Lippmann's shift from philosophical liberalism to cultural conservatism and indicative of an intent to be less of an activist and more of a detached observer. He explained his new stance in an address before the Phi Beta Kappa chapter at Columbia University (he had won his own key in 1910). The talk, given in 1932, dwelt on the theme that an impalpable barrier existed between the "demands of the contemplative life and the active life." If one were a partisan in politics, it would be, he professed, much more difficult to be a genuine patron of the "invisible empire of reason." Many academicians disagreed with him. They claimed one's political participation need not interfere with scholarly objectivity. That would mean, to use an example, an historian could treat dispassionately the administration of President for whom he had campaigned.

It was Lippmann's belief that a columnist must constantly strive for objectivity and, like Caesar's wife, be above suspicion. For his self-appointed role as *jurisconsultus* for the people, he laid down the following prescription:

"The world will go on somehow, and more crises will follow. It will go on best, however, if among us there are men who have stood apart, who refused to be anxious or too much concerned, who were cool and inquiring, and had their eyes on a longer past and a longer future. By their example they can remind us that the passing is only a moment; by their loyalty they will have cherished those things which only the disinterested mind can use."

Chapter VII

THE NEW DEAL

The troubled 1930's brought financial ruin, economic collapse, and misfortune to millions. Conservatism became disgraced by 1932 and the very name of President Hoover was used to christen "Hooverville" hovels that grew up on vacant lots. Passions ran high, first against the G.O.P. and then in favor of the New Deal and Franklin D. Roosevelt. In this milieu of misery it was difficult to obtain objective political analysis of any kind, especially from liberal commentators. They felt confident reform and recovery would take place only after reactionary policies of Republicans had been reversed. Intellectuals and crackpots alike proposed many plans for refashioning society. It was an era when almost any idea could get a hearing if it but promised the return of prosperity.

Commenting critically on the events of the day, Lippmann made no attempt to placate either liberals or conservatives. In a period of extreme partisanship, his independent stance alienated some and attracted others. British Laborite, Harold Laski, complained privately to Justice Holmes that Lippmann had become "one of the main voices of American conservatism." The eminent literary critic Edmund Wilson addressed an open letter to his former friend containing the reprimand, "You are a long way now from the days when you wrote for the *New Republic*. . . ." William Allen White, on the other hand, applauded him by writing, "Your leadership in these days is unquestioned among the people who think." This nationally known editor of the *Emporia Gazette*, who had himself been an outstanding leader in the Progressive movement, respected Lippmann's judgment. Bernard A. Weisberger rendered yet another opinion of Lippmann's role as a critic. The Washington columnist was, it appeared to him, "Always proudly independent but always seeming to brood magisterially over a political scene in which the actors did not understand their roles nearly as well as did Lippmann himself."

In his columns of the 1930's and a 1931 publication entitled *Notes on the Crises*, Lippmann chided Hoover for his many failures. But he also censured those pejorative pessimists who wanted to abandon capitalism prematurely. History, he explained, moved in patterns of "crisis and renewal." The catastrophic nature of the depression was

an incontestable fact. Economic breakdown was "not a collapse of our
system," went his argument, rather it constituted a "furious purge"
of its ills. Those radicals who lauded the Soviet Union as the only
"land of the future" were deluding themselves. Surcease of prosperity
was caused by human mistakes made during the last decade and recovery was possible when those errors were rectified. All was not hope-
less by any means.

What caused the Great Depression? A whole array of faulty postwar
policies set the stage for the debacle. To begin with, America's refusal
to join the League of Nations had contributed to European instability.
Lippmann listed other causes such as the incredibly high Hawley-
Smoot Tariff of 1930, refusal to cancel Allied war debts, lack of action
in stabilizing international currency, and an overall withdrawal into
isolationism which helped to weaken the economic foundation of the
Western world. Being a creditor nation, he averred, the United States
had been "extracting tribute" from Europe without fulfilling corollary
responsibilities. Lowering tariffs and working for international adjustments would have stimulated world trade and provided a base for
prosperity. America's attitude on reparations and war debts, he aptly
described, was the "trademark of a fool." They should have been can-
celed immediately after the war.

In *A New Social Order*, a small volume published in 1933, Lippmann
predicted a trend away from the "loose, individualistic, and acquisi-
tive democracy" of the previous quarter century toward a "planned
and managed" economy of the future. He agreed that compelling reasons existed for bringing to fruition a more "ordered society" and yet
he made it clear this should not involve "drafting five year plans."
Regulatory measures were needed to control the chaotic business cycle
and reforms were needed for economic stability. Still he feared the
pendulum of planning would swing too far toward some form of collective regimentation. Recovery and reconstruction in a democracy could
not be achieved by emulating either the Soviet Union or fascist states;
it would come, he predicted, through "long effort, by trial and error"
and via the "hard discipline of experience."

Lippmann's assessment of the New Deal varied over the years, as
did his evaluation of Franklin D. Roosevelt. He advised the President
in 1933 to use the "widest administrative and ministerial powers possible under the Constitution." Latitude for experimentation was needed.
When F.D.R. utilized executive power to the utmost he applauded the
action. Approval was given to such bold ventures as the Agricultural
Adjustment Act, the National Recovery Act, and monetary devalu-

ation. Although he would have preferred use of an international method of solving the depression, he defended the "national approach." Circumstances warranted it. Whereas the New Deal seemed radical, Lippmann considered it merely a "lineal descendent of the reforming enthusiasm of Theodore Roosevelt's New Nationalism and Woodrow Wilson's New Freedom." F.D.R. was proceeding on a course well within the American political tradition.

Nevertheless an apprehensive feeling gripped Lippmann over the possibility that Franklin D. Roosevelt might at any time depart completely from the free enterprise system. This haunting fear, which was actually groundless, may have been induced by the plethora of radical proposals then in circulation. Many intellectuals were captivated by the roseate promise of total scientific planning. Such works as *A Planned Society* by George Soule; *The Economy of Abundance* by Stuart Chase; *Technics and Civilization* by Lewis Mumford; *New Frontiers* by Henry A. Wallace; and *The Battle for Democracy* by Rexford G. Tugwell all appeared to be ominous indicators of an imminent departure from capitalism. In point of fact they did not influence F.D.R.'s thinking. Lippmann had compounded his worries by misinterpreting what Wallace said, since the Secretary of Agriculture at no time favored the idea of collective farms; and by overestimating Tugwell's importance, even though the latter was close to Roosevelt. Tugwell, an original member of Roosevelt's Brain Trust, was a prolific writer but had little actual influence on the course of the New Deal. Much radical rhetoric camouflaged the cautious character of the President's policies. Roosevelt at no time thought in terms other than of saving the capitalistic system.

The *Method of Freedom*, written by Lippmann in 1934, was his version of what the New Deal ought to be. Because a copy was sent to him, Roosevelt was aware of this appraisal. Lippmann's main line of argument was that the "true method of freedom" lay in implementing a "compensated economy." He was sure an application of John Maynard Keynes' theories were in order. The British economist popularized the concept of government spending to stimulate the economy. This meant federal intervention for the purpose of furthering the general welfare even though the national debt increased. Lippmann pointed out that this practice also had American antecedents. Alexander Hamilton advocated it in the 1700's. Laissez-faire minded Herbert Hoover had, in fact, anticipated the New Deal with the Reconstruction Finance Corporation and the Federal Farm Board. "The modern state cannot endure unless it insures its people their

standard of life," Lippmann reasoned, therefore "compensatory policies" were actually conservative in nature. They were aimed at insuring the preservation of capitalism by reforming the economic system
through democratic means.

The temptation to resort to undemocratic procedures in an effort to
hasten recovery was strong, he admitted, but a "Compensated Economy or Free Collectivism" stood in contradistinction to the "Directed
Economy or Absolute Collectivism." The former was indigenous to the
American scene, argued Lippmann, while the latter was alien and
dangerous. It was difficult for him to specify just when the line had
been passed from a compensated to the directed approach. Defining
the basic precepts which should guide reform, he wrote: "Its ideal is
to prevent excess; its general principle is not to impose a social order
conceived by officials but to maintain in a changing order, worked out
by the initiative and energy of individuals, a golden mean."

A compendium of Lippmann articles published in 1935 as *The New
Imperative*, once again viewed the New Deal sympathetically in overall terms. Here he developed the theme that whereas the "old imperative" of government involved defense of national interests abroad, the
"new imperative" imposed an obligation to protect the domestic
economy. This intervention was justified both as a means of regulating abuses and stimulating business. Welfare and public projects were
considered desirable as devices for serving the needs of the people.
Although the arch-conservative Liberty League denied the validity of
his assumption, he believed it was salutary that "the business cycle
has been placed within the orbit of government, and for laissez faire
and individual adjustment and liquidation there has been substituted
conscious management by the political state." No longer would the
federal government allow the chaos of capitalism to disrupt the national economy.

In 1936 Lippmann surprised Roosevelt, to put it mildly, by coming
out for the election of Alfred M. Landon. Before going into the reasons
for this drastic decision, let us examine one of his major works, *An
Inquiry into the Principles of the Good Society* (1937). Again, his
concern for reform within traditional guidelines prompted him to elaborate upon the historical constructs of the liberal philosophy and the
necessity for adhering to them. At the outset he renounced his earlier
acceptance of certain liberal tenets which ignored tradition and continuity. He admitted:

"The general scheme of the human future seemed fairly clear to
me . . . [in 1914]. So in my *Preface* [*to Politics*] I assumed without

question that in a regime of personal liberty each nation could, by the increasing exercise of popular sovereignty, create for itself gradually a spaciously planned and intelligently directed social order.

"For more than twenty years I have found myself writing about critical events with no better guide than the hastily improvised generalizations of a rather bewildered man. . . . My personal confusion reflected the fact that in the modern world there is a great schism; those who seek to improve the lot of mankind believe they must undo the work of their predecessors."

Lippmann then presented his case for what he called "historic liberalism." It constituted another step in his attempt to fuse progressivism with cultural conservatism. By tracing the origins of American political and economic liberty back to their early English antecedents, he aptly demonstrated their reliance on the ideas and actions of Adam Smith, John Stuart Mill, Edmund Burke, and William Gladstone. The economic theories of Smith and Mill held that free enterprise unencumbered by government restrictions was conducive to industrial greatness. It was the Liberal party in England which linked economic liberty to personal freedom, thus furthering the cause of democracy. From then onward their mutual development was interrelated and intertwined as part of the fabric of history. The British experience proved that change was best when it took place slowly. Stability was preserved when both constitutional and common law were modified gradually to accommodate them to the legal prerequisites of an evolving industrial age. Since free enterprise and democratic institutions had developed simultaneously, while adjusting constantly to the dynamics of the industrial revolution, they were an integral part of the same historical process. "So it is not accident," he concluded "that the division of labor, common law, the ideal of social justice, the restraint of prerogative and privileges, the conception of international law and of peace as the paramount policy of states should have all evolved together in the same regions of the earth."

The contours of Western culture contained many facets and yet possessed a distinct form. Variance in developmental patterns merely constituted "different aspects of the same momentous changes in which men have been passing out of their primitive self-sufficiency into the intricate interdependence of the Great Society." Complexity increased and institutional accommodations had taken place together with economic practices, politics, and juridical procedure; thus, in his judgment, capitalism, democracy, and the tradition of common law were

"organically related and must stand or fall together, because they are
different aspects of the same way of life."

Communist and fascist systems of the twentieth century were actually premised on reactionary principles, reasoned Lippmann, because
Karl Marx, Adolf Hitler, and Benito Mussolini (he had a personal
interview with the latter in Rome), had misinterpreted the dynamics
of the industrial revolution. By coping with their domestic problems
through totalitarian means, maintained Lippmann, dictators were not
moving forward but were returning to older repressive methods.
Liberalism had freed men from the "authoritarian collectivism" of
monarchies and mercantilism, yet these leaders insisted upon regi-
menting their populations through total planning. They were, in his
judgment, guilty of propagating a "gigantic heresy" in terms of the
liberal "tradition of the West."

Any totalitarian regime must by its very nature presume a "static
and inert" society, since the omnipotent state must arbitrarily control
all human endeavor. Such an assumption, warned Lippmann, was
totally "unsuited to the highly dynamic character of the industrial
revolution." Regimentation was in fact a reversal of the historic trend
toward more individual freedom. Stifling controls would only serve to
debilitate a vibrant society and impede its normal development. Doing
away with personal initiative was the "rock on which the whole conception founders." The lessons of history proved, he thought, that the
road of progress did not lie in returning to the "heresies of absolutism,
authority, and the dominion of man by man." Historical liberalism,
on the other hand, opened the avenue for future advancement because
it was a superior political system. "No government planned, no political authority directed, the material progress of the past four centuries,
or the increasing humanity which has accomplished it. It was by a
stupendous liberation of the minds and spirits and conduct of men
that a world-wide exchange of goods and services and ideas was
promoted. . . ."

Was Lippmann then advocating a return to a laissez faire type of
capitalism? No, he was also critical of those wanting to maintain a
pristine liberalism. They made the fatal error of adhering rigidly to
a set of abstract principles and thereby ignored the historical transformation of the liberal philosophy. Herbert Spencer's theories had
created a "hypothetical social order." This famous Social Darwinist
claimed the government should not regulate the economy by interfer-
ing with personal freedom. There never was a time when capitalism
lay completely outside the perimeter of law or governmental legisla-

tion. For businessmen to claim immunity from regulation, and to do
so in the name of liberty, denied the realities of history. Arguments for
keeping capitalism totally unregulated were both false and fallacious,
he explained:

"Were there any question about the thesis that capitalism developed in a context of historic law and not in a free realm of Nowhere,
the conclusive evidence would be found in the fact that the substance
of law has been continually modified.

"What is it that the courts and legislatures have been doing these
hundred and fifty years if not defining, amending, and supplementing
the laws of property, contract, and corporations, and of human relations . . . they have never been letting alone [i.e. *laissez faire*], on the
theory that they are not within the jurisdiction of the state. . . .

"Now the progress of liberation was, I am convinced, halted by the
wholly false assumption that there was a realm of freedom in which
the exchange economy operated and, apart from it, a realm of law
where the state had jurisdiction."

Obviously Lippmann was neither defending rugged individualism
nor equating historical liberalism with this philosophy. He believed
economic conservatives, as distinct from his own brand of cultural
conservatism, had perverted the tenets of historical liberalism by fus-
ing classical economics with Social Darwinism to defend exploitive
methods. That conceptual system was then frozen into immobility and
falsely cloaked with immutability by linking it with natural law. The
only "really inexorable law of modern society," he countered, was "the
law of the industrial revolution." Conditions made it imperative for
democratic institutions to adjust to societal changes caused by industrialism. Translated into political reforms this meant approval of such
innovations as Keynsian monetary theories, collective bargaining,
social security, and federal action to stimulate the economy. Lippmann, by the way, knew John Maynard Keynes on a personal basis.
The brilliant economist spent many hours at his Woodley Road residence in Georgetown as a welcomed guest. One of the interesting items
in the category of memorabilia in the Walter Lippmann Collection at
Yale University is an old cloth cap his British visitor inadvertently
left behind.

To reactionary conservatives then, Lippmann admonished, "Liberalism is the normal philosophy of the men who live in the Great
Society"; to impetuous liberals overly eager to impose reform by force,
he warned, the "logic of liberalism" equalled the "logic of law over
men." Whether those drastic changes included dreams of a planned

society or the destruction of democratic institutions to allow for total freedom (which would be anarchy), both violated the basic principle of orderly transition inherent in the Anglo-American tradition. "The denial that men may be arbitrary in human transactions," he vowed, "*is* the higher law." Monarchs submitted to law thus abrogating absolutism and tyranny as a legitimate system in the West. Why then return to it? Modern man as the legatee of a valuable heritage has a "moral commitment" to preserve "human rights" even while working to reconstruct society. What he said, in the final analysis, was that progressive change could neither be stopped by doctrinaire roadblocks or promulgated by arbitrary decrees. It had to evolve within the historical confines of the American way of life.

In retrospect, on a CBS television program in 1960, Lippmann admitted his attitude toward the New Deal had been an ambivalent "in-and-out feeling." An apparent vagary was due, he explained, to his dislike of certain aspects of the Roosevelt program. Those measures involving excessive planning were labeled "very bad" and features which "had to do with compensated economy" were considered "very good." In a quantitative analysis of T & T (counting articles for and against), David E. Weingast concluded that seventy-one per cent of them were critical of the New Deal compared to fifty-one per cent which expressed adverse attitudes toward the President. Favorable response to the New Deal constituted only nine per cent of the columns while Roosevelt got eleven per cent. Another twenty per cent of the content expressed a neutral feeling toward the New Deal as did thirty-eight per cent with regard to Roosevelt. If this type of evaluation has validity, since it does not take into account any qualitative criteria, then it did reflect a predilection on Lippmann's part to be critical of both President Roosevelt and his overall domestic program.

His personal reaction to F.D.R. was mercurial to say the least. In 1924, when the young Roosevelt fought for Al Smith's nomination, Lippmann hailed him as a "gallant and generous figure." After the election of 1928, in which Roosevelt won the gubernatorial race while Smith lost the presidency, he wrote admiringly: "Franklin D. Roosevelt more than any other man in this nation today has shown in what spirit the defense of the American system should be conducted."

Once the Squire of Hyde Park became Governor of New York, Lippmann's attitude altered drastically. When Roosevelt vacillated in his actions relative to the conduct of Mayor Jimmy Walker, he commented tersely that by doing nothing the Governor "will continue to disappoint his friends." Since no decision in Albany had been made by 1932 concerning the allegations of municipal corruption on Walker's part, Lippmann increased the intensity of his criticism: "This squalid mess is due to nothing but Governor Roosevelt's own weakness and timidity . . . The trouble with Franklin D. Roosevelt is that his mind is not very clear, his purposes are not simple, and his methods are not direct."

Although Roosevelt's reelection by a substantial margin in 1930 automatically made him a top contender for the 1932 Democratic presidential nomination, Lippmann opposed him and gave his support to Newton D. Baker. Irked when rumors began circulating that the former Secretary of War was physically incapable of being a nominee, he wrote privately to Colonel House and charged, "Those who are very close to Governor Roosevelt, and probably the Governor himself, are spreading the report that Newton Baker is disqualified because of his health." This led, furthermore, to the public accusation that Roosevelt had simply adopted enough of the "key phrases of the progressives" to sound liberal, when in fact his position was "quite indistinguishable from that of Mr. Hearst." Being compared to newspaper publisher William Randolph Hearst, the notorious opportunist, was a damning indictment. After F.D.R. unexpectedly lost the Democratic primary election in Massachusetts, he scoffed, "These results dispose completely of the Roosevelt propaganda that he is the idol of the masses." His most disparaging evaluation of Franklin D. Roosevelt was made just prior to the national convention in Chicago.

"The art of carrying water on both shoulders," he declared, "is highly developed in American politics, and Mr. Roosevelt has learned it. . . . Franklin D. Roosevelt is a highly impressionable person, without a firm grasp of public affairs and without very strong convictions. . . .

"For Franklin D. Roosevelt is no crusader. He is no tribune of the people. He is no enemy of entrenched privilege. He is a pleasant man who, without any important qualifications for the office, would very much like to be President."

Once F.D.R. won the Democratic nomination, Lippmann did support him against Herbert Hoover. As previously stated, he approved many early measures of the New Deal including a favorable reaction to the Triple-A and NRA programs. Rexford G. Tugwell, a Brain Truster who had become the Assistant Secretary of Agriculture, claimed some credit in selling these programs to Lippmann through personal contact. There appeared to be some indication that the columnist's endorsement of the AAA stemmed from this influence. It was certain that Lippmann never was an expert on agriculture. He has either ignored this field or commented only sparsely on it.

Lippmann maintained a relatively detached position *vis-à-vis* Roosevelt even though the President sought to cultivate his support. White House invitations came frequently and access to the Chief Executive was accorded him whenever desired. In 1934, he sent a congratulatory letter to F.D.R. telling him: "I haven't anything in my mind that you can't afford to hear. . . . I was very happy about the election. The vote of confidence which you got was as magnificent as it was well earned." But by 1935 he was advising the administration to slow the pace and take "time to digest, to harmonize, to co-ordinate the immense projects already started." Now was the time for a "restoration of the normal process of government," since, in his opinion, the "great crisis" was over. We are a "society based on law" and thus the improvisation and experimentation should cease, he maintained. Criticisms were also leveled at the administrative confusion that seemed to pervade the New Deal.

Roosevelt did not succeed in winning Lippmann's endorsement for reelection in 1936. The President complained in private correspondence to Norman Hapgood that the columnist was "not always consistent." It would be good for him to "come more into contact with the little fellow all over the country and see less of the big rich brother." Lippmann was persuaded that Governor Alfred Landon of Kansas, a onetime Bull Mooser, could provide a government of "national union" to stabilize the American society. The nation needed "solidarity" and an end to "unreal and unnecessary divisions." Justifying his decision, he wrote: "I think that this is the most important thing to be gotten out of this election. And because I am convinced that Governor Landon is in a political situation where he must conduct a government of national union, because I believe that by temperament and by his views he is disposed to such government, I shall vote for him."

Oddly enough, Alfred M. Landon did not capitalize fully on this support. Ballard Dunn, his press secretary, sent him a special memorandum notifying him of Lippmann's endorsement, but apparently it never reached him. O. Glen Saxon, a National Committeeman from Chicago, also informed Landon, via Carl Ratt (the Governor's secretary), that his chances for victory were enhanced "with Walter Lippmann and the *Baltimore Sun* swinging away from Roosevelt." This communication also got sidetracked. Eugene Meyer, a prominent

party member, thinking Lippmann might well serve as an adviser to
the G.O.P. nominee, tried in vain to arrange a meeting between the
two men. It seemed incredible, but many years later Alf Landon
confessed:

"I'm sorry I didn't have an opportunity of conferring with Mr.
Lippmann in the 1936 campaign, or either before or since then.

"I wish I had. I have great respect for him. As a matter of fact,
I didn't know he was supporting me in that campaign until Arthur
Schlesinger, Jr. told me when he was here two years ago going
through my letters at the [Kansas] Historical Society [in 1951].

"That's what happens to a candidate frequently at both national
. . . and state levels. His attention is not called to important factors."

F.D.R. was more than a little annoyed at Lippmann's support of
Landon even though it became less enthusiastic as the campaign progressed. "I always hate the frame of mind which talks about 'our
group' and 'my group' among liberals," the President again confided
to Hapgood. Whereas Landon's speech writers might well have borrowed excerpts from Lippmann's excellent prose, they did not; but
Thomas Corcoran, a Brain Truster and presidential aide, did do so.
He used the columnist's phrase "appointment with destiny" and con-
verted it to the famous passage, "rendezvous with destiny" used by
President Roosevelt in his acceptance speech at Franklin Field in
Philadelphia. In retrospect, the issue was never in doubt as F.D.R.
won the plaudits of the people wherever he spoke. Roosevelt received
an overwhelming mandate to continue the New Deal. To his credit the
President did not chide Lippmann for his action; rather, he sought to
reestablish a cordial relationship. The columnist responded to this
friendly overture by replying: "It was very kind of you to write me
as you did, and I greatly appreciate it. I do most sincerely wish you
good sailing in the four years to come."

No sooner had F.D.R. taken the oath for his second term, than he
launched his drive to reform the Supreme Court. Lippmann denounced
the effort as a brazen attempt to pack the court. Reprimanding the
President for his "audacity without parallel in American history," he
regarded the court packing proposal as tantamount to a "bloodless
coup d'etat which strikes a deadly blow at the vital center of constitutional democracy." His columns were filled with strong words of
castigation for those "shortsighted zealots" who have insisted "that
there must be no limits upon the power of the New Deal majority."

The political differences between himself and F.D.R. now seemed irreparable. But as the second term neared its end, the peril of war brought them together again. That episode will be taken up in detail in the following chapter. At the time of President Roosevelt's death, even though he had been his constant critic on domestic affairs, Lippmann paid him simple tribute: "Under his leadership, the debates on . . . fundamentals were completed, and he left a stronger America."

Chapter VIII

THE ATLANTIC COMMUNITY

Woodrow Wilson's famous Fourteen Points remained haunting symbols to the post-World War I generation. For many Americans the idea of a League of Nations capable of developing a universal code of justice for world brotherhood had been a cause worthy of the sacrifice made by many American soldiers. A promise of utopia, which ardent idealists thought was within grasp, faded into oblivion. Unwilling to discard their dream, despite the betrayal at Versailles, yet with the United States playing no role in the League, some disenchanted liberals resorted to a form of isolationism. Others sustained their faith in the new order to come by advocating a kind of moralistic internationalism.

The first group seemed desirous of preventing the United States from becoming tainted with any guilt by associating with the supposedly wicked nations of Europe. Those of latter type, with equal fervor, insisted on condemning aggression wherever it occurred, but without a corollary commitment of military force. Each was driven by conscience to work for world peace, but neither condoned the use of military power to enforce international obligations. A wide discrepancy existed therefore between foreign policy aspirations and the means to be used for attaining these goals. Universal amity and moral rightness were American ideals, but they had no relevance to world affairs without the will to make them meaningful in practice.

There was also a negative reaction on the part of conservatives, who, by and large, rallied around a program of economic isolationism and insular nationalism. Nationalist sentiment was bifurcated; some desired total retreat from all international responsibilities while others, though willing for the United States to participate on an advisory level, preferred noninvolvement. It must be said that some Americans during the twenties and thirties did see the need for active assumption of obligations to preserve the balance of power on the international scene. They, as a small minority, protested futilely against the drive for unilateral disarmament and the reliance upon meaningless treaties. Relatively few experts concerned themselves with realistic solutions for international problems, other than to demand repayment of war debts, and fewer still were fully aware of the dangers inherent in the ostrich-like posture of their nation.

Public sentiment became divorced from reality. Britain was blamed, and to a lesser degree France, for their alleged treachery and deceit in enticing U.S. participation in World War I. Expectations had been raised unduly by President Wilson's grandiose rhetoric and when these beautifully stated aims were not fulfilled, public disillusionment was disastrous. The United States, in the popular mind, was imagined an innocent country seduced by wily European nations. America paid dearly for its involvement and received nothing in return. War itself was associated with the old world. Americans, according to this mythical explanation, emerged morally unblemished from the conflict since they had been duped by Britain. This rationalization was given substance when historical revisionism by renown scholars tended to exonerate Germany from its guilt in starting the war. It was no wonder the mass mind came to believe U. S. intervention in 1917 was a terrible mistake; and when the Allies were unable to repay their war debts, they were regarded as unscrupulous ingrates. "Never again," went the slogan. The public mentality was dead set against future involvements that implied sending troops or lending money.

The illusory mirage which equated peace with pacifism was another menace that added to the national paralysis. The Carnegie Endowment for International Peace, a movement led by Edward W. Bok, and the American Committee for the Outlawry of War were also manifestations of widespread repugnance against repeating the events of 1917. Since it was assumed that war itself was an aberration and could be eradicated by rational agreements among nations, naive idealists placed great faith in the World Court and on international law. They did not, however, consider the details of enforcement. This gave a quixotic quality to all of their endeavors. Peace could not be acquired by merely signing parchments. It was a day to day task involving readiness and risks.

The appeasement mood at Munich allowed Hitler to win a cheap victory over Czechoslovakia without firing a shot. Americans did not react with alarm to this Nazi triumph. There was no public outcry for rearmament. Revulsion against military preparation during the thirties debilitated the American will. Repeated failure to engage in realistic diplomacy propelled the United States along a dangerous course of misdirected aloofness from the problems of the world. This journey of folly came to an end suddenly during the 1940's when the nation's very survival was in jeopardy.

The ordeal of the first World War and its agonizing aftermath also had its effect on Lippmann. His discomforture over the final peace treaty, abetted by an innate dislike of military conflict, made him susceptible to the isolationist temper of the times. This did not mean he approved of a policy of utter seclusion, but an unusual dichtomy was apparent in his thinking during the twenties and thirties. At times it reflected the realism of Theodore Roosevelt while on other occasions it resembled the moralistic idealism so evident in the thought of Wilsonian internationalists.

In the first instance Charles Evans Hughes was praised as an "able" Secretary of State who had conducted the Washington Disarmament Conference (1921-1922) with "force and determination." Lippmann reacted favorably to the various multilateral treaties, which reduced the navies of the United States, Great Britain, and Japan, to a 5:5:3 ratio. Upon reflection, he thought it might have been better to deal with Japan on a bilateral basis, since active friendship with the Japanese was vital for preserving peace in the Pacific. Japan wanted naval parity. When that was denied them, Japanese leaders harbored a deep resentment against the West. Thus whatever gain was achieved by naval limitations was nullified by the alienation of Japan.

Again, when Frank Kellogg, Coolidge's Secretary of State, labored for approval of a treaty to outlaw war, Lippmann initially thought it a noble venture. He indicated his approval to Kellogg, but his suggestions relative to a specific definition of what constituted a violation were rejected.

"I greatly appreciate your very generous words of commendation about my negotiations for the Multilateral Treaty," Secretary Kellogg replied. "At the same time I wish to thank you for your uniform support of the principles of the Anti-War Treaty. . . .

"I am unable to agree with your second point. There is nothing in the Treaty which expressly justifies wars of self-defense. That question must of necessity be left for each country to decide, but it must justify itself to the world and to the other signatories."

The Kellogg-Briand Pact of 1928, often referred to as the Paris Peace Pact, contained no enforcement machinery—just pious disclaimers. All signatories, and every major nation approved it, agreed they would not use military force to resolve international disputes. Pacifists, idealists, and even the general public were deluded into thinking war had actually been outlawed. Lippmann had to concede that in its final form the pact was a "masterpiece of ignorance."

With no means of determining the aggressor and with the absence of a provision calling for collective action against transgressors, it was a meaningless document. Deep down, however, he wanted the machinery of international law to replace military force as the means of settling world problems. When Aristide Briand died in 1932, he eulogized the French Foreign Minister with these words: "The name of Briand will remain of good report, because he made hatred a little less patriotic and good will a little more fashionable." What Lippmann did not know then was that the co-author of the Paris Pact aided and abetted the growth of the Maginot Line mentality of his nation. The groundwork was laid for the disastrous military defeat of 1940.

Oftimes Lippmann wrote of the need for a realistic foreign policy. His support of John W. Davis in 1924 was justified on the basis he was the "only one of the three candidates whose mind actually deals with the postwar world." He felt Davis, unlike either Coolidge the Republican nominee or LaFollette the Progressive, was "willing to cooperate with Europe in organizing the peace of the world." American foreign policy changed little even after Herbert Hoover assumed the presidency. High tariffs continued and until economic conditions made adjustments necessary, Hoover sought to collect war debts. The Iowa Quaker harbored deep seated isolationist sentiments. He did nothing concrete to shake the nation from its trance-like position regarding international responsibilities. Once prosperity declined, Americans were even less inclined to look beyond their own borders.

Taking into account the economic depression and America's pre-occupation with its own recovery, Lippmann urged European countries to do more for themselves. Having visited the continent he believed, despite U. S. shortcomings, that European "disunity" more than anything else had "bedeviled" and impeded postwar reconstruction. In a sense he was givng tacit approval for a U. S. policy of isolation and detachment from Europe.

No diplomatic arrangement was ever concluded to mollify French fears of German revenge. When British Prime Minister Ramsay MacDonald also sought closer ties with the United States, Lippmann urged frankly that such an accord not be in the form of a binding military agreement. Despite his previous advocacy of an Anglo-American entente to preserve the balance of power in Europe, he now advised that such cooperation merely take the form of a "common understanding of universal principles . . . to maintain peace." Europe must go it alone. He explained unconvincingly: "The practical problem is to find a substitute for the armed superstate which will provide a sufficient sense of security to justify a French government in consenting to some amendments to the status quo. The only conceivable substitute is a renewal of the Franco-British entente."

When President Herbert Hoover continued the policy of working for arms reduction, Lippmann commended him. He wrote approvingly about the efforts of Secretary of State Henry L. Stimson to further reduce naval tonnage at the London Naval Conference of 1930. The United States, by the way, had not even maintained fleet strength permitted under the 1922 agreement. At the same time Stimson was working for greater limitations on construction of capital ships, he personally considered Japan's activities in Manchuria to be overt aggression. The Secretary of State wanted his nation to take positive steps to check Japanese expansion, but Hoover vetoed that proposal. As an alternative Stimson thought some form of nonrecognition of the Nipponese spoils might prove effective. Such moral censure might possibly force Japan's leaders to alter their expansionistic course. According to Elting E. Morison, Stimson's biographer, the Secretary was influenced by Lippmann:

"On December 22 [1931], however, it was brought to Stimson's mind again by a letter from Walter Lippmann. The commentator suggested that since 'all resort to force is barred to us' it was unwise to take any measure short of it 'but in that direction.'

"Why not, therefore, do something that would leave Japan 'indicted and on the defensive?' If Japan took Chinchow, why not try to persuade the signatories of the Nine Power Pact to declare that they could not recognize as legal any agreements which may result from Japanese action since September 18th?

"Thus confronted, time and economic circumstances would work against Japan and, concluded Lippmann, 'it would be fair to hope the military party would eventually be overthrown'."

Stimson subsequently promulgated the nonrecognition doctrine whereby the conquests of Japan were not to be acknowledged as legitimate acquisitions of territory. There was no threat, explicit or implied, either to forceably stop the Japanese or to punish them for their plunder. Great Britain refused to make the declaration a joint one since their foreign office did not place much faith in proclamations as deterrents. Moral condemnation without a commitment to force had two adverse reprecussions; first, it lured the Chinese to instigate a boycott of Japanese goods for which they were punished by a naval bombardment of Shanghai; and secondly, such censure made the Japanese feel like international lepers. When they sought to expand into frontier areas at the expense of weaker nations, as the United States did *vis-à-vis* Mexico in 1845, their actions were sternly rebuked. They resented the double standard of morality implicit in that code of conduct. Because Lippmann defended the woefully inadequate Hoover-Stimson doctrine as "one of the greatest moments in the evolution of international law," it truly depicted how the mood of the times had influenced him. Note his peculiar ratiocination:

"The world has in effect announced a campaign of passive resistance against the Japanese aggression. Such a campign requires a higher morale, more understanding and more enlightened patience than the application of sanctions. . . .

"The world has entered upon a fascinating and perhaps momentous experiment. . . . The American principle of not recognizing the results of aggression . . . is the direct opposite of the procedure of the Covenant. It is in its implications the most absolute pacifist principle imaginable; it carries into international law something of the philosophy of Mahatma Gandhi.

"In place of a superstate maintaining international order the nations are to ignore and ostracize the consequences of law-breaking. The principle is novel and far-reaching. . . ."

The false line of reasoning that prompted Lippmann to accept this frail theory was soon shattered by the force of events all around the globe. Italy's brutal assault against the hapless Ethiopians in 1935 awakened him to the extreme danger of substituting moral epithets for bullets. Appropriately entitled, "The Shattered Dream," he wrote an article admitting U.S. diplomacy had been totally "impotent" in dealing with Germany, Italy and Japan. Americans had deluded themselves by believing in ephemeral "wishes," he wrote, and that in turn "invited the results we are now witnessing." Obviously he was indicting himself also. Casting aside his own aversion to war, he made the following admonition: "In the last analysis, however, the defense of civilized ideals today must depend, not on protests, but on far-sighted policy. For those nations which are threatened with aggressive violence, the only defense is diplomatic combination backed by military force and a willingness, when deeply challenged, to use it. It is the old-fashioned remedy, expensive, dangerous, and unsatisfactory, but there is no cheaper or easier way."

After the advent of hostilities on a major scale in 1939, Lippmann called for prompt mobilization, repeal of the neutrality acts, and immediate assistance to Great Britain. With great verve, he sought to undue the damage done by isolationist Senator Gerald P. Nye, whose investigations of the munitions industry made manufacturers appear as calculating warmongers. Column after column endeavored to counter the nativist arguments of the America First Committee. One such hard-hitting article, "The Generation That Was Duped," strove to refute the many misconceptions about America's participation in World War I.

"The postwar generation," he wrote, "has been duped by a swarm of innocent but ignorant historians, by reckless demagogues, and by foreign interests, into believing that America entered the other war because of British propaganda, the loans of the bankers, the machinations of President Wilson's advisers, and the drummed up patriotic ecstacy.

"They have been told to believe that anyone who challenges this explanation of 1917 and insists that America was defending American vital interests is himself a victim or an agent of British propaganda."

It was doubtful whether Woodrow Wilson actually ascertained so keenly just what American interests were at stake in 1917. Essentially he had regarded German submarine warfare as basically immoral and this, not hardheaded considerations of national interest, drove him along a path leading to war with Germany. Although the President was not oblivious to other factors, his innate idealism forced him to justify the intervention on moral grounds. Once in the war he elevated it into a crusade for humanity—thus obscuring even further the real reasons why an Allied victory was desirable for the United States. Lippmann did point out correctly, however, that revisionist history and popular myth were blinding the nation to the peril it now faced.

Not only did Lippmann utilize his column to alert Americans to the need for a drastic change of attitude, he contributed his talents to the Committee to Defend America by Aiding the Allies (often referred to as the William Allen White Committee). By means of a speech written for the aging General John J. Pershing, which the World War I commander gave on radio under the auspices of the William Allen White Committee, Lippmann defended President Roosevelt's so-called destroyer deal of September 2, 1940 (which transferred fifty allegedly overaged destroyers to Britain for long-term leases on air and naval sites). When asked for assistance by Benjamin Cohen, an aide to F.D.R., in the drafting of a resolution to be presented to Congress by Senator Claude Pepper, he volunteered his service. This measure, which anticipated what later became the lend-lease act, met defeat amid an atmosphere of frenzied fear that the United States would once more became involved in Britain's battle. Lippmann was by no means the only columnist to champion aid to Britain and its Commonwealth, but Lord Robert Casey, the Australian Minister to the United States, recalled having frequent meetings with Lippmann, whom he attested as being "wholeheartedly on our side and did everything possible to help before . . . the time of Pearl Harbor. . . . He was, I think without a doubt, the most highly regarded pressman (or more properly writer in the American press) in the United States."

The years from 1938 to 1940 were unusually somber ones for Lippmann because the international scene became one perpetual crisis. His personal life also was a cause of inner turmoil when his first marriage ended in divorce. A remarriage, to Helen Byrne Armstrong, was to be a happy one. The orderly life and domestic serenity needed for his writing was enhanced immeasurably. Their home in Georgetown was essentially a scholar's study for him. The regimen of his life was a strict schedule of research and writing, meetings with other columnists or officials of various kinds, and taking trips abroad to keep abreast of foreign affairs. He and his wife led a quiet life in social terms entertaining only intimate friends. Their favorite vacation spot was Maine, although they did travel periodically to other parts of the country. When war erupted in Europe, his attention was focused almost entirely upon the rapid sequence of events that was propelling the nations of the world into a conflict of massive proportions.

In calling for intervention on behalf of Britain and France, Lippmann revived his earlier concept of the Atlantic Community. Viewing the Atlantic Ocean as a "bridge and not a barrier between natural allies," he wrote, "We should declare that . . . our policy is to keep the Atlantic Ocean under the control of ourselves and of our friends." France lay in defeat, but the Free French under General Charles de Gaulle were to be acknowledged as truly "representing the French people." The very future of Europe, with its democratic freedoms, depended on the survival of Great Britain. It now stood alone as a beleagured bastion against Naziism. Americans could not afford to stand idly by and watch Western civilization collapse. Nor could the U.S., for selfish reasons, exist as an island of freedom amid an ocean of totalitarian states. America's duty was clear. In Lippmann's judgment it had to come to the aid of those nations to which its history was linked by so many tangible bonds of tradition and mutual interests.

Speaking in somber tones, he told the thirtieth reunion of his 1910 Harvard class they were facing the "most solemn hour of the history of the modern world." The defenses of Western civilization lay prostrate, professed Lippmann, because certain European nations, along with the United States, "decided to disarm." That seemed the "easy way," he admitted, since "it saved money [and] it saved effort." Other mistakes were catalogued: "We indulged ourselves in the inflationary boom and let it run. . . . We maintained the tariffs, we maintained the wage costs, and the overhead expenditures of the boom, and thus made it impossible to recover from the crash." Dividends that appeared so great were nothing compared to the delayed premiums now due.

With a tinge of self-incrimination, he acknowledged that although "organized mechanized evil" ran rampant, the American people acted as if nothing had gone awry in the world. The momentum of militarism and overt aggression went unchecked. "We heard it threaten the things we believe in," he lamented. "We saw it coming, year after year, savage crimes. We disliked it all. But we liked better our easygoing ways, our jobs, our profits, and our pleasures, and so we said: it is bad but it won't last; it is dangerous but it can't cross the ocean. . . ."

Why had totalitarian regimes been so successful in conquest? In sermon-like words, Lippmann answered:

". . . what has made possible its victories is the lazy, self-indulgent materialism, the amiable, lackadaisical, footless, confused complacency of the free nations of the world. They have dissipated, like wastrels and drunkards, the inheritance of freedom and order that came to them from hard-working, thrifty, faithful, believing, and brave men.

"The disaster in the midst of which we are living is a disaster in the character of men. It is a catastrophe of the soul of a whole generation which had forgotten, had lost, and had renounced the imperative and indispensable virtues of laborious, heroic, and honorable men."

There was only one option available; Europe's people must be "liberated, and the lands that are subjugated redeemed, and the world we live in purified and pacified once more." This was, he declared, the "American destiny, and unless we fulfill that destiny we shall have betrayed our own past and we shall make our own future meaningless, chaotic, and low."

Lippmann's concern for miliary preparedness was so great he admonished F.D.R. to assert even bolder leadership. "The world is on fire," he exhorted in print, "The alarm has to be rung, kept ringing, first and without stopping by the President, until the fire is put out." The American people "cannot sleep through the fire," he forewarned, "or they too will be trapped in the flames." Despite President Roosevelt's attempt to mobilize the nation in the face of strong protests from isolationists, he nevertheless rebuked him for his charade-like performance: "Listening to Mr. Roosevelt has been [the equivalent of] listening to a radio station from which the announcer gives forth epoch-making news and appeals to patriotism, interspersed with advertisements for soft mattresses and efficient laxatives." This was an unfair charge, since the President had to cloak his defense efforts to avoid undue opposition.

The presidential nomination of Wendell Willkie in 1940 struck Lippmann as a political phenomenon. Spontaneous support for the Hoosier candidate materialized from nowhere. "It is a popular uprising of men and women who have responded, as free people ought to respond, to good leadership when good leadership is available." The Republican nominee, he thought for a time, could do a better job of unifying the nation for the trials and tribulations that lay ahead; but as the campaign progressed, many factors caused him to doubt whether the G.O.P. candidate could rule his own party— let alone run the affairs of state. Because of the harsh, obstructionist tactics of Republican congressmen to block a draft law, Lippmann called them "reckless". In his August 19 column, he commented, "Mr. Willkie cannot make speeches advocating conscription and the policy of extending to Great Britain 'the material resources of the nation,' and expect the people to follow him if his own party does not follow him. . . . The party cannot offer the country a national leader for the next four years if in the weeks after he accepts the nomination they reject and repudiate his leadership."

President Roosevelt, meanwhile, had taken steps to attract independent Republicans by bringing Henry L. Stimson (as Secretary of War) and Frank Knox (as Secretary of Navy) into his cabinet; and had moved forward to prepare the country's military defenses. Administration policy makers sought and succeeded in getting a Selective Service Act passed, a joint Canadian-American Board on

Defense established, and Latin American unity was furthered by the Pan-American Foreign Ministers Conference in Havana. Likewise the destroyer deal was comsummated over the vociferous objections of isolationists. Henry A. Wallace, the Democratic nominee for the vice-presidency, hammered away at the G.O.P. as the party of appeasement while F.D.R. practiced a bit of political mendacity by telling a Boston crowd: "I have said this before, but I shall say it again and again and again: Your boys are not going to be sent into any foreign wars. . . . The purpose of defense is defense."

Lippmann did not challenge the President's credibility but a phalanx of American First orators did. They interpreted each of F.D.R.'s moves as a calculated step to move the nation closer to war. Executive leadership in this instance was given good press by Lippmann, since the objectives to be achieved were considered vital to national security. Gaining confidence in Roosevelt's leadership, his doubts about F.D.R. disappeared and his enthusiasm for Willkie waned. In the end he was glad the President won reelection. Writing in 1944, he declared: "Although Willkie never succeeded in converting the 'old guard' and in restoring the party to its great federalist position, he was able to hold in check its tendency to sink into know-nothingness and reactionary obstruction. . . . If the ideas of his [Republican] rivals in 1940 had prevailed, we should be today not on the slopes of victory, but isolated, divided, and desperately hard pressed."

Certainly the shock of Pearl Harbor demesmerized those still clinging to the hope America could remain safely isolated from the contagion then engulfing the world. The suddenness of it all and the devastation left in its wake appalled Lippmann. Had the Japanese gone mad? Had madmen taken over the world? He was terribly distressed by the repeated symptoms of savagery stemming from warfare that had become so commonplace among the so-called civilized nations. For that reason, when asked to speak to the American Catholic Philosophical Association, only a few weeks after the nation was plunged into war, he utilized the occasion to reflect soberly upon underlying reasons for the widespread reversion to barbaric behavior. A regression had occurred, he reasoned, because modern men "rejected the culture of their civilization." In the new order of things "they no longer think of themselves and their children in the tradition which comes to them from the prophets and the saints and the teachers and philosophers and the discoverers who raised Western man out of barbarism." Everything seemed reversed now, "The cultural tradition and the great central institutions of the Western world came down to us from men who would have regarded what is now the fashionable image of man as the image of an uncivilized barbarian."

What had caused this upheaval? It was attributed directly to the liberation of man from the "bonds of tradition," which left him a creature with "no rational command over . . . [his] desires." Being slaves to primitive instincts, he maintained, "men's subjective expectations, which, because they are unlimited and insatiable, cause violence, inequality, hatred and frustration." This led ultimately to a logic of lunacy:

"Though we like to tell ourselves that our purpose is to solve the social problem by ministering to men's needs, in practice we have a conception of human nature, and derived from it an educational system and a commercial and political propaganda, which treat all needs as unlimited. No income can therefore be sufficient to satisfy men's needs.

"For the appetite merely grows from feeding it. . . . No prosperity is rich enough . . . no nation can be big enough and no state can be powerful enough. For until someone has conquered the whole world, it is always possible to be bigger and greater than you are."

Covetous and conscienceless individuals sought "refuge among the masses of their fellow beings, becoming anonymous, faceless, and no longer persons in some one of those mass movements which are so characteristic of our times." This description categorized the Nazi hordes perfectly. Depersonalized and products of ideological zeal, they were absorbed into the "formless mysticism of an irrational collectivism." Brutal, cruel, and without moral restraint, these robots of the Third Reich were like dumb beasts "contained within the discipline of an ordered existence." As ideological monsters and inspired automatons, they did, he conceded, make obedient soldiers. But the price of this mechanical efficiency was "moral blindness" and the "intellectual error" of not knowing that true freedom involved "personal responsibility." Totalitarianism was the "supreme heresy of our enemies," since it destroyed traditional values and carried "ruthlessly to the logical conclusion the denial of man's personal responsibility, and therefore of his personal dignity. . . ."

The frightening consequences of totalitarianism included not only conquest and subjugation of vast populations, but the deliberate purge of ideas and ideals stemming from the Judaic-Christian, Greco-Roman heritage. This was a portent of even greater havoc for the future because the retention and transmission of the West's ancient wisdom was the only means of preventing widespread historical amnesia. Once that happened a new Dark Age would occur and a race of primitive vandals would be propagated. Western man must again find his way back to civility for "in this tradition," Lippmann elucidated, "man does not fulfill his destiny except as his is ruled by the reason within him which transcends that which is only animal, because it is attached to that which is universal."

What should be the punishment for war criminals who inspired shouting masses to indulge in unimagined horrors and atrocities? An eye for an eye? No! A restoration of rational order made it imperative that the "rule of justice" be applied in spite of the desire for pure vengeance. He did not think the German people were entirely blameless, not sufficiently so to declare them "innocent victims" of Hitler's madness; nor were they to be "forever cursed" for their collective guilt. Obviously culpable practitioners of tyranny were not to be allowed to evade the chastisement they deserved. They had violated basic principles of law. In advocating this procedure his conscience bade him to ask that justice be "tempered with mercy." It was for this reason he supported the Nuremberg Trials but opposed the Morgenthau Plan. Morgenthau, Roosevelt's Secretary of the Treasury, wanted to eliminate Germany's industry and reduce the nation to a land where the people would have to farm for a living. Lippmann attended several of the sessions of the trials at Nuremberg as a special observer. There he saw the faces of Nazi leaders as they stood before the bar of world justice. But before that scene took place, he was solicitous lest pent up hate make a mockery of the judicial process. Not hesitating to reprove those who would let might determine right, he expostulated: "The constant knowledge must be with us that our power, like all power, is good only within the moral order. Therefore, when we send forth our men to kill or be killed, let us not in moral inertia and laziness of spirit refuse the effort of making sure their battles are not meaningless and their sacrifices are not in vain."

Observations like these found their way into Lippmann's columns frequently over the years. By so doing he could place contemporary events into their proper perspective through detached reflections. Always probing deeper aspects of contemporary occurrences as the disinterested observer, he stimulated many to think seriously about mankind's predicament. Upon Sinclair, for one, appreciated these in-depth explications. Writing to Lippmann, the perpetual *défenseur* of the Socialist cause in America expressed the fine sentiment: "You and I have had our fights and they were not polite ones, but what you have been writing about the present crisis puts them all in the past. They are handsome pieces of writings, representing a great service to our country in this dreadful crisis."

During the war years Lippmann paid close attention to diplomatic efforts because, as with World War I, the results would determine the course of postwar events. Very early he came to the conclusion that Roosevelt had mastered the art of wartime leadership. Roosevelt, needless to say, took special care to keep Lippmann informed through private interviews and secret briefings. A global conflict on the scale of World War II required the coordination of vast amounts of men and materiel, plus close cooperation among the United Nations allies. From the intelligence data he received and from his own observations Lippmann felt F.D.R. was doing an excellent job as leader of a vast coalition. He was confident the United Nations possessed ample power and sufficient unity to be "masters of the war." Never for a moment did he doubt the inevitability of military victory, but occasionally the course of wartime diplomacy troubled him.

Political and diplomatic decisions made while the war was in progress would determine whether concerted agreements and specific postwar settlements would be in effect when the fighting stopped. This was the issue that really concerned Lippmann. With Wilson's mistakes in the back of his mind, he felt compelled to issue periodic warnings to members of the Roosevelt administration. Secretary of State Cordell Hull was predisposed to enunciate lofty principles, often getting the Soviet Union to subscribe to them, but he seldom secured hard and fast agreements. Equally idealistic was Vice President Henry A. Wallace, who gave speeches that echoed the Wilsonian hopes for a universal peace through the instrumentality of a United Nations. Sumner Welles and others in the State Department (though not all by any means) also seemed overly captivated by the prospect of bringing to fruition what Wilson had failed to accomplish.

In a column entitled "To Certain Idealists," he cautioned these men against allowing an "ardor for an all-embracing [international] association to keep the world peace" from obscuring the need to secure "practical measures by which their hopes may eventually be realized." Still another article, written just before Hull's departure to the Moscow Conference of Foreign Ministers in 1943, offered a reminder that it was "absolutely essential" to temper unrestrained idealism "if we are not once again, as we did in 1919, to build a house of cards." Secretary of State Hull did indeed return with the Moscow Declaration, stating vaguely that all problems would be amicably settled

by the proposed international organization. But negligible concrete
negotiation was accomplished and this upset Lippmann. When he
queried the President about the results of the meeting, Roosevelt
replied with reassuring words: "Moscow was a real success. Sometimes, however, I feel that the world will be mighty lucky if it gets
50% of what it seeks out of the war as a permanent success. That
might be a high average."

Statements of guarded optimism made Lippmann feel confident
F.D.R. meant ultimately to engage in hard bargaining with the
Soviets, but he still felt uneasy about the neo-Wilsonians in the administration. To counter their thinking and to educate the public on the
subject of international realism, he wrote two books on diplomacy.
The first, *U.S. Foreign Policy: Shield of the Republic* (1943) was
theoretical in scope while the second, *U.S. War Aims* (1944), contained concrete recommendations. In the earlier work he set forth his
basic premise:

"The thesis of this book is that a foreign policy consists in bringing
into balance, with a comfortable surplus of power in reserve, the
nation's commitments and the nation's power.

"The constant preoccupation of the true statesman is to achieve
and maintain this balance. Having determined the foreign commitments which are vitally necessary to his people, he will never rest
until he has mustered the force to cover them.

"In essaying ideals, interests, his measure of their validity will be
the force he can muster at home combined with the support he can
find abroad among other nations which have similar ideals, interests,
and ambitions."

Using an historical approach rather than proposing model solutions, Lippmann took the position that the "Founding Fathers
understood the realities of foreign policy" because they understood
the easily "forgotten principle" that "commitments" and "power"
must be kept in "balance." One example used was the formation of
the Monroe Doctrine. Basing his arguments on Dexter Perkin's *Hands
Off: A Study of the Monroe Doctrine*, he pointed out that those who
promulgated it understood what was involved. Since the United States
could not possibly protect the Western Hemisphere in 1823, the obligation was announced with the clear understanding that a "concealed
source of power" was available by an "informal alliance with British
sea power." Subsequent generations "lost the prudence" and realism
of earlier times, he added, thus encouraging "idealists who habitually
rejected the premises of the politics of power." American diplomats

assumed mistakenly that national self-interest could be served "verb-ally—by promises, threats, and exhortations" without resort to some residue of force. Kellogg and Stimson during the 1920's exemplified this tendency par excellence.

Referring to his former idol, Theodore Roosevelt, he now explained what real diplomacy was all about:

"Theodore Roosevelt had . . . the elements of a genuine foreign policy. Aware of the American commitments, he sought to develop—though tentatively, unsurely and without making the matter plain to the nation—the elements of American power; our strategic posi-tion by constructing the Panama Canal, our armaments by enlarg-ing the navy, our alliances by adhering to those powers who were our friends and opponents of our opponents.

"But these rudimentary beginnings of a true foreign policy were not carried forward by Theodore Roosevelt's successors."

Contravening his own role in the Wilson administration, he criti-cized the wartime President for not fully understanding the reason for U.S. intervention in 1917. Winning the war prevented German "mas-tery of the Atlantic Ocean" while the idealistic aim was "to make the world safe for democracy." The first goal was quite unattainable but failure to achieve the second gave rise to the cynical belief America was "maneuvered into a non-American war by the international bank-ers and the British diplomats." Wilson's fundamental error was in not delimiting U.S. commitments to those objectives where American power could be brought to bear. The result was tragic:

"The legalistic, moralistic, idealistic presentation of the war and of the League obscured the realities—caused it to appear that for what we were asked to give to our allies, we were receiving nothing from them.

"It was made to seem that the new responsibilities of the League flowed from President Wilson's philanthropy and not from the vital necessity of finding allies to support America's vast existing commit-ments to the Western Hemisphere and all the way across the Pacific to the China Coast."

The nation's "unearned security," when it was protected by dis-tance and the British navy, gave rise to a mode of thought that regarded armaments and alliances as both evil and unnecessary. In turn this led to a feeling that the balance of power system was "mili-taristic, imperialistic, reactionary, and archaic." This myth rose to the status of a "national ideology" that, in turn led to a greater mis-conception of national destiny:

"It caused us to forget that man has to earn his security and his liberty as he has to earn his living. We came to think that our privileged position was a natural right, and then to believe that our unearned security was the reward of our moral superiority.

"Finally we came to argue, like the idle rich who regard work as something for menials, that a concern with the foundations of national security, with arms, with strategy, and with diplomacy, was beneath our dignity as idealists."

Looking back at his own record, Lippmann later confessed he felt "ashamed" for having once praised the Washington Disarmament Conference of 1921, an action he considered tantamount to having "celebrated the disaster as a triumph." Deep regret for having supported the "reckless conduct" of American foreign policy during the interlude between the wars was freely acknowledged. "Since I have lived through this period, and have for thirty years been writing books and articles about current events, I have been troubled because, with the advantages of hindsight, I am criticizing others for holding views which at the time I may myself have shared, or for lack of foresight of which I was also guilty." Further proof of his remorse was evinced in a portion deleted before publication which read: "And when I think of the men who were lost on Bataan and of General Wainwright at Corregidor, I find it impossible to forgive myself."

"Experience of history," Lippmann wrote, revealed that the "fundamental subject of foreign policy is how a nation stands in relationship to the principal military powers . . ., [since] no great power can be indifferent to any of the other great powers." Diplomacy thus concerned itself with such matters as balance of power, spheres of influence, supporting allies, and isolating potential adversaries. No major power could live in isolation and simultaneously enjoy national security. Vital interests demanded attention be paid to regional imbalances, military alignments, and territorial changes. Diplomacy denoted involvement. In its classical sense, as it evolved from Italian city-states of the sixteenth century, diplomatic negotiations were used to adjudicate differences or, if need be, to form power blocs to maintain international equilibrium. Here is where U.S. failures stood out. Nothing had been done to check or contain the aggression of either Germany, Italy, or Japan.

The League of Nations had not fulfilled idealistic expectations about replacing balance of power diplomacy. Realists never believed it would do so. In point of fact collective security failed primarily because peaceful nations overlooked the power realities involved in international relations. Lippmann had seen the need for such alignments within the League at the time of its formation. He again revived and elaborated upon his idea of an Anglo-American entente. This time he labeled it a "Nuclear Alliance" or in other words a "nucleus of force" within the Atlantic Community. It would exist to assure the effectiveness of collective security, that is to give substance and power to a future world organization.

To Lippmann it was both natural and necessary to form regional alignments or power blocs. Western Europe and the United States constituted a group of "nations allied with one another by geography, history, and vital necessity." The Atlantic Community, so denoted by him, was linked by a historic highway of water which facilitated the transfer of commerce, people, and culture from the Old World to the New. All Western nations were legatees of Greco-Roman, Judaic-Christian culture. Their institutions bore the imprint of a common tradition. A natural unity existed, he argued, "by geography, by strategic necessity, and by historic formation . . . their permanent interests are, when tested in the fires of total war, inseparable."

The emergence of a regional group led by the Soviet Union was taken for granted by Lippmann. His interest centered not on ways to prevent such a coalition, which constituted a Russian sphere of influence, but how to prevent a collision of this Soviet bloc with the Atlantic Community. "Russia and the Atlantic Community," he declared, "have . . . a profound interest in a European settlement which will maintain itself without bringing them into conflict." Precisely here, on this issue, diplomacy entered the picture. It was his basic contention that East-West relations should revolve around concrete issues and not be centered on vague talk about perpetual friendship or universal amity. Future accord would be secured by candid discussions and frank settlements.

Negotiating from a position of strength, the Atlantic Community (with the nuclear alliance as the inner core) could protect the vital interests of the West. His thinking, at the moment, envisaged the erection of a *sanitaire cordon* or buffer zone to separate the Atlantic Community from the Soviet bloc. A balance had to be struck between the two and maintained. "Combined action by America, Britain, and Russia," he repeated, was the "irreducible minimum guarantee under which it is possible even to begin to establish any wider order of security." More specifically a mutually acceptable power arrangement and not reliance on a United Nations Organization *per se* would keep the peace. Without agreement among the super powers there would be no concord anywhere.

Lippmann interpreted F.D.R.'s personal diplomacy to be a reversal of the "Wilsonian procedure." He considered Big Three summit conferences, where Roosevelt, Churchill, and Stalin met personally to parley, most realistic. These negotiations, while the war was still in progress, avoided Wilson's mistake of waiting until hostilities ceased before arriving at any agreement on peace terms. While praising the President, he nonetheless remained critical of Cordell Hull. The Secretary of State had the disconcerting habit of substituting "high sounding, imprecise generalizations" for specific "definitions" of American war aims. Hull revelled in declarations of principle and mistakenly assumed assent to them constituted a hard and fast agreement. Secretary Hull, in Lippmann's estimation, also placed far too much trust in the United Nations as the sole instrument for preserving peace. This "super idealism" ignored the incontestable fact that "regional groupings were devised by the geography of the earth and the course of history."

The Wilsonian oriented Secretary of State was not oblivious to Lippmann's observations. He received a critique of *U.S. Foreign Policy* from his State Department aide, Stanley K. Hornbeck. It was in many ways a refutation rather than a reflection on the contents of the book. Hornbeck took issue with Lippmann on whether foreign policy should be "initiated solely on the basis of military and international considerations" by claiming mistakenly it was a concept never before advocated by an American statesman. His summary of Lippmann's position was correct: "He makes it clear that he would build up from the bottom, on the basis of local interests, through *regional organizations* in the presence of which an international organization *might* perform a useful function; but that he does not believe in relying upon a world organization as the first and the sole instrumentality for security."

Vice President Henry A. Wallace, due to his many speeches describing World War II as a crusade for the abolition of war and want, became for all intent and purposes a second Woodrow Wilson. His vision of a new world was based almost entirely on the belief Soviet-American friendship was permanent and that some form of world government would emerge from the global struggle. Wallace dreamed of a "century of the common man," which would come to fruition when nations based their foreign policy on altruism and principles of cooperation, rather than continuing policies of exploitation and imperialistic diplomacy. Lippmann described him as a "mystic and isolated man to whom the real world is not clear." The Vice President's calling was "that of a prophet" and not one of a politician. He bluntly reminded the idealist from Iowa that "In international relations politics is called diplomacy, and we must not imagine . . ., having created the world organization, diplomacy will disappear."

Not only did Hull and Wallace resent Lippmann's negative attitudes, but supporters of the Roosevelt administration often reacted even more adversely. Any criticism, whether it be on foreign policy or domestic programs, reasonable or unreasonable, was interpreted as a political attack to be repulsed. While not comprehending either the essence of his argument or the significance of his criticism, the *United Mine Workers Journal* lambasted Lippmann's writings by charging he "has been making $40,000 a year for passing out this kind of whang-doodle to the snobby readers of the daily press." Personal attacks of this kind completely ignored the issues being discussed.

Unperturbed by such allegations, Lippmann pressed his case for international realism by coming out with another book. With great skill, he again challenged the veracity of Wilsonian idealism in foreign policy. The thesis of *U.S. War Aims* (1944) was stated forthrightly:

"The Wilsonian principles are prejudices formed in the Age of Innocence, in the country of American isolation. Wilson wished America to take its place in a universal society. But he was willing to participate only if the whole world acted as the United States acted when it enjoyed isolation during the nineteenth century.

"The United States had no need to arm, no need to find alliances, no need to take strategic precautions; Wilson's principles were a demand that the whole world take vows to live forever after on the same terms. He supposed that international relations could then be conducted verbally by meetings at Geneva."

To be sure, the facts of international life were undeniably selfish and sordid. But the enunciation of moral principles would not prevent nations from seeking their self interest. Acknowledging realities rather than ignoring them, a sounder procedure was to seek effective "checks and counterchecks" among "great regional constellations of states." Through diplomatic negotiations these respective power blocs could arrive at "compromise, bargains, [and] specific agreements." The Atlantic Community was one such power block of which he had already spoken. Under conducive circumstances, he envisaged its ultimate circumference to include Latin America, Germany, and "perhaps all of Europe to the borders of the Soviet Union." He also foresaw the formation of other "orbits" or groupings:

"Russia is the nucleus of another is clear, and China will form another. Eventually one or more constellations will probably form in the Hindu or Moslem worlds, but that is more distant.

"What we can recognize in detail even today is the grouping of the Atlantic Community on the one hand and of the Russian Orbit on the other. The settlement with Germany will be cemented by these two groups of states, with Japan by these two and China."

Anticipating the rise of the United States to the rank of a super power, Lippmann held it was "American destiny" to forge the free world into a powerful, unified community. "Fate" decreed that America was "at the center, no longer at the edge of Western civilization." Idealism was dangerous and isolationism dead. International realism dictated a change in policy. His concept of an Atlantic Community was still somewhat nebulous, and perhaps an idealized description of the occident, but it represented a fundamental framework for collective security.

By way of summary, Lippmann concluded his book with fundamental guidelines for realistic conduct of American foreign policy during the immediate postwar period:

"1. Consolidate the strategical and diplomatic connections . . . of the Atlantic Community.

"2. Recognize as valid and proper the strategical system of the Russian orbit [the Soviets have designated this a Socialist Commonwealth].

"3. Recognize that China will be another center of a third strategic center.

"4. Recognize that in time the Moslem and the Hindu nations of North Africa, the Middle East, and Southern Asia will form regional systems of their own.

"5. Make the cardinal principle . . . that Japan shall not hold the balance of power in the Far East [and] Germany shall not hold the balance of power between the Atlantic Community and the Russian Orbit.

"6. Recognize that the general aim of any lasting settlement of a war of aggression is to extinguish the war party and to protect the peace party, by making the defeat irrevocable and the peace acceptable."

With the end of the European war imminent, Lippmann credited

Roosevelt with doing a superb job in keeping the Grand Alliance functioning with a minimum of friction. Maintaining wartime coalitions demanded skill and he praised F.D.R. as a "great war leader." A fourth term for the President seemed necessary to him so that final negotiations might be completed successfully. When President Roosevelt met with Stalin and Churchill at the Crimean Conference, he looked with favor on this method of engaging in substantive talks. Reacting favorably to the announcement of Soviet participation on the Far Eastern front, he stated in his column, "Since so large a part of the Japanese power is on the mainland of Asia, a conclusive victory over Japan is difficult to achieve without the intervention of the Soviets in collaboration with the Western powers and with China."

This opinion, although then substantiated by the best military judgment, proved to be erroneous. It was an honest miscalculation. After the advent of the Cold War, however, the Yalta agreements were subjected to severe condemnation. Critics claimed Roosevelt yielded too much for Russian aid that was not really needed. This hindsight ignored the circumstances under which Soviet assistance was sought. Assessed fairly, Lippmann believed the concessions made to the Soviets for their promise of military intervention were warranted. Thus he defended what was done at Yalta. By and large the accord reached there was "very favorable to the Western powers," he concluded. In 1955, after the full text of the secret protocol was published, anti-Russian critics again claimed the agreement was a "sell out" and a "giveaway." Amid the clamor of anti-Communist hysteria, Lippmann calmly reiterated his conviction that the Crimean Conference represented legitimate diplomatic bargaining at its best. Eleanor Roosevelt took note of his defense of F.D.R. and wrote him: "I read your third column on the Yalta papers and thought it admirable. I want to thank you warmly for having written it."

During the final phase of the war in Europe, Lippmann remained convinced President Roosevelt had avoided the pitfalls that ensnared Woodrow Wilson. Not knowing Stalin's true intentions, he gave considerable credit to the Big Three for their exemplary wartime diplomacy:

"This is the great lesson which Churchill, Stalin, and Roosevelt have learned and are applying. They have seen to it that the coalition has become closer and larger, the alliance more firmly knot. . . . The Conference at Moscow and then at Teheran and now at Yalta show an impressive progress from general promises of united aspiration to more and more concrete measures of united action. . . . Unless we remain united . . . in the task of dealing with Germany, we cannot make a lasting peace. . . .

"Of all the manifestations of power, says Thucydides, 'restraint impresses men most.' There has been no more impressive international conference . . . none in which mighty states have so explicitly . . . sought to prove that they wish to exercise the power they wield as a trust for the peace and welfare of their peoples and of mankind."

Franklin D. Roosevelt's sudden death shocked Lippmann. He, like millions of Americans, had relied on his leadership and had grown accustomed to him. A relatively unknown man from Missouri was suddenly elevated to the free world's most powerful office. Harry Truman journeyed to Potsdam to meet with his peers. Churchill met unexpected defeat at the hands of his electorate and was replaced by Clement Attlee. Important decisions were made that seemingly laid the groundwork for amicable relations with Stalin. Japan ignored the warning sent to her and within weeks two atomic bombs forced total capitulation. The year 1945 thus brought to an end the greatest global conflict yet known to man. Once again, at least momentarily, the world was at peace.

CHAPTER IX

THE COLD WAR

Upon learning the nation had a new Vice President, Admiral William D. Leahy expressed in his own salty way what many Americans wondered: "Who the hell is Harry Truman?" Relatively little was known about the Missourian. Washington news correspondents, to be sure, were familiar with his outstanding work as the Chairman of the Senate Special Committee to Investigate the National Defense Program, but to the public at large he was an obscure figure. His selection as the vice-presidential candidate came only after key important party leaders had decided to use him as an alternative to Henry Wallace. When thrust into the presidency on that fateful day of April 12, 1945, it was with practically no preparation that Truman assumed the responsibilities of this high office. Not only did he possess no administrative experience, he had never been briefed on any of the crucial matters of state.

Truman's man-on-the-street, commonplace appearance contrasted sharply with the impressive, almost majestic, bearing of his predecessor. A provincial accent and country manners marked him as a man possessing little formal education and lacking in urbane sophistication. Sans elegance and without affectation, he seemed like a small-time politician completely out of place in the White House.

This lackluster image was misleading. Under the surface, Harry S. Truman was tough and tenacious. He had graduated from the school of hard knocks, not Harvard, and his understanding of politics came from experience, not textbooks. If he was plain spoken, it was because he said what was on his mind without benefit of fancy adornment. Communication with common people came natural to him, but he seldom impressed intellectuals or learned academicians. Simple and yet complex, the Missourian knew history and recognized the responsibilities of his position. He was determined to do his level best to succeed.

The pace of events did not slow down. Even before the new President could familiarize himself with Roosevelt's policies, he had to make momentous decisions. Should the atomic bomb be used against Japan? Must the Yalta Agreement be carried out? Could U.S. troops be stationed in Europe? All of these questions had to be answered

105

within a very short time after Truman entered the White House. If he floundered momentarily, it was understandable. And yet through it all he withstood the pressures that were his daily companion. "The first five days as President," Truman observed during retirement, "seemed like five lifetimes."

When Truman began to comprehend what was going on, he discovered some things not to his liking. His instincts as a hard-nosed politician made him feel U.S. efforts to conciliate Russia were a one-way affair. Certainly he wanted to get along with Stalin, but the President harbored no illusions about Kremlin intentions. He did not rationalize Russian behavior in apologetic terms nor did he believe America must lean over backwards to prove its friendship. During the first month of his presidency, he spoke sternly to V. M. Molotov about the failure of the Soviet Union to conduct free elections in liberated Poland. According to Admiral Leahy (who was present), the President used "blunt language unadorned by the polite verbiage of diplomacy." Lend-Lease supplies to Russia were cut off, but this was reversed after a mission to Moscow by Harry Hopkins. Although the latter was in the "let's be friends with Russia" category, Truman sent him to see Stalin in the hope that amicable Soviet-American relations could be restored. Desiring post-war cooperation, the President was willing to extend to hand of friendship to Stalin.

Few in the Roosevelt cabinet stayed to serve Truman. To him, idealists, do-gooders, or one worlders were "professional liberals" who promised much and delivered little. His dislike for impractical dreamers was equaled only by his distaste for those guilty of personal disloyalty. Henry Wallace, former Vice President and now the Secretary of Commerce, was pushed out for meddling in foreign policy; Secretary of State James F. Byrnes got the same treatment for failing to keep the White House adequately informed. Truman liked political realists. Aides were invited to speak frankly about specific issues; his mental faculties reacted best to concrete facts—not abstractions.

When convinced he was right, the President acted with intrepid boldness. Critics sometimes interpreted this as recklessness. Yet the policy of firmness he initiated toward the Soviet Union was not the result of hasty or headlong decision. At Potsdam, for instance, he did not join Churchill in taking a hard line against the Soviets. He tried to establish a working rapport with "Uncle Joe," but Stalin seldom responded to his overtures. The President gave the Russians enough rope, in Missouri parlance, to hang themselves and then he reacted swiftly. Lessons of the Kommandatura in Berlin convinced him not to allow the Soviets an opportunity to disrupt the occupation of Japan. Since the Russians were determined to take advantage of American weakness, Truman was not about to make them a present of anything.

The arbitrary actions of Stalin in establishing the Oder-Neisse boundary for Germany, his refusal to negotiate peace treaties for Eastern Europe, and the subversive activities of Communist guerrillas in Greece all served to force Truman into a "get tough" policy toward the Russians. When Prime Minister Attlee, because of economic difficulties at home, decided to withdraw British troops from Greece, the President had no alternative but to fill the void. And by massively increasing financial and technical aid to friendly nations of Europe, Truman bolstered the defenses of the Atlantic Community and, in so doing, prevented much of Europe from falling behind the Iron Curtain. All pretense of Soviet-American friendship ceased as wartime cooperation turned suddenly into postwar confrontation.

Tensions rose. Most liberals were dismayed at the turn of events and some New Dealers blamed Truman for the Cold War. Henry Wallace, now editor of the *New Republic*, attacked the President as a warmonger and of deviating from Roosevelt's policy of peace. The 80th Congress, whose leadership was conservative and markedly anti-Communist, also joined in on the political assault. Such Republican stalwarts as Robert A. Taft, John Bricker, and Kenneth Wherry spearheaded a neo-isolationist drive to prevent the United States from becoming involved in European affairs. It is an ironical twist of fate that Truman's hard-nosed foreign policy garnered the opposition of both G.O.P. isolationists and one world internationalists.

President Truman's advisers knew that the Greek-Turkey aid program and the loan to Great Britain, which were approved by Congress only after prolonged and rancorous debate, were not sufficient in and of themselves to prevent the collapse of Europe. Germany lay prostrate and the economies of England, France, Italy, and other continental countries were nearing collapse. Ensuing chaos would have made it comparatively easy for the Soviet Union to gain dominance over all of Europe. Improvised reaction to Russian moves was no longer feasible.

At this point the Under-Secretary of State, Dean Acheson, suggested the need for overall coordination of a policy to check Soviet expansion. Following up on this advice, Secretary of State George C. Marshall acted quickly to establish a planning staff. Headed by George Kennan, a scholarly diplomat with many years experience, the

State Department Policy Planning Staff assessed carefully all the strategic considerations involved in stopping a Soviet takeover in Europe. Recommendations were made to implement containment of Russia by rebuilding war devastated economies of the several European nations. This was to be done through massive financial aid and mutual political cooperation.

Secretary Marshall's address at Harvard University, on June 5, 1947, contained the essence of what became the European Recovery Program. The Marshall Plan, as it was popularly called, involved huge U.S. expenditures for the reconstruction of Europe. Satellite countries of Eastern Europe were asked to participate, but Soviet pressure prevented them from accepting. European recovery should have been a dream come true to liberals who wanted to remake the old world; yet pro-Wallace supporters, including Senators Claude Pepper and Glen Taylor, labeled it a thinly disguised manifestation of American imperialism. Wherry-type isolationists, on the other hand, attacked the proposal as a mad adventure to involve the United States in a giant giveaway program. An economy minded Congress was in no mood to appropriate the huge sums needed and to make matters worse Truman's prestige was at an all-time low. The President faced an upcoming election with his own party divided (Wallacite and Dixiecrat factions were in the making) and he faced domestic problems that compounded his troubles. It was extremely doubtful whether he could secure the necessary support for congressional approval of the Marshall Plan.

Joseph M. Jones, in his book *The Fifteen Weeks*, a detailed chronicle of how the European Recovery Program was ultimately passed, credits Walter Lippmann with doing much to prepare public opinion for its acceptance. Lippmann's column of April 5, 1947, according to Jones, was "one of the most consequential . . . he has ever written." (*Today and Tomorrow* was by then syndicated in over two hundred newspapers and reached a reading audience of approximately thirty million persons.) This particular column helped coalesce support for economic aid to Europe as well as influence the thinking of George Kennan. Under-Secretary of State Acheson emphasized an identical theme in his address to the Delta Council of Cleveland, Mississippi, which prepared the way for Marshall's famous Harvard speech. The impact of Lippmann's column, Jones pointed out, was unusual for the following reasons:

"Lippmann did not say anything that was new to many in the State Department. But he simultaneously informed the whole staff of the State Department, from the Acting Secretary on down [Secretary Marshall was attending the Moscow Conference and Dean Acheson was Acting Secretary], the entire government hierarchy, the Congress, of his own estimate of the proportions of an adequate solution: peacetime Lend-Lease and economic union of Eurpe.

"Most important, he so informed the readers of scores of newspapers throughout the country, including the nation's most influential citizens . . . His proposal that the European countries be asked to get together and agree upon a common recovery program and present us with a consolidated deficit was, so far as this writer can discover, original."

On a nationally televised interview in 1960, Lippmann described the Marshall Plan as "probably the greatest single act of constructive statesmanship since the war." Yet, strangely enough, on the same CBS program he also stated, "I was not a supporter of Truman at any time." Why this apparent contradiction? Knowing the ordeal of Harry Truman, it seemed incredible he would take this stand. A closer examination of Lippmann's thought solves this apparent enigma.

In his books *U.S. Foreign Policy* (1943) and *U.S. War Aims* (1944), Lippmann had predicted a Soviet orbit in Eastern Europe. Its existence was not so much an alarming fact as it was a natural turn of events. Truman reacted too impulsively, he thought, talking tough about Eastern Europe when he should have been negotiating peace settlements in Western Europe. To him the Truman Doctrine and containment were too much a reflection of the anti-Communist hysteria gripping most Americans. The United States, somewhat panic stricken at the idea of a Soviet sphere of influence, was driving itself into a frenzied flurry of fear to stop Communism all over the globe. Thus, he observed, the Truman administration was falling prey to the Wilsonian spirit of world crusading. This course, he predicted, would lead ultimately to over commitments and involvements far beyond the nation's military or natural resources.

Lippmann decried the "war psychosis" which prompted all manner of measures to check the expansion of Communism. Cold War psychosis affected not only foreign but domestic policies and seemed to justify witch hunting at home and ideological warfare abroad. American proclivity for elevating international disputes into holy wars should not be encouraged. The primary goal of American foreign policy was to solidify the Atlantic Community and this should be done with calm dispatch. This involved primarily economic and not military aid. It was possible, through the Marshall Plan, to "transcend the cold war and clear the air for European recovery." Rehabilitation of the nations of Western Europe would lead to a "restoration of the balance of power" and such an achievement would by its very nature preclude Soviet hegemony over Atlantic Community countries. Lippmann insisted: "A settlement with Russia does not depend upon an abandonment of Russian imperialism and a renunciation of the Communist ideology." Only by war could that be accomplished and Lippmann advised against such a perilous course of action.

In 1947 he examined Soviet-American relations at length in a book titled significantly *The Cold War: A Study in U.S. Foreign Policy*. His use of the term "cold war" fostered its popular usage and made it part of the lexicon of international diplomacy. Lippmann reiterated his support for a straightforward policy of joining with "natural allies" to "consolidate" the Atlantic Community. It would be a horrendous mistake, he warned again, to "expend our energies and our substance upon . . . dubious and unnatural allies of the perimeter of the Soviet Union." That would be tantamount to a "gross misuse" of American power. The consequences of trying to contain Communism all over the world constituted futile "globalism," asserted Lippmann, and it would lead to an "unending series of insoluble dilemmas." With decisive finality, he penned this axiomatic asseveration: "The earth is much too large, and its troubles and disorders much too extensive for us to regard ourselves as the ultimate fixers of everything everywhere."

Two themes were constantly stressed: a resurgent Europe would force the Soviet Union to regularize its relationship with the Atlantic Community; and the United States should avoid vast military commitments it could not honor. No presumption was made that it was America's moral responsibility to liberate all the iron curtain countries nor its duty to prevent Asiatic nations from entering a Chinese orbit. Lippmann's overriding anxiety stemmed from his feeling the U.S. would, as a self-proclaimed defender of democracy, intervene on the Asian mainland. Red China would extend its sphere and American encroachment might have severe repercussions. Quite literally the specter of a nuclear war with Russia or a land war with Communist China haunted him. In his opinion the Truman Doctrine came perilously close to resembling a world-wide Monroe Doctrine. If that were true it would only be a matter of time, he projected, before the United States, as paladin of the free world, became involved in hostilities with the red dragon of China.

President Truman regarded Lippmann's argumentation as abstract speculation. The Chief Executive did not envision his policies as too grandiose since he had only reacted to Russian provocations with firmness and caution. When asked about Lippmann's views, the President often replied with curt comments such as "Mr. Lippmann is entitled to his opinion" or "hindsight is a great thing." A few choice expletives must have been uttered by Truman after reading the *Washington Post* of March 11, 1948. That day Lippmann wrote, "I myself believe, though few may agree with me, that a very large part of the tension, and indeed hysteria, is due in the last analysis to the fact that on the one hand the Truman administration has no confidence in itself because it was never really elected, and on the other, that the will of the majority was frustrated in 1944." Another column in April contained this strident judgment:

"It is not, I think, an alarmist exaggeration to say that the condition of the Truman Administration is a grave problem for the Nation, not merely for the Democratic Party. The problem is not whether Mr. Truman can be nominated and elected. It is how in the perilous months immediately ahead the affairs of the country are to be conducted by a President who has not only lost the support of his party but is not in control of his own Administration."

Lippmann not only endorsed the Republican presidential nominee in 1948, he went out on a limb by predicting Thomas E. Dewey was "as good as elected." By late October he supposed the Governor of New York held such a commanding lead that one of his columns contained the rhetorical question, "Has it not become clear Dewey will be chosen over Truman?" Lippmann, like almost all political forecasters at the time, went amiss on that particular election. So did the pollsters.

John M. Redding, who helped plan the campaign strategy for the so-called miracle victory, kept a file of Lippmann's columns during the campaign. When the Democratic National Committee no longer had use for them, he sent the file to President Truman with the following remarks:

"After writing for more than seven months that Truman could not possibly win the election, Lippmann had this to say about his clouded crystal ball on November 4, 1948, in the *New York Tribune*:

" 'As one who did not foresee the results of the election I can say, as of the morning after, that I went wrong because I did not expect the Democrats to bring out their full vote. . . .

" 'That is what all of us who went wrong thought was happening; that Dewey could win decisively, not because he had a popular majority but because the Democrats could not or would not bring out their majority.'

"And then Lippmann announced that he was leaving the country for a few weeks to take a trip through Europe!"

Harry Truman must have gotten considerable satisfaction from this memorandum and no doubt grinned gleefully after reading the last sentence.

Despite his election gaffe, Lippmann continued to voice disapproval over Truman's foreign policy. Administration supporters sometimes thought the columnist's criticisms resembled personal carping. Truthfully Lippmann did not think Truman possessed the qualifications for the high office he held. The President's penchant for quick action and, using Speaker Sam Rayburn's words, "shooting from the hip" seemed brash and ill-advised for the head of a powerful nation. Differences between personal bias and rational dislike cannot always be discerned readily, but basically Lippmann's displeasure stemmed from honest disagreement with foreign policy. He felt the President was committing the United States to a disastrous course.

Those within the Truman administration who helped formulate the policy of containment reacted to Lippmann's public strictures in various ways. George Kennan, a major contributor, actually agreed with some of the columnist's criticism. Kennan had remained silent while a member of the State Department, but many years later acknowledged there were glaring faults to which he had objected. He wrote: "Actually, . . . I distinguished clearly in my own mind between areas that I thought vital to our security and ones that did not seem to me to fall into this category. My objection to the Truman Doctrine message revolved largely around its failure to draw this distinction . . . Mr. Lippmann . . . mistook me for the author of precisely those features of the Truman Doctrine which I had most vigorously opposed. . . ."

Dean Acheson, who succeeded General Marshall as Secretary of State, considered himself a thorough realist in foreign policy matters and could never fathom why Lippmann was so captious in regard to the Truman administration. Resenting what was in his mind unfair fault finding, especially since it came in the wake of much unjust abuse from political adversaries, it was the Secretary's firm belief that the United States had to stand up to the Soviet Union. Yet he always counseled restraint lest a full-scale war be triggered off. For instance, the United States did not seek to liberate Czechoslovakia in 1948 after a Communist *coup* overthrew the democratic government of

Jan Mazarek. Even the Berlin airlift, to circumvent Russia's attempt to drive the U.S. from the German city, was a cautious response to a warlike blockade. Even the North Atlantic Treaty Organization, which Acheson helped to create, was purely defensive in nature. By strengthening nations of the Atlantic Community, a balance of power in favor of the free West was achieved. Reaction to Communist aggression in Korea met force with counterforce, but in the measured terms of a limited war. The cautious character of U.S. actions was ignored or overlooked by critics. Even now, while in retirement, Acheson can muster some caustic words when asked his opinion of Walter Lippmann.

Disagreement between these two men merely underscored the fact that realists can differ in their appraisals. Since Acheson bore responsibility for national security, he could not afford the luxury of detached speculation. His policies, not unlike Lippmann's viewpoint, envisaged the restoration of a balance of power in Europe and Asia, with special emphasis upon strengthening Western Europe. Norman Graebner, a diplomatic historian at the University of Virginia, attested that Acehson's concept of foreign policy was based strictly upon power realities. What mattered to him, wrote Graebner, "was the power and unity of the Atlantic Community." It was Acheson himself who defined the prime objective of American foreign policy in terms which Lippmann might well agree: "Its purpose is to protect and further the deepest and most vital interests of the United States and those states which are working toward the same end of safeguarding our common civilization." As a public official the Secretary of State could not take for granted what a critic presumed to be true; namely, Russia was willing to negotiate. Acheson had to cope with their warlike behavior. He learned to distrust what the Soviets said because their actions often contradicted their avowals for peace. Using a press conference for his forum, Acheson explained the practical basis of Truman's foreign policy:

"We must realize, however, that the world situation is not one to which there is an easy answer. The only way to deal with the Soviet Union, we have found from hard experience, is create situations of strength . . . I don't need to go over again with you the fact that, growing out of the last war and between wars, there have been created all over the world these situations of weakness . . .

"Therefore, we go to work, as I said, to change these situations of weakness so that they won't create opportunities for fishing and opportunities for trouble."

Some of President Truman's advisors, far from believing U.S. policies were too firm, came to the conclusion they were too weak. Militant anti-Communists believed Lippmann did not place enough importance on ideological factors. James Forrestal, the first Secretary of Defense, was such a person. Responding to a T & T article which stressed the need for a workable *modus vivendi* with the Soviet bloc, he made the following notation in his diary: "Walter Lippmann's suggestions [imply] that the task of statesmanship is not necessarily to secure democracy for all the world, but to discover the means by which . . . democracy and Communism . . . can find a way of living together."

Following up on this pertinent suggestion, the Secretary asked Professor Edward F. Willet of Smith College to analyze the "nature of the Russian state philosophy" for determining any "possibilities of accommodation between the democratic and communistic systems." A study was prepared. Forrestal sent the findings to Lippmann with the comment, "Your piece last month . . . is responsible for the enclosed notes." The results, however, contradicted what the columnist had recommended since coexistence seemed possible only if the United States strove to contain the Soviet Union both territorially and ideologically. Similar conclusions were also reached by George Kennan. In "The Sources of Soviet Conduct," published in the July, 1947 issue of *Foreign Affairs* (under the pseudonym of Mr. X), Kennan advised a "vigilant application of counter force . . . corresponding to the shifts and maneuvers of Soviet policy." After his retirement, Kennan revealed his disagreement with some aspects of the Truman foreign policy, but he still took more cognizance of idological factors than did Lippmann.

Obviously a crucial point of difference existed between Lippmann and many of those advising President Truman. Lippmann consistently held that Russian foreign policy was formulated primarily to serve Soviet self interest rather than to further the cause of international Communism. He did not think Soviet leaders would ever subordinate the vital interests of their country in order to be the defender of Communism all over the globe. Translated into practicalities that meant ideological rhetoric notwithstanding the Kremlin would not jeopardize national security merely to champion Communism everywherein the world. The August, 1968 invasion and occupation of Czechoslovakia by Russian troops (and those of other Warsaw Pact nations) indicated anew that Communism and Soviet national interest may not be so compartmentalized as previously thought true.

While going on the assumption the Soviets had not ordained themselves the international guardians of Communism, Lippmann spoke disparagingly of U.S. attempts to be the knight errant for world democracy. America's self-designated role as defender of the entire free world would lead to certain calamity. Speaking to a group of students from William and Mary College, he stated: "A diplomacy for the world as it is, which is not to expend itself in verbal declarations on the one hand, and on crusades of annihilation on the other, must deal with the balance of power and the determination of spheres of influence." In this 1948 address, sponsored by the Phi Beta Kappa, he went on to condemn the "all or nothing" attitude so prevelant in American public opinion. There was no millenium of peace awaiting mankind nor should there be an atomic holocaust because the choice was not one of being either "red or dead." This only appeared to be the case since U.S. leaders too often predicated their policies on "high and hopeful declarations" rather than on realistic assessments of actual situations. "Rivalry and strife among nations, communities, and factions are the normal conditions of mankind," he maintained, and these continual conflicts were handled best by recourse to the "classic procedure of diplomacy."

Quite frankly Lippmann accepted the situation as normal when big powers dominated certain geographical areas. Just as the United States has traditionally controlled the Western Hemisphere, and intervened when events dictated (expecting no interference from other nations) so the Soviets controlled their satellites and tolerated no meddling from without. With Red China growing in power yearly, Lippmann took for granted that they would seek paramountcy on the Asian mainland. Southeast Asia would in a matter of time become part of their sphere of influence. Thus he feared the United States, in its role as protector of democracy, would become hopelessly entangled in the Far East. "What could suit the Russians better," he asked, "than to have the only land army in Western Europe fighting guerillas in Indo-China?" This question was raised in February, 1960, just four months before the U.S. was to commit itself to the defense of South Korea; and a full decade before American involvement in Vietnam.

On June 26, 1960 the United Nations Commission in Korea reported to the Secretary-General, Trigvie Lie, that the North Korean Peoples Republic had launched an invasion by crossing the 38th parallel. Reacting to this unprovoked aggression, which he presumed to be inspired by the Kremlin, Truman issued orders to American air and naval units to halt the onslaught from the North. Meeting in emergency session, the Security Council, with the representative of the Soviet Union absent (Jacob A. Malik had been boycotting U.N. meetings), called for an immediate cease fire. Designated by the U.N. to be its police force, U.S. troops were to defend South Korea. General Douglas MacArthur, American Far Eastern Commander, urgently informed Truman that only a large commitment of men and materiel would stave off a collapse of the entire front. Authorizing a drastic increase in the number of soldiers to be used in combat, Truman escalated the level of fighting with the justification, "If we are tough enough now, there won't be any next step." The Truman Doctrine was being implemented in Asia even though formulated originally to protect Western Europe.

Noting the quick action by the United Nations, Lippmann endorsed the decision to intervene. The multilateral nature of the police action made it appear to be a genuine exercise of collective security by member nations. "But for their obligations in the Charter and their interest in avoiding a general conflagration it would be hard to interest most of Asia in the fate of that Korean government." Setting aside his own dismay at the thought of fighting a land war in Asia, he agreed, "If a wretched little satellite government in North Korea can thumb its nose at the U.N. then all hope would be lost that through that universal society the nations of Asia and the nations of Europe and the Americans can find a way to work together."

Within a week after writing those words, he had second thoughts about the wisdom of sending such large contingents of American forces to Korea. Widespread support of other U.N. members did not materialize as he had expected. Token troops showed up, but in insufficient numbers to prevent the Americanization of the conflict. "Both the League and the U.N. have shown that you cannot rally all the nations to a collective war to enforce peace," Lippmann contended, "when the issue is less than the survival of the great nations, the method of collective security will not be used because it is just as terrifying to the policemen as it is to the lawbreakers . . ." Had not the United States gotten involved in a "dirty little war" because of its role as defender of the free world? Apprehension increased due to the close proximity of the fighting to Red China. America was courting danger by venturing into the Chinese sphere of influence and ignoring its own national survival.

Momentarily the tide of battle changed for the better. General MacArthur stood on the banks of the Yalu River with total victory, seemingly, close at hand when suddenly the vast expanses of Manchuria disgorged hordes of Chinese soldiers. Red China had intervened in the war. Their entrance forced an American retreat back to the 18th parallel and beyond. Then MacArthur, with his pride hurt and fury aroused, wanted to turn the defense of South Korea into a full fledged war with Communist China. Despite the public furor, Truman was forced ultimately to relieve General MacArthur for insubordination because he did not want the war turned into a crusade for the total destruction of China. Conceivably that would have involved the use of atomic weapons and may well have provoked the Soviet Union. Fortunately, the new American Commander, General Matthew B. Ridgeway, understood the concept of limited war; defining it, in his excellent work *The Korean War,* as "a war in which the objectives are specifically limited in the light of our national interest and current capabilities." Within this context the U.S. intervention was a success, since it achieved the objective, namely, the preservation of the territorial integrity of South Korea.

Continued conflict in Korea plagued Truman during his final years in office, but he was determined to keep the struggle from escalating into an irrational Armageddon for the annihilation of Communist China. But by so doing, he was handicapped in not being able to rally the American people to a grand crusade. Since his speeches were guarded rather than flambuoyant, opponents of a limited war could make effective use of ringing slogans as General MacArthur's dictum, "There is no substitute for victory." By not using the techniques of Wilson or F.D.R., Harry Truman opened himself to charges that he was unequal to the task of war leadership. Even while opposing Communism, extremists on the right of the political spectrum made him out to be everything from a incompetent dupe to a crypto Communist. Caught in a bind, the prestige of the President declined as the war in Korea waged on. Because he refused to either withdraw American troops or expand the scale of war, Truman reaped a harvest of public censure.

Truman's memoirs refer to this period as the *Years of Trial and Hope,* but to Lippmann they were the bungling years. "Instead of leading the people, the administration spokesmen have relied upon the bastard art of manipulating opinion by sloganeering and shock." Singling out the Secretary of State for special reprimand, Lippmann said: "I hope that Mr. Acheson will write a book explaining how he persuaded himself to believe that a government conuld be conducted without the support of the people." Perhaps to answer his critics, though not just Lippmann, Acheson did write a book, *Power and Diplomacy*, which in turn revealed a unique blend of classical diplomacy with traditional American idealism. The Korean War, for instance, was justified in terms of stopping the advance of Communism, but embodied within that explanation was the object of preserving a balance of power in Asia. American self interest was at stake, vowed Acheson, in that a red inspired takeover in Korea might entice other Communists to try for one in Europe or somewhere in Latin America. All in all, Truman's foreign policy, which in part was formulated by Acheson, was a pragmatic blend of *realpolitik* with moralistic justification for engaging in a struggle to contain Communist power.

Naturally Truman resented Lippmann's attacks and thought his criticism gave respectability to allegations made by less rational opponents of administration foreign policy. Truman's friends did not think the President was being given enough credit for his restraint and refusal to enlarge the war. Right at the time when the going was rough, they thought it ill-advised for Lippmann to undermine the President's power and prestige. World peace had to be purchased at a price, if it was to be attained at all, and the Truman administration saw no alternative other than war.

Invited to present a lecture in 1952 at Oxford University in England, Lippmann placed his opposition to the Korean War in broad historical perspective. This resulted in a book, *Isolation and Alliances: An American Speaks to the British*, which traced the earliest origins of U.S. foreign policy and the dynamics that fashioned it. He once again hammered home the lessons of history. Centuries of isolation and non-involvement with overseas countries conditioned Americans to think in terms of "pacifism and withdrawal." Beguiled into believing the United States attained greatness without acting as other nations, the legend arose that Amrica was morally pure. Its "struggle for the continent" was rationalized by a "moral conviction" that the area of freedom was being expanded. Manifest Destiny, even though it justified conquest of Mexican territory in 1845, was not thought of as outright aggression. Expansionist minded Americans ran roughshod over nation-tribes of Indians with whom it had peace treaties but American history contained no account of moral wrongdoing. Later generations were shielded from the realities of power. When the American eagle unsheathed its talons for battle, popular myth enshrined this predator in a halo of righteousness for rendering its victims helpless. America could do no wrong.

An idealistic aura of moral innocence still pervaded American thought, Lippmann explained, because of the distortion of history. The public failed to understand that "America is one nation among other nations with whom it must deal as rivals, as allies, [and] as partners." By preserving the tale of its pristine purity, American actions were always justified in terms of mission or morality. This outlook, he claimed, "shaped the arguments of those who have favored intervention, participation in the League of Nations and the United Nations, the Truman Doctrine, the Marshall Plan, the North Atlantic Treaty, the intervention in Korea, [and] the Mutual Security Act."

Because of their tradition bound idealism, U.S. leaders outwardly abhorred the creation of spheres of influence or the use of power diplomacy. Contrary to their oft repeated condemnation of such practices, the nation did have a sphere and it did practice power diplomacy. The Monroe Doctrine was not promulgated so much to help Latin America as to keep other countries out of our orbit. By conquering much of the North American continent early in our history, the U.S. dominated its neighbors without seeming to practice power diplomacy. Thus contemporary Americans came to believe we alone had never initiated hostilities for territory or selfish gain. According to this fallacious interpretation of the past, our nation fought for the rights of humanity and to extend the blessings of democracy. The idea of a free world versus a Communist enslaved world was an extension of this line of thought. Lippmann considered it unrealistic for President Truman to pledge American support in the defense of all so-called democratic governments. Thus the public was told that by protecting the Republic of South Korea, we were actually defending democracy. After Korea then what? Would not the United States again have to wage war in the defense of another small nation? Obviously American aims had to be tempered or else U.S. soldiers would be dying on Asian battlefields for decades to come.

Because of being mired down in Korea, the United States was neglecting its natural allies. Primary attention must go to Europe to strengthen its "partnership" with the Atlantic Community. Europe was the fulcrum of power in the world and the security of each constituent member depended upon collective cooperation. More consultation with the governments of Western Europe, particularly Britain, and less action on a unilateral basis would lead to less mistakes. European experience, with its residue of "old world wisdom of mankind," he opined, would temper the crusading zeal of the United States and furnish a "fresh appreciation of the new realities." Quite obviously Lippmann considered Europe, not Asia, the focal point for U.S. concern. Rather consistently, he made it seem as if American concern for allies in the Far East must always take second place to those within the Atlantic Community.

Even though armistice talks began at Kaesong on July 10, 1951 (they moved to Panmunjom in August), it was not until 1954 that the Korean conflict was officially terminated. Despite Truman's belated action in seeking an end to the fighting, Lippmann thought the President had discredited his party and disorganized the nation. In his judgment it was time for a change to a Republican administration.

One of the arguments Lippmann arrayed in defense of his support for Thomas Dewey in 1948 was that the G.O.P. had been out of power for too long a time. Republicans were becoming negative and irresponsible in their perpetual role as representatives of the minority party. "McCarthyism," he pointed out, was evidence of such behavior. To correct this situation he believed the Republican party needed new leadership and a chance to demonstrate its ability to govern. His 1952 choice for the presidency was Dwight D. Eisenhower; for this man, he thought, would be able to revitalize and remold the party. Antics of the junior Senator from Wisconsin, Joseph McCarthy, would of necessity be curtailed with Republicans in control of the government. General Eisenhower, Lippmann conjectured, was best qualified to be a "restorer of order and peace after an age of violence and faction."

"Ike" won his mandate with relative ease. Korean negotiations came to a conclusion and Senator McCarthy was indeed censured by his peers in the Senate. The new President did not ask for repeal of New Deal measures which would have turned back the clock to the days of Herbert Hoover. In general, the Eisenhower administration moved ahead with a moderate program, but most of all it provided a period of pause and consolidation. Although the President satisfied neither radicals nor reactionaries, he did appeal to moderates. By 1956 Eisenhower was the most popular political figure in America with a vote getting appeal far greater than that of the Republican party. The broad grin and upraised arms were irresistible and the phrase, "I like Ike" was not merely a cleverly contrived campaign slogan. It was literally true for millions of Americans.

Despite his achievements, Eisenhower's first term did not fulfill Lippmann's sanguine hopes. Rebuilding of the Republican party along the lines he expected did not materialize; hence, he dramatically shifted his support to Adlai E. Stevenson in 1956. It was with amazement that Lippmann watched Senator John Bricker of Ohio and other conservatives seek to delimit the authority of their own leader. Many columns were written urging Eisenhower to uphold the prerogatives of the presidential office to prevent congressional usurpation of power. Ike was repeatedly taken to task for his supposed failures in defending the "balance of the Constitution, the powers of the Executive, its responsibilities and duties in dealing with foreign affairs, the dignity of the government, and the rights of individual Americans." Stevenson, it was presumed, would correct this vacuum in leadership.

Why did not Eisenhower contest the old fashioned ideas of congressional leaders? This was a question Lippmann continually put to the President. Midwestern Republicans in particular seemed intent on reducing the executive office to a mere figurehead. They linked a strong presidency with the evils of big government and, thus, were opposed to anything that took from Congress its right of restricting the scope of the administration's programs. It struck Lippmann as ludicrous that much of Eisenhower's legislative program ran into opposition from his own party. Only the efforts of Lyndon Johnson and Sam Rayburn salvaged it and they were leaders of the opposition.

Lippmann rejected the Jeffersonian political theory which held the best government was that which governed the least. Modern problems remained unsolved because of congressional inactivity, and without strong executive leadership, the legislators resolved little. Their claim to supremacy over the executive department was an old heresy resurrected to stop progress. It was erroneous, he disputed, to think, "Majorities can do no wrong, that there is no higher truth than the transient opinions of contemporary majorities, and that there is no higher law than the ambitions and the maneuvers of the persons they are persuaded to elect."

According to Lippmann's assessment, congressmen too often represented the selfish and provincial interests of their localities. Without executive leadership their attention could not be focused on those issues affecting the national welfare. Consequently, the country was drifting and people were being lulled into a false sense of security under the stewardship of a president who did not act aggressively. Eisenhower either lacked comprehension or determnaition to move the nation forward. If this were not true, how could civil rights have remained a dormant issue until the Supreme Court took the initiative? Why had space exploration lagged until the Russians led the way with their Sputnik? Why did foreign policy seem to be in the hands of an erratic Secretary of State rather than those of the president? The nation had found itself in the contradictory position of taking on more commitments abroad while cutting the budget at home. Chiding the President for not correlating domestic and foreign policies more adequately, he wrote:

"The overriding emphasis on balancing the budget at a lower level of taxes, does much to raise the question of whether the determining principle of the military policy has been military security or fiscal policy.

"Nor would it be a serious exaggeration to say that . . . the exigencies of the cold war receive hardly more than token recognition."

Taking all things into consideration, it was Lippmann's contention that Eisenhower had "fumbled the ball in the contest of armaments with the Soviet Union," especially regarding parity of missile strength, thereby forcing the United States to "negotiate from a second rate position." Lippmann blamed the President for America's dilemma, i.e. a missile gap and a lagging economy, because of a lack of expertise. He did not honestly think Eisenhower fully understood what was going on at home or abroad. Not only did the Chief Executive's political ineptness trouble him, but Ike's over reliance on the army style staff system failed to produce results. "When nothing much needs to be done," Lippmann professed, the method had merit, but it failed miserably as a means to formulate "new policies" or to "meet the demands of the critical time we are living in." Not many newsmen ventured such strong criticism of the venerable war hero. Whether that evaluation of President Eisenhower's administrative technique was fair or not can be debated. It was true, however, that this method was more effective in the military than for government usage. Like most generals Eisenhower relied heavily on close aides. This forced presidential assistant Sherman Adams to handle affairs not normally within his province. More than once Adams became irritated when his Chief was on the golf links and he was forced to delay matters of state while White House telephone operators sought to catch Ike on the ninth green.

Dwight D. Eisenhower's memoirs dismiss the opinions of Lippmann with a terse comment that the columnist "consistently opposed me." James C. Hagerty, presidential press secretary and a former columnist of the *New York Times,* claimed "Mr. Lippmann and President Eisenhower, as well as members of the President's cabinet, talked privately," but he did not know the substance of those conversations.

Sherman Adams, in retrospect, was certain that "Mr. Lippmann's influence upon the Eisenhower administration was nil."

One cabinet member in particular who provoked much dissent from Lippmann was Eisenhower's Secretary of State, John Foster Dulles. He disagreed with almost all of Dulles' ideas. His misgiving increased after analyzing the Secretary's foreign policy and discovering they were predicated upon what he deemed a fallacious set of premises. These included a belief the Soviet system would ultimately collapse or be overthrown; the desirability of breaking up the Communist bloc by replacing containment with a daring plan for liberation; and a quasi-religious conviction that the United States should strive constantly to prevent Communism from spreading anywhere in the world. Dulles did on occasion speak rashly about liberating Soviet satellites or of recapturing the mainland of China for Chiang Kai-shek. The Secretary also introduced a new phrase into the lexicon of military intimidation; namely the missile-rattling statement about "massive and instant retaliation." Such verbal overkill by Dulles was best illustrated with his truculent remark, "If you are scared to go to the brink you are lost."

Harsh as Dulles' rhetoric sounded, it had a Wilsonian tone about it. All the ingredients were there: the crusading zeal, a universalism, and moral righteousness. Enunciating goals impossible of attainment seemed to Lippmann not only folly but a flirtation with catastrophe. The United States by no means possessed the ability to defeat Communism everywhere and it certainly could not liberate satellite nations or overthrow the Communist regime of Mao Tse-tung in China. In fact, when Chiang Kai-shek took such talk seriously, he had to be rebuffed. Formosa could be no embarkation point for an invasion of China for such a move would have initiated a war of great magnitude. By the same token when the Hungarians expected assistance in 1956, they were denied help and their revolt was crushed by Soviet troops without U.S. interference. Their fight for freedom was valiant, but American intervention would have been tantamount to a declaration of war on the Soviet Union. Bombastic pronouncements by Dulles were responsible, he charged, for the "vascillation between idealism and realism" in American foreign policy relative to both "theory and practice."

Hastily seeking to make West Germany a bastion against Communism, John Foster Dulles moved to give armaments to the Bonn government. This did not set well with Lippmann for he opposed making Germany a pawn in the Cold War. Once rearmed the Germans would be able to play off East against West; it would be wiser, he argued, to have it absorbed into a unified Europe. Proposing the creation of a "great buffer belt from Scandinavia to the Mediterranean," with Germany the nucleus of a *sanitaire cordon* between the Soviet bloc and the Western democracies, he wanted Germany neutralized in a "Commonwealth of Europe." By remaining nonaligned, so went his syllogism, the Germans would be able to develop a stable, democratic government along the lines of Sweden. Resolution of reunification problems and determining ultimate borders had to be accomplished without drawing the two major power groups into conflict.

Permanent prospects of East and West living in two armed camps and shouting threats at each other seemed untenable to Lippmann. Under these conditions any minor incident might touch off a nuclear confrontation. Immediate steps to establish a *modus operandi* or working relationship with the Soviet Union was imperative and two books, *America in the World Today* (1957) and *The Communist World and Ours* (1958), delved into the prospects for such an arrangement.

The brunt of Lippmann's argumentation for a live and let live approach to Communism was presented in *The Communist World and Ours*. This work was written after he visited the Soviet Union to interview Chairman Nikita Khrushchev. A second such session with Khrushchev in 1962, by the way, garnered him a Pulitzer Prize in journalism. Lippmann's first meeting with "Mr. K.," the way he referred to Khrushchev, convinced him the Russian leader was interested in lessening international tensions. While the Communist party chief "regard[ed] the United States as a military power to be treated with the utmost respect," he related, Mr. K. also made it clear that "neither country can defeat the other in direct conflict." This was taken to mean the Kremlin was conceding the existence of a nuclear stalemate insofar as an arms race was concerned.

Using an indirect way of advocating coexistence, Mr. K. told Lippmann, "Communism . . . is indeed a great danger to you as an ideology and as doctrine, but it is not a danger to you as a military policy of the Soviet government." Khrushchev's "central thesis," he proffered, was that the "Soviet economy will in the near future surpass ours in productivity per capita, and that this achievement will cause the poor countries of the world to turn to the Soviet Union as an example and for material help." Boastful, yes, but at least it put Communism and capitalism in competition within acceptable limits by excluding military confrontation. Lippmann sized up his host with this description: "Mr. K. has for the most part a pragmatic and earthy temperament, and he is not so much given to utopian speculation. But he has in him also the basic revolutionary faith that a new history has begun, and that a Communist man is a new kind of man. Along with this, he has an infinite faith that technology and applied science can solve all human problems."

The second portion of *The Communist World and Ours* was devoted to Lippmann's own analysis of East-West differences and ways of resolving them. At the outset he claimed the basic "cause of the bad relations . . . [was] the suspicion, felt on each side of the Iron Curtain, that the other side intends to commit aggression." This feeling was exaggerated every time bellicose language was used in mutual denunciation. Mr. K. and Secretary Dulles were needlessly guilty of much truculent rhetoric. Not only loose talk but "our policy of military containment with its forward positions on their own borders is in their minds conclusive proof that Lenin was right." To achieve a diplomatic *detent*, that is a relaxation of tensions, a frank recognition was needed that neither side could attain a victory over the other. Through such a policy the Soviet Union and United States could reach accord in many areas.

There are "many worlds," he maintained, and recognition of this pluralism would lessen the messianic urge on each side to convert the world to its particular brand of political faith. Admittedly the Russians were "misreading . . . the reality of things" to assume Communism would ultimately triumph all over the world. But Lippmann acknowledged a tendency for the Soviets to artificially harden their stand because of the "propensity of Mr. Dulles, and in lesser degree of the President himself, to treat the conflict, not as one of empires and great states but as a religious war in which the contending positions are absolute." Any prelude to disengagement had to invlove the cessation on both sides of bluff, bluster, and blatant propaganda.

Termination of the Cold War thus depended upon U.S. recognition that "We have to live on the same globe with the Communist powers." Providing the nation kept ready with a "balance of deterrent power," it had nothing to fear from the Soviet Union. Lippmann expressed doubt whether the monolithic character of the Communist bloc could be sustained for long. "I feel sure that the Soviet domination of Eastern Germany, of Poland, Czechoslovakia, and Hungary is precarious and impermanent." Events such as the Hungarian revolution, the schism with Red China, and the independent attitude of satellites bore out that prediction for a time. Sudden Russian occupation of Czechoslovakia in 1968, however, indicated there was a limit to the amount of freedom and latitude the Kremlin would tolerate among the so-called Socialist system of states.

No one should expect that Communism would simply die and disappear. Yet their ideology itself was not the chief cause of concern. "We delude ourselves if we do not realize that the main power of the Communist states lies not in their clandestine activity," cautioned Lippmann, "but in the force of their example, in the visible demonstration of what China has achieved in about ten years." Expectations that Communist countries would collapse where chimerical and unrealistic. Efforts had to be made to win over emerging nations not with guns or military alliances, but through concrete economic assistance. U.S. officials were exhorted to "make an heroic effort of statesmanship to demonstrate that there is an alternative to . . . [Communism], that there is another way to overcome the immemorial poverty and indignity of the life of the Asian masses." That endeavor would require more than mere anti-Communist cliches or hyperbolic moralisms; it involved energy and expenditures.

President Eisenhower assumed personal control of foreign policy during the latter part of his second term and some of the changes Lippmann desired did come to pass. Ike took the initiative and met Soviet leaders at a summit conference in Geneva. Likewise he invited Khrushchev to visit the United States in 1959. Informal discussions between Eisenhower and Mr. K. at Camp David did much to pave the way for lessening of tensions. A fruitful dialogue was initiated and even after the U-2 affair, in which an American overflight wrecked the scheduled Paris summit conference of 1960, lines of communication were kept open. Christian A. Herter, who became Secretary of State after the death of John Foster Dulles in 1959, continued policies aimed at thawing the Cold War.

During the summer of 1960 when the two major parties were in the process of selecting their respective presidential candidates, Lippmann authored a column called, "The Country Is Waiting for Another Innovator." A desire was expressed to see a new leader rise to power in order to redefine the national purpose, "not as a mere restatement of our ideals," but as part of a positive and dynamic "innovation of the political formulae, the concrete measures, the practical program, by which our ideals can be realized in the greatly changed world we now live in." There had been a discernable pause in progress toward domestic reform during the Eisenhower years.

The concept of a compensated economy had been slighted in favor of balanced budgets; abortive launchings of rockets symbolized the lag in space technology; slow implementation of the 1954 Supreme Court decision outlawing segregation in schools had allowed its foes to organize; and a recession on the domestic scene indicated a slackening in the Gross National Product. Executive initiative was again needed to start the cycle of reform. Such inventiveness and leadership, Lippmann predicted, "will appear with the new generation." And indeed there was a young man from Massachusetts, born in the twentieth century, about to win his party's nomination for the presidency. His name was John F. Kennedy.

CHAPTER X

KENNEDY'S NEW FRONTIER

The calamitous nature of world history since 1914 once prompted Winston Churchill to cry out in anguish, "This terrible twentieth century!" Hardly representing the furthermost reach of mankind's evolutionary progress, the last fifty years represented an epoch of considerable savagery. Wars were waged on a magnitude and with weapons never before imagined. Science, the supposed savior of modern man, became the handmaiden of death and destruction; while education, heretofore the hope of humanity, failed to bring forth the promise of universal understanding and peace. Man's collective genius had brought forth the creation of a great technological society, but, paradoxically, while it gave birth to widespread affluence it also produced an age of unprecedented anxiety.

Fallen rubble of brick and mortar in war stricken countries could be quickly rebuilt after World War II, but to reconstruct old value systems was not so easy. Theologians strove to revive religious orthodoxy and philosophers devised existential truths, but neither succeeded in re-establishing a firm foundation for moral absolutes. Materialism simply ignored the existence of God and intellectuals declared the deity dead. Eternal verities, then, rested upon the shifting sands of uncertainty. Twentieth century man had little cause for celebration as the modern malaise of spiritual alientation afflicted him and his society.

Whereas the church once provided answers to profound questions, people now sought advice from social scientists—from psychologists, psychiatrists, sociologists, and educators who attained a status of infallibility usually attributed to the physical sciences. Quantitative studies were used to verify the validity of social mores; environment was made the villain when human behavior took on anti-social attributes; and a couch replaced the confessional.

Several generations of children were raised according to the dictums of Dr. Benjamin Spock and then educated in conformity with the doctrines of John Dewey. Methodology, life adjustment, and permissiveness supplanted the older emphasis on subject matter, inner directed behavior, and discipline. The schools adhered closely to the principles of psychology, and great stress was placed on learning by experience. Experimental methods were wedded to methodology; history, for example, became merely a handmaiden of social studies. Group projects, designed to encourage sociability, supplanted solitary study and reflection. Functional activities became supreme. Courses devoted to Latin, ancient history, or logic were discarded in favor of dancing and driver training. "School was life," said John Dewey, and that slogan justified a multitude of new learning by experience activities.

With cities towering higher and factories turning out goods like a magical cornucopia, modern civilization was a marvel of man's technological inventiveness. These great advances resulted because of a heritage that included a tremendous fund of scientific knowledge. The rich legacy of the past also supported a magnificent culture. Contemporary civilization rested on pillars of history and the American way of life stood atop the entire structure. If the basic constructs of western civilization crumbled, would not American institutions be endangered? So much depended upon continuity and knowledge of what had gone on before. Schools bore the responsibility for transmitting this precious cultural heritage.

Writing for *Commonweal*, Lippmann struck out at "Education Without Culture." Decrying the replacement of classics with "incidental improvisations," he urged restoration of basic courses in the curriculum. Learning about democracy involved more than practicing group methods and social adjustment. Survival of the democratic way of life depended upon self-restraint, knowledge of its historical development, and an appreciation for the traditions of Western civilization. Scholarship and reflective study were more important on the scale of priorities than group activities or social skills. Educators were reminded: "Men cannot remain civilized when they have rejected the culture of their civilization; that is to say when they no longer think of themselves and their places in the universe, when they no longer discipline themselves . . . in the tradition which came to them from the prophets and the saints and the teachers and the philosophers who raised Western man out of barbarism."

By lectures, articles, and books, Lippmann continued to dwell on the vital necessity for transmitting the cultural heritage to young people. Because secularism replaced religion and the "prestige that once adhered to those who speak by revelation today belongs to the scientist," he wondered what would happen to the manners and morals of those unacquainted with the moral precepts of the Judaic-Christian tradition? Liberal thinkers of the 17th and 18th centuries "were themselves the adherents of a public philosophy which is inherent in the central tradition of the classical and Christian world"; and it "never occurred to them," he remarked, "that the public philosophy which they regarded as self-evident would become lost to educated men." Ironic as it was, "The founding fathers inherited this belief. For modern secular men, who have been taught to reject it, an act of faith is needed."

Complete absence of a public philosophy or a commonly held set of beliefs augured ill for humanity, especially Western man. Speaking before the United Nations, a rare privilege accorded to no other journalist, he outlined somber prospects for the rest of the twentieth century:

"The future of the United Nations is bound up with the agonies and the hopes of a great historical process. This process is the dissolution of the ancestral order of power and authority under which mankind has been accustomed to live.

"An anarchy of emptiness has followed this dissolution. Amidst violence and frustration and disappointment, we are living through the attempts to create in this vacuum a new and acceptable order."

During the 1950's, paralleling the Eisenhower administration, Lippmann and other cultural conservatives attempted to reconcile traditional values with contemporary needs. Although they were divergent in viewpoint and acted independently, such seminal thinkers as Clinton Rossiter, Peter Viereck, Russell Kirk, and Peter Drucker were part of an intellectual movement dedicated to the promotion of a New Conservatism. It coincided roughly with the efforts of Arthur Larsen to promote "modern Republicanism" (elaborated upon in his *A Republican Looks at His Party*). Viereck best described the broad principles of this movement as: "Self-expression through self-restraint; preservation through reform; humanism and classical balance; a fruitful nostalgia for the permanent beneath the flux; and a fruitful obsession for unbroken historic continuity."

Other ideas emanating from the new movement reflected concern with positive government, preservation of cultural values, and progress within a stable society. This related it in political terms to the Federalist-Whig-Progressive tradition identified with such historical figures as Alexander Hamilton, John Adams, Abraham Lincoln, and Theodore Roosevelt. Very few of its principles were business oriented, hence it had little in common with economic conservatives who dealt exclusively with cutting the budget and limiting the role of government. Perhaps the most serious blunder of President Eisenhower was his failure to champion modern Republicanism or even to take advantage of the intellectuals' endeavor in seeking to inaugurate a conservative renaissance. Inasmuch as the Republican Party and American conservatism were essentially the same after Ike's departure—he could hardly be considered a great conservative leader. When such G.O.P. stalwarts in the Senate as John Bricker, William Knowland, and Barry Goldwater established themselves as spokesmen for the party, it made Republican principles synonymous with reactionary do-nothingism. Because Ike's cabinet was composed of such businessmen as Ezra Taft Benson, Charles Wilson and George Humphrey, to name a few, newsmen were quick to describe it as "eight millionaires and a plumber." The latter term referring to Martin Durkin, president of the plumber's union, who remained as Secretary of Labor only a short time. This failure to rebuild the Republican Party was, in part, the reason Lippmann opposed the President's reelection in 1956. It also prompted him to write another book.

Walter Lippmann produced his most important work, *Essays in the Public Philosophy*, as the culmination of thirty years of political thought. It was indeed his *magnum opus*. The direct antecedent of this work was an address, "Man's Image of Man," given to the American Catholic Philosophical Association in 1941. This cogent exposition on various interpretations of human nature was intended to be the theme of a book when wartime events forced a postponement. After resuming work on it, the scope of his study was broadened to include both an examination of reasons for the decline of democracies and why moral authority in the West was decaying. Surveying history once again he wrote, "I believe there [has been] a public philosophy of civility . . .," and that "public philosophy [was] the premise of the institutions of the Western society, and they are, I believe, unworkable in communities that do not adhere to it." Lippmann elaborated on his thesis trying to establish its validity. To do this he utilized metaphysical arguments.

What was the origin of the public philosophy? Its authenticity involved knowledge of its source, an epistemological question, and the veracity of that genesis. The guiding principles or "laws of a rational society," Lippmann claimed, could be deduced from the "imponderable authority which [was] derived from tradition." Encapsulated within long-established custom resided a wisdom of the ages. By virtue of its survival, having been tempered by time and tribulation, this cumulative sagacity of the past acquired an inherent authenticity constituting a vital "natural law." By enduring—it transcended the kaleidoscopic flux of immediacy and gave mankind a body of permanent verities. These lasting values did not represent the whim or caprice of any one generation or even any one century because it formed an aggregate of "higher generalities," according to his logic, and thus attained a status of self-evident and universal truth. Constituting a sapiential consensus of countless centuries of Western civilization, this tradition represented the insights and mature thought of untold numbers of philosophers, prophets, saints, and sages from time immemorial. American society was the direct beneficiary of this collective wisdom or "traditions of civility," using Sir Ernest Barker's concept, since it provided the philosophic foundations for all of the nation's legal and political institutions.

There was a spiritual aspect to the public philosophy and Lippmann set about to prove it. Immediate environment and events did mold individual behavior patterns, none the less, he insisted in the final analysis the past gave meaning to the present. Drawing from George Santayana's *The Realm of Being*, he set forth the proposition that man lived simultaneously in a "realm of existence" and a "realm of the spirit." The ontological bridge between the temporal, with its transitory change, and the permanent, which encompassed man's rational and spiritual life, was the "realm of essence." This realm of essence, referring to the body of abstract truths as refined and preserved by tradition, constituted the only available means for man to interpret the ultimate meaning of life in relationship to the universe. These essences provided man with absolutes, transcendent values, and idealized concepts necessary to fathom the unknown reaches of reality. Armed with this realm of purified truths it was possible to live in the material world and yet be guided by rationality. Without them there was only "being and nothingness," and the institutions of society could not long rest upon such philosophical nihilism. Man was an animal to be sure, but he also had a spirituality in need of a value system.

Throughout history a creative tension existed between the realms of existence and spirit which resulted in the dynamic achievements of Western civilization. Neither aspect of man's life, his material or spiritual, need be destroyed by the other; to the contrary, the lives of great men from classical antiquity to the medieval era were an example of maintaining a delicate balance between the two. Only now in modern times did it appear that the spirit of man would be crushed and with it the very basis of Western morality. The quality of man as both a moral and materialistic entity had to be preserved because this

allowed for the co-existence of earthly grandeur with a higher morality; empirical science with philosophical speculation; poetry with technology; and universal truths with relativisitic change. It could not be
"either/or" but both—for this was the genius of Western man.

What practical application did Lippmann's philosophical postulates
have? The "principle of right behavior in the good society," he posited,
was "governed by the Western traditions of civility." Communities
were bound together by a "continuum of public and private memories [that] transcend[ed] all persons in their immediate and natural
lives and it tie[d] them all together." Knowledge of and participation
in this continuous whole linked the quick and the dead, the young
and the old, and transformed cultural aliens into full fledged members
of society. If the "seamless web of memory," was rent asunder or, for
some reason, the "cultural heritage was . . . not transmitted," the
result, he cautioned, was to condemn each new generation to the difficult task of "rediscovering and reinventing and relearning, by trial
and error, most of what the guardians of society need to know." Youth
not conversant with what transpired in the past would know nothing
of the traditions of civility. In their ignorance they would lose their
orientation and locus within the confines of Western civilization.
Without a "mirror of history," using theologian Karl Jasper's phrase,
modern man cannot recognize himself or his environs. Left to welter
in a labyrinth of uncertainty with no positive guides for life, young
people would wander aimlessly suffering from self indulgence and
spiritual anxiety.

Lippmann held that "a nation divided irreconcilably on 'principle,'
each party believing itself pure white and the other pure black, cannot
govern itself." Principles of the public philosophy served to unify the
nation even when political dissent appeared. Unwritten but generally
accepted rules guided behavior simply because everyone accepted the
traditions of civility. This in no way meant differences of opinion
could not exist, but it did mean diversity was both possible and necessary within the general acceptance of the public philosophy. "Democracy can be made to work only when the bonds of the community are
inviolate, and stronger than all the parties and factions and interests
and sects." Lippmann elaborated:

"The civilized man is conservative in that his deepest loyalty is to
the Western heritage of ideas which originated on the shores of the
Mediterranean Sea. . . .

"The civilized man is liberal because the writing and the administration of the laws should be done with enlightenment and compas-

sion, and with affection. And the civilized man is progressive because the times change and the social order evolves and new things are invented and changes occur."

Prior to the second World War many democracies succumbed to the lure of totalitarianism. This defection, he asserted, was attributable to radical departures from the West's public philosophy. Without restraints imposed by traditional morality, entire populations were organized into barbaric phalanxes. Since the days of the French Revolution, he maintained, "The Jacobins and their ancestors made a political religion upon the reversal of civility. Instead of ruling the elemental impulses, they stimulated them. . . . Upon this gospel they founded a popular religion of the rise of the masses to power.

"Lenin, Hitler, and Stalin, the hard totalitarian Jacobins of the twentieth century, carried this movement and the logical implications of its gospel further and further towards the very bitter end."

Maximillien de Robespierre, the leader of the Jacobin faction in the tortuous upheaval that shook the French nation, believed in using fire and sword to attain political goals. Robespierre ended his revolutionary career on the guillotine, a victim of the very Reign of Terror he helped unleash. Instability ensued and France forever after has lived in the aftermath of that bloodbath. Ideological hatreds remained so that parliamentary government frequently became paralyzed in the French Republic. Only with the advent of Charles de Gaulle in modern times has France attained a workable democracy. Revolutionary zeal, the barricade and mob violence were not harbingers of a stable society. To the contrary, self restraint in politics yielded results that were both beneficial and lasting.

Since sound government was the product of institutional stability, this accounted for Lippmann's great emphasis on schools as transmitters of the cultural heritage to train leaders who would in turn be custodians of the public philosophy. Those who governed or assumed roles of responsibility in society had an unwritten obligation to strengthen the fundations of democracy.

"For that reason," Lippmann declared, "society must demand of those who have the ambition to lead it a higher standard of disinterestedness than they would live up to if they had no public ambitions.

"Noblesse oblige. This . . . [was] not, though some may think so, a 'highfalutin' and perfectionist view of the obligation of leadership. In the case of the captain of the ship, for example, who must save all other lives before his own, so high a standard of conduct is regarded not as fancy and foolish but as indispensable to the discipline and safety of the ship."

Leaders in every facet of American life, he told the graduating class of the New School for Social Research, must themselves lead a "dual life." They, as scholars, had to "seek the truth dispassionately," but as men of action were compelled to engage in "rational debate" and reasonable compromise. Within the basic principles of the public philosophy a consensus was possible, because the democratic process depended upon debate not demagoguery, and it thrived on ideas not ideological conflict. Lippmann believed that a dialogue between leaders could take place both privately and in the public arena. Because of his own contacts, he discovered discussions and exchanges of opinion were possible in such social organizations as the Century Association of New York or the Metropolitan Club in Washington, D. C. Here men of various professions, such as government officials, journalists like himself, and businessmen, could exchange ideas on an informal basis. Argumentation was useful, but more important was the adjudication of differences within the confines of the American political system.

Reactions to *Essays in the Public Philosophy* were mixed. Charles de Gaulle informed Lippmann the work was "filled with ideas, reflections, [and] . . . depth of thought." The General, who would become President of the Fifth French Republic within three years after he wrote Lippmann, commented:

"What, in my opinion, shakes the democracies is that they mingle themselves with the representative parliamentary system, that is to say with the usurpation of the people's sovereignty by some professional politicians.

"There results from it that the latter do not have the adequate authority or credit to [solve] problems and that the people no longer are in democracies but [only] the organization and representation of particular interests."

A different response, somewhat negative in character, came from the eminent theologian Reinhold Niebuhr. Before he launched into a critical review of the work, he prefaced his statement with a friendly remark: "I heartedly agree with everything he has written journalistically and in his occasional writings in an effort to alter the inadequacies of our 'public philosophy'." Having said that, Niebuhr outlined two major areas where he disagreed with Lippmann:

"His political answer is the establishment of a stronger executive power. This is not convincing. . . . If our executive power were stronger than it now is, it would become irresponsible (or partly irresponsible, as the power of the president in the Fifth Republic of France now is).

"His moral answer is the restitution of 'natural-law' norms. Traditional conceptions of natural law presupposes a classical ontology, which equates history with nature and does not allow for the endless contingencies of history and the variety of its configuration.

"If we do full justice to these contingencies, our norms are bound to be no more precise than the general feelings that there are standards of justice which transcend any conceivable positive law."

Because of his views in *The Public Philosophy*, some critics again claimed Lippmann was advocating some type of rule by a cultured oligarchy. What he had in mind was no more than that implied in Thomas Jefferson's desire to see the nation ruled by an "aristocracy of talent," meaning well educated leaders. Lippmann's critical attitude toward all presidents was due to the high level of performance he expected of them. Since they were the captain of the ship of state, he evaluated their political behavior in a very hypercritical manner. His criteria for excellence rose as the responsibility of the position increased. With this in mind one can fathom why he was so critical of Truman and Eisenhower. Lippmann did not think either acted wisely in using executive power or the moral authority of his office.

During the latter portion of the fifties, Lippmann perceived the existence of a "defensive" attitude on the part of the general public. At a time when presidential leadership should have been imaginative, innovative, and inspiring, it tended, in his opinion, to lull the American people into an unwarranted sense of well-being. Speaking on a nationally televised interview in 1960, "Lippmann on Leadership" (which earned him a Peabody Award) he voiced concern over the inertia of the Eisenhower administration. Wanting to "hold on and to conserve" had to be overcome with a driving desire to "push forward and to create." Real conservatism, however, involved preservation through adjustment—not by resisting all reforms. He claimed it was not the nation that was old and incapable of change, "but only its leaders."

When the time came for the political parties to select their respective nominees in 1960, Lippmann did not think Richard M. Nixon possessed sufficient stature for national leadership. It was impossible for him to attain the "exalted position" of Eisenhower in terms of popular esteem and trust. The Vice President was a talented politician but lacked character. Governor Nelson A. Rockefeller of New York impressed him; although he was considered a "man of the future." His opportunity for the presidency would come later. The

Democrats were the best instrument for change, since their "historical function" has been "innovation," he explained, while that "of the Republican party consolidation." Among the Democratic contenders he liked Adlai E. Stevenson best. Although twice beaten, the former Governor of Illinois and titular head of the party deserved another opportunity. Everything about Stevenson qualified him for the presidency. A young Senator from Massachusetts also caught Lippmann's attention, but when it appeared the religious issue might plague John F. Kennedy, as it had Al Smith, he thought the vice-presidency might be a better goal for the youthful contender. After the nominating conventions, when it became a contest between Nixon and Kennedy, Lippmann favored the election of the latter.

As part of the research for this work the authors inquired of the late Senator Robert F. Kennedy just what influence the writings of Walter Lippmann had upon his brother's political thinking. We presumed it to be considerable. Robert Kennedy's reply, dated September 22, 1967, confirmed this opinion:

"Your conclusion that 'while serving as the Senator from Massachusetts, John F. Kennedy did consider the views of Mr. Lippmann as worthy of consideration, is indeed correct.

"And while he was President, he had a great respect for him, and although he frequently disagreed, he had great respect for the fact that Lippmann took a position and gave his views with courage, unlike many others. President Kennedy always read his column."

In the Pulitzer prize winning book, *Profiles in Courage*, written while convalescing from a serious operation on his back, John F. Kennedy set the tone of the work with a quote from Lippmann's *Essays in the Public Philsophy*. Kennedy, who, in this study, gave historical recognition to political figures demonstrating resolution and integrity, wrote:

"Walter Lippmann, after nearly half a century of careful observation, rendered in his recent book a harsh judgment on the politician and the electorate: 'With exceptions so rare they are regarded as miracles of nature, successful democratic politicians are insecure and intimidated men. They advance politically only as they placate, appease, bribe, seduce, bamboozle, or otherwise manage to manipulate the demanding, threatening elements in their constituencies. The decisive consideration is not whether it is popular—not whether it will work and prove itself, but whether the active-talking constituents like it immediately'."

J.F.K.'s library in the Senate building contained many of Lippmann's works. The Senator was fond of quoting the columnist. In one particular Senate speech, given on January 1, 1960 and included in his book *The Strategy of Peace*, Kennedy called for a new approach to end Cold War tensions. During the course of his address, he declared: "Certainly it is time for a change—time for us, in the words of Walter Lippmann, 'to come alive and to be alert and to show vigor, and not to keep mouthing the same old slogans, and not to dawdle along in the same old rut'." It was clearly obvious from this and other expressions of opinion that Kennedy agreed with Lippmann's basic outlook on the future direction of American foreign policy.

After his election to the presidency, John F. Kennedy's new policy took a course parallel to the one advocated by Lippmann. J.F.K. accepted the concept of an Atlantic Community and sought to use it as a basis for increasing Western unity. This became evident, when in his "Report to the Nation on the Berlin Crisis," which was delivered over television on July 25, 1961, J.F.K. said:

"The Atlantic Community, as we know it, has been built in response to the challenge; the challenge of European chaos in 1947; of the Berlin blockade in 1948; the challenge of Communist aggression in Korea in 1950.

"Now, standing strong and prosperous, after an unprecedented decade of progress, the Atlantic Community will not forget its history or the principles which gave it meaning."

Elaborating further on his own plans for solidifying the Atlantic Community, Kennedy told Congress in his State of the Union Message of January 11, 1962, and again following a position championed by Lippmann, that Western Europe was no longer concerned with "purely military aims." What it wanted now was "common understanding" and this could be accomplished through cooperation as "partners in aid, trade, defense, diplomacy, and monetary affairs." A union of free nations working for the attainment of common interests provided a realistic foundation for success. Time and tenacity were needed, since differences among the Western nations had to be resolved by mutual assent. "It is a matter of undramatic daily cooperation in hundreds of workaday tasks," the President explained, since, "The Atlantic Community grows, not like a volcanic mountain, by one mighty explosion, but like a coral reef, from the accumulating activity of it all."

Figuratively speaking, the distance between Woodley Road (Lippmann's residence) and the White House was less during the Kennedy

administration than it had been since the days of World War II.
Receiving both official invitations for events at the White House and
private requests for consultation, Lippmann was a frequent guest at
state dinners or concerts, such as the featured appearance of Pablo
Casals. There were differences of opinion between Lippmann and
Kennedy (or with presidential advisors), but the Chief Executive
possessed the intellect and inclination to appreciate rational dissent.
New Frontiersmen generally admired the dean of Washington's press
corps and listened attentively to what he had to say. Perhaps Lippmann identified Kennedy in his mind's eye with Theodore Roosevelt.
T.R. did not resemble J.F.K. physically, but there were similarities.
Both the statesman from Sagamore Hill and the young President
from Hyannis Port wrote history, read widely, appreciated culture,
were energetic, possessed attributes of both conservatism and liberalism, and viewed foreign policy in realistic terms.

J.F.K.'s boldness in exerting moral leadership for advancing civil
rights; awareness of urban problems; applying the principles of the
new economics to increase the Gross National Product; and pushing
the space program forward were given editorial support by Lippmann.
Likewise, he thought Kennedy's foreign policy objectives, in the main,
were correct. Moves toward a *détente* with the Soviet Union; general lowering of tariffs at home and abroad; steps to further economic
unity in Europe; and a test ban treaty preventing nuclear explosions
in the atmosphere were all written about with hearty approval. Because of opposition from the radical right loudly objecting to overtures toward the Soviet Union and a negative attitude on the part of
Congress, which prevented enactment of many administration proposals, his columns tended more and more to defend Kennedy while
criticizing the President's political opponents.

There were other reasons why Lippmann found J.F.K. an ideal
leader. For instance, the President exemplified *noblesse oblige* at its
best. Born into wealth, Kennedy nevertheless devoted his talents to
government service. He was well educated, knew the art of politics,
and possessed traits of leadership. His mature tastes and appreciation
for culture were hallmarks of an administration that did more for the
performing arts than any previous one. J.F.K. strove to upgrade public taste. Borrowing another of Lippmann's concepts, it was President
Kennedy who said: "The 'Great Society' asks not how much, but how
good; not only how to create wealth but how to use it; not only how
fast we are going, but where we are headed." To bestow public honor
on those persons who had made distinguished contributions to the

quality of American life, J.F.K. established the Medal of Freedom. This award was presented to Walter Lippmann in 1964, by President Johnson, with the citation: "Profound interpreter of his country and affairs of the world, he has enlarged the horizons of public thinking for more than five decades through the power of measured reason and detached perspective."

In 1960 Lippmann shifted the origin of his syndicated column from the *New York Herald Tribune* to the *Washington Post*. Shortly thereafter he began to contribute regular bi-monthly articles to *Newsweek* in as much as both publications were owned by Philip and Katherine Graham. Featured as a cover story, his first piece for *Newsweek* was an evaluation of the Kennedy administration in which he praised the President for his handling of the Cuban missile crisis. "John F. Kennedy knows how to learn by experience . . . In October 1962, he showed he has not only the courage of a warrior, which is to take risks that are necessary, but also the wisdom of the statesman, which is to use power with restraint."

When Kennedy sought to stimulate the national economy by implementing theories from the so-called new economics, it aroused opposition in Congress. Lippmann charged that Southern reactionaries, Senator Harry Byrd of Virginia in particular, "talk as if they had never read a book on economic matters which had been written since the great depression of 1929." The "nub of the theory" was "not to balance the government budget itself but to balance the economy." Explaining its origins, he said: "The Kennedy domestic program is based on the same economic philosophy as the reports of the Rockefellers Brothers Fund. Both go back to the pioneering works of the great modern economists, notably Wicksell and Cassel in Sweden and John Maynard Keynes." Lippmann considered this economic philosophy conservative in application, not radical, because it strengthened the capitalistic system. This new mode of thought simply recognized the totality of the economy, both public and private sectors, and utilized appropriate techniques to induce general prosperity. Such innovation in economic thinking was merely a concomitant to vast changes that had already occurred in the circles of high finance.

Lippmann visited London and other European capitals in 1962 to assess the status of the Atlantic Community. "Seen in its historical perspective," wrote Lippmann, "Prime Minister Harold Macmillan's decision to apply for membership in the European Economic Community and President Kennedy's proposal for a trans-Atlantic low-tariff partnership were joint efforts to set the Western world on a liberal course." The development of the common market, to which the United States was linked through the Trade Expansion Act of 1962, was in his judgment "one of the greatest movements of our century." After returning to the United States, he wrote a series of T & T articles on what he had learned. These were subsequently published in book form as *Western Unity and the Common Market*, which was dedicated to his friend, and one of the main architects of European unity, Jean Monnet. "I set out with a strong conviction," he wrote, "that the [common market] project was desirable, indeed, necessary, that it was part of the manifest destiny of the Western world." Success in this venture would integrate the economies of the Atlantic Community to such an extent it would create true unity; and if that could be accomplished, it would perhaps end forever Europe's destructive, internecine warfare.

To Lippmann's great disappointment, the Atlantic Community was not completed because Charles de Gaulle did not favor Great Britain's entry into the common market. Why? In Lippmann's view it stemmed from French dislike of American nuclear supremacy and its hegemony over Europe. President De Gaulle did not want the English to be a Trojan horse for its commonwealth or U.S. interests and thus opposed Anglo-American dominance in Europe. Through a Franco-German treaty, he challenged America's Atlantic Partnership with a concept of Europe extending from the Atlantic to the Ural Mountains. Though De Gaulle prevailed, Lippmann still thought the Atlantic Community concept more valid than dreams of "French grandeur." Consequently, he did not think it advisable for the U.S. to deliberately proliferate nuclear weapons by giving them to France. "We do not have a divine right to have in our hands, rather than European hands, the ultimate decisions," he concluded, "but it is in our interest to hold on to the ultimate decisions, if we can, and we must not be beguiled and bemused by any sentimental adulation of venerable statesmen who are not moved by sentimentality."

Growth of the American economy was not only linked to problems of foreign policy, e.g. trade expansion and the common market, but many other reforms were contingent on the success of expanding the scope of business activity. Kennedy's attack upon hard core unemployment and fostering of equal opportunities for Negroes hinged on an ability to increase the number of domestic jobs. Lippmann regarded the administration's efforts in civil rights as truly commendable. Long overdue, he thought, "Negroes are asking for their lawful rights which are the normal prerogatives of non-colored American

citizens." Such a desire was not a "rebellion," but a legitimate appeal
for "redress of grievances." Therefore his advice to J.F.K. was to act
"resolutely" in the "enforcement of equal legal rights." Since Southerners were labeling this movement both un-constitutional and Communist inspired, he defended Kennedy against these excessive charges.
Integration would, in fact, head off real racial disturbances; and the
black moderates, in this case Dr. Martin Luther King, Jr. and the
leaders of the National Association for the Advancement of Colored
People, were working completely within the framework of democracy.
They had been patient and reasonable in their demands and J.F.K.'s
endeavor to both move Congress and enlighten the public on this
issue were lauded by Lippmann.

Lippmann viewed J.F.K. as the prime example of a political moderate. Not since Theodore Roosevelt had he been so generous in his
acclaim of an American President. Repeatedly, he pointed out the
stellar qualities of J.F.K.'s statecraft. "Though Mr. Kennedy is a progressive and a liberal, he is also a profound conservative, and only the
befuddled theorists find that strange and hard to understand." On
another occasion he wrote: "To be a man of the center is to be at
once conservative, liberal, and progressive. Mr. Kennedy has always
been a man of the center and, in leading the Democratic administration in the center-position, he has led the Democratic party to the
place where the big majority lives."

Appearing on television in 1964, for a special interview program on
CBS, Lippmann described Kennedy as the prototype of a "new kind
of American politician." His achievements were fourfold, he asserted,
even though the work started by the assassinated President was essentially unfinished. In this evaluation of Kennedy, he credited him with:
(1) bringing "to an end the threat, for the foreseeable future, of
nuclear war"; (2) initiating a "new fiscal policy"; (3) starting a
"really serious attack on the problem of Negro rights"; and (4)
formulating a positive "campaign against poverty." The slain President perceived what needed to be done and provided the nation with
an agenda for action.

That dismal day at Dallas brought an abrupt end to the life of a
vibrant and exciting leader. His brief moment on the stage of history
was dramatic albeit shortlived. Having begun his writing career before John Kennedy was even born, Lippmann mourned the death of
the President as a great tragedy. History had taken a cruel course
with no rational explanation for it. The life breath of a magnificent
leader was snuffed out in an instant by the wicked act of another

human being. On December 1, 1963, while in a pensive mood during the advent of Christmas, Lippmann penned this thoughtful sentiment:

"In the presence of a young man's death and of his brilliant promise cut short by the terrible evil of mankind, the better course of man was for a time in command. When next we work ourselves up into a tantrum about something or other, let us remember how small it is in the perspective of the first and last things of human experience."

Chapter XI

JOHNSON'S GREAT SOCIETY

Lyndon Baines Johnson had built a solid record of achievement while serving as Majority Leader in the Senate. Skilled in the parliamentary techniques of a floor leader, he knew how to maneuver and cajole his colleagues for votes. But after the election of 1960, while Vice President, he was somewhat relegated to the wings away from the center of the political stage. It was no secret that L.B.J. did not feel at home among the New Frontiersmen. The Texan's rough-cut manners and folksy style seemed out of place amid an atmosphere of intellectual conversation and sophisticated wit. Johnson liked plain talk, the personal touch, and plenty of action. Leadership to him did not involve consulting critics or enlightening public opinion; it meant making deals and maneuvering legislation through the labyrinth of Congress.

When the fortunes of fate suddenly placed him in the White House, Lyndon Johnson intended to be known in history as a great President. Relying on his own legislative experience, L.B.J. began to operate in the style to which he was accustomed. He persuaded, pressured, scolded, and charmed Congressmen. Whichever technique suited the occasion was utilized to secure enactment of a huge backlog of bills worked out previously by Kennedy task forces. Before long, countless measures were passed and brought to him for presidential signature.

In less than a year, Congress enacted a Civil Rights Act, a foreign aid appropriation, the Economic Opportunity Act (the antipoverty act), a Housing Act, funds for the "impacted areas" (money for schools), extended the National Defense Education Act, and reduced taxes to stimulate economic growth. Medicare and massive assistance to the Appalachia region missed on this occasion, but his record was, nevertheless, impressive. Democrats were elated at their prospects of electing Johnson to a full four-year term in 1964. L.B.J. had aptly demonstrated to the American people his ability to get things done in a hurry.

Until after the California primary, which saw Governor Nelson Rockefeller go down to unexpected defeat, few political forecasters expected Barry Goldwater to win the presidential nomination. Since the Arizona Senator represented right wing Republicanism, according to the normal rules of coalition politics, it should have ruled him out. No one ever questioned the sincerity of Goldwater's stand on important issues—just their wisdom. Essentially, he stood for a return to *laissez faire* capitalism, high tariffs, and limited government; all of which were more appropriate to nineteenth rather than twentieth century America.

Regarding foreign policy, the Arizonan opposed any action that might be considered being soft on Communism. Using emotional appeals to morality and red blooded Americanism, he spoke of achieving "total victory" over Communism everywhere in the world. This was advocated, seemingly, without considering the repercussions of his remarks. By calling Russia and Red China our "sworn enemies," and promising to eradicate the Communist challenge in Europe and Asia, his bellicose rhetoric made it appear he was ready to mount a full-scale war against the enemies of democracy.

With the nation watching over TV, the Republicans at San Francisco nominated Barry Goldwater and ran roughshod over liberals while doing so. To make matters worse, the nominee made no conciliatory gestures toward them and in fact right-wing delegates went out of their way to show their disdain for the so-called Liberal Establishment of the East. Goldwater supporters felt the communications media were biased and some were even convinced that such large publications as the *New York Times* reflected socialistic ideas. During one frenzied outburst against the press, a delegate from North Dakota was heard to shout: "Down with Walter Lippmann! Down with Walter Lippmann!" A huge crowd at the Cow Palace went wild with delirium when Goldwater, in his acceptance speech, uttered the defiant words, "Extremism in the defense of liberty is no vice." This convention, resembling a congregation of true believers, wanted to wage a campaign against what they deemed to be corrupting influences in American life and Goldwater was their prophet.

To Walter Lippmann the Republican nominee was a man of principle, but also a political figure with doctrinaire and outmoded views. "The paramount fact is that a great many of our greatest problems cannot be resolved without a higher rate of growth," he maintained. "The national economy was no longer plain private enterprise," as Goldwater presumed, but an "organic mixture of public and private money, public and private management." In contrast, the political philosophy of the G.O.P. candidate seemed to be a mixture of Jeffersonianism, Social Darwinism, and rugged individualism of days gone by. Such beliefs, if implemented, would render the government ineffective exactly when positive action was urgently needed. He would, Lippmann contended, "disavow and disown the whole heritage of Hamilton, Lincoln, and Theodore Roosevelt." Contrary to Goldwater's conservatism, the Federalist-Whig-Progressive tradition "stood for strong and evolving federal power, not for a loose and impotent confederation of states."

Within the context of his own political philosophy, Lippmann did not consider Goldwater a true conservative at all but a "radical reactionary" who wanted to return to a "crude and primitive capitalism." The Arizonan mistook his own state for the United States. He liked the open country, unrestricted freedom, and individualism borne of the sparsely settled West. But the environment in which most Americans lived, however, was urban and industrial. Simplistic formulas of frontier days were no longer applicable to the complex problems caused by huge enterprise and crowded cities.

Because he regarded the new economics of Keynes as a form of socialism rather than a means of stabilizing capitalism, Senator Goldwater talked constantly of the need for government to leave business alone and to stop meddling in economic matters. Radical rightists, the core of his support, applauded statements about the vigor of free enterprise while not really understanding modern economics. Typical of their arguments against government intervention was an allegation by Zygmund Dobbs, of the Veritas Foundation, who claimed: "Keynesianism is not an economic theory. . . . It is a weapon of political conspiracy." Because Lippmann knew John Maynard Keynes and accepted the British economist's proposals, he was therefore presumed to be guilty of propagating subversive ideas.

Other right wing ideologues were quick to point at Lippmann's college affiliation with socialism as proof he was a Marxist. Some ardent members of the John Birch Society were not above calling him a crypto Communist. Even his graduation from Harvard and later association with its Board of Governors was used to make him out a leftwinger, since in their twisted thinking that institution was a hotbed of Communism. John A. Stormer, in his controversial *None Dare Call It Treason* (which was circulated in paperback edition before the election) labeled Lippmann a "long-time leftist." He too called attention to his youthful flirtation with socialism; and, because of his foreign policy views, claimed the columnist was an "apologist for Castro" and one who "rather consistently opposes any action to free the captive peoples behind the Iron Curtain." Senator Goldwater simply referred to Lippmann as that "radical columnist." All in all Lippmann was the recipient of more abusive attacks than he had ever before experienced during his long career as a political commentator.

"If, while Goldwaterism were being applied at home, we were also practicing Goldwaterism in foreign affairs," Lippmann countered in his column, "the country would be in the crazy position of risking a very great war while it was disorganizing itself at home." By engaging in a total war to the death, which was a logical result of his desire for a complete victory over Communism, federal power would of necessity have to be increased—not decreased. Whatever controls were used in the second World War would indeed seem minor in comparison to what a third global conflict would demand. Goldwater was a grand idealist who deduced unrealistic solutions to real problems from a set of abstract doctrines. Lippmann considered his proposals dreamlike in their grandeur because they possessed an "unworldly divorce from reality." The G.O.P. presidential candidate's foreign policy ideas were based on a naive assumption the "United States must be obeyed by all the rest of the world." What a "cruel fallacy." Goldwater gave voice to the "unreason of the dreamer: the illusion of Superman that all opponents can be commanded to disappear." His final assessment of Barry Goldwater and William Miller struck at their oversimplified version of conservatism:

"What is their remedy for all our moral evils? To liberate the individual from the tyranny of government and the constraints of society, to deny and reject the belief—which is the central conviction of genuine conservatism—that the individual is part of a community of the dead, the living, and of the unborn, to which he is bound, as Edmund Burke said, by 'ties which, thought light as air, are as strong as links of iron.'"

Because of the ill-conceived program put forth by the Republican nominees, Lippmann endorsed Lyndon Johnson as the candidate most likely to win allegiance of a "vast majority of prudent men in both parties." L.B.J. had already displayed astuteness in office and he seemed the distinctly better choice in 1964.

Lippmann attributed Johnson's tremendous victory to the weakness of the opposition. It had been no contest. Relating this "Republican disaster" to its historical contexts he wrote: "For over 50 years, since the great Roosevelt-Taft schism in 1912 the established and continuing leadership has been misunderstanding the internal state of the union and its relations abroad. Once again the Republican Old Guard had, in effect, asked the American people to make a "revolutionary break with the foreign and domestic policies . . . established over the last three decades." A Goldwater triumph would have been "dark indeed," he asserted, because the Great Society needed an imaginative, forward looking leader.

Lack of rational debate on foreign policy was an unfortunate omission. Inasmuch as Barry Goldwater took such an extreme position, L.B.J. did not have to comment on problems abroad other than to allege his opponent was "trigger happy." Highly damaging to Goldwater was his image as a Western he-man with six guns and atomic bombs looking for Communist villains. Because of this absurd stance, matters of international relations were hardly mentioned by the Democrats. America's future role in Vietnam, for instance, was not given the serious deliberation it deserved. Lippmann decried this state of affairs, but he asked seriously: "How could these unsettled problems be debated with a man who starts out with a dogmatic prejudice that all who call themselves Communists from Yugoslavia to North Vietnam are identical and should be treated with the same implacable hostility?"

Lyndon Johnson won a massive mandate on the basis of his short but impressive record. Having acquired the presidency in his own right, he sought an appellative term to distinguish his administration from that of his predecessor. Since the President considered Lippmann "his friend," and had counseled with him when he first assumed office, he now made use of a phrase popularized by the columnist. Lippmann used the term "Great Society," which he acquired from Graham Wallas (one of his professors at Harvard), to mean the complex, urban-industrial way of life which had evolved because of vast technological changes. L.B.J. thought such an expression was an excellent replacement for New Frontier, for it adequately reflected the focus of domestic reforms he had in mind. Presidential assistant Bill Moyers related how the Great Society was formulated:

"Several members of the President's staff participated in the many deliberations which led to the crystallization of the Great Society concept. The ideas of Walter Lippmann were among many that influenced the staff.

"This is not to say that Lippmann's writings gave birth to the Great Society. They did not. It is much more the product of the President's long experience in public service and his thinking about government.

"The ideas and thoughts of many men were considered in defining the whole concept. Mr. Lippmann was one of them."

"There are three central places where we must begin to build the Great Society," President Johnson proclaimed in a campaign speech, "in our cities, in our countryside, and in our classrooms." Then he went on to define what he meant:

"The Great Society rests on abundance and liberty for all. It demands an end to poverty and racial injustices. But that is just the beginning. The Great Society is a place where every child can find knowledge to enrich his mind and to enlarge his talents.

"It is a place where leisure is a welcome chance to build and reflect, not a feared cause of boredom and restlessness. It is a place where the city of man serves not only the needs of the body and the demands of commerce, but the desire for beauty and the hunger for community."

These were sentiments Walter Lippmann could endorse wholeheartedly, because the nation was rapidly becoming a sprawling urban civilization and its future course depended upon wise planning and government guidance. Quantity had to be transformed into quality; material abundance into cultural excellence; and slums into dwelling places where the human spirit would not be stunted. It appeared that President Johnson was dedicating his administration to making metropolitan areas livable and bringing all minorities into the good life that awaited all Americans. This commitment to action prompted Lippmann to make the optimistic prediction:

"In an environment of relative peace and increasing affluence, there is no reason whatever to throw up our hands and say that a city like New York is ungovernable. Thus far, the great cities have not really been governed.

"They have been too busy growing to think much about being governed. But now at last in the biggest of the great cities the way is open to a new beginning."

Johnson's Inaugural Address appealed for harmony and a unified determination to proceed with plans for building a better nation. He called on all Americans to "join reason to faith and action to experience, to transform our unity of interest into a unity of purpose." A national consensus existed and the circumstances for major reforms were favorable. L.B.J. knew it. The time was ripe, he affirmed, to "achieve progress without strife and change without hatred: not without differences of opinion, but without the deep and abiding divisions which scar the Union for generations."

Writing for *Newsweek*, Lippmann lauded L.B.J.'s avowed intention of dealing with domestic problems. "The Great Society, as President Johnson is using the words, is much more than a mere collection of

necessary or desirable programs making life more livable in this country," he declared, "it is an attempt to open a new chapter in the
annals of popular government." Because the "scientific breakthrough
in modern economics was prepared in the years between the two
world wars, the result of this change is a benign revolution which
makes it possible that the costs of improving schools and colleges, of
reducing poverty, of rebuilding slums, can be covered by calculated
increases in the national output of wealth." Prognosis for success was
bright. All was set. Lippmann sounded but one somber *caveat*:

"The Johnson conception of the Great Society rests on the two
pillars of controlled affluence and of political consensus. If the conception were to fail, it would not be because the conception is false.

"It would be because of some external cause—possibly because we
had become diverted by some entanglement in another continent."

Asia was the area Lippmann had in mind. Both Eisenhower and
Kennedy had involved the United States in Vietnam, but only in a
limited manner. Now he deemed it vital to national interest for the
United States to keep from getting further embroiled in Southeast
Asia. Any large scale intervention would be a dangerous intrusion
into the sphere of Red China. Rather than to think along the lines
of trying to defeat all advances of Communism, essentially Goldwater's position, he felt it was necessary to work out "some kind of
coexistence" between "Asians and Westerners."

When it occurred, Lippmann did not interpret U.S. retaliation for
the Gulf of Tonkin incident as undue escalation. Congress approved
a resolution condoning air bombardment of North Vietnam installa-
tions to prevent gunboat assaults on American naval vessels. Apprehensive as he was, Lippmann did not object strenuously when more
U.S. troops were sent in small numbers. He presumed all along
that force was being used only to induce the North Vietnamese to
come to a peace conference. "The test of any extension of the war,"
he maintained, "is whether it produces a negotiation."

When escalation increased dramatically, so did Lippmann's opposition. Such a policy, asserted Lippmann, was fraught with danger and
should be reversed promptly. Gradual withdrawal would create a
favorable climate, lessen tensions, and prepare the way for Vietnamese settlement of their own internal problem. It was "possible to post-
pone and then to avoid a mortal confrontation with Red China," he
predicted, if the United States used prudence by recognizing that
nation's predominant position on the mainland. What should America's
role be in Asia? Lippmann answered: "In my view, our true power in

the Pacific, which is unequaled and unquestioned, is diminished because we have become entrapped in a land war. Our true interest, then, is to negotiate a settlement which releases us from the trap and frees us, as the paramount power on the sea and in the air, to work toward a general settlement in Asia."

Exactly one month later, Lippmann revealed the extent of his disquietude over L.B.J.'s war policy in Vietnam. "All through January the focus of attention was the Great Society," he noted, then "the situation of Vietnam took a dramatic turn for the worse, a victory of the Viet Cong seemed probable and to this the administration responded by becoming an active belligerent." As a result the attention of Congress was diverted from programs of the Great Society. If reforms ceased, internal chaos was inevitable. Lack of funds would result in the continuation of "violence and bitterness, the squalor and the crime which trouble our domestic peace." In a sharper tone, but still speaking like a friendly adviser, he bespoke of dire consequences:

"The Johnson administration will not be allowed to devote itself to the Great Society here at home unless it develops a foreign policy which faces lucidly and deals constructively with the pressing problem of the over-extended commitments of the United States.

"To develop such a policy will require as high degree of intellectual and moral courage at home as the physical courage we expect of the soldiers who risk everything abroad."

On April 28, 1965 President Johnson suddenly ordered American troops to occupy the Dominican Republic. This surprising move was prompted by the likelihood of a Communist takeover. Some 20,000 U.S. Marines landed on the Caribbean island and only after intervention was a *fait accompli* did L.B.J. seek aid from the Organization of American States. The onus of unilateral action was thus ameliorated to some extent. From the immediate evidence given him, Lippmann deemed the move a justified reaction on the part of the United States. After a provisional government was established and still no withdrawal took place, he became more critical. "The President's initial decision to intervene in the Dominican Republic was correct, so I believe," he wrote on May 23, "because on the information available to him in the emergency he had no time for a thoroughgoing investigation and could not take the risk that the rebellion might be captured by Communist agents." His objection related to the prolonged nature of occupation. By remaining, "we in effect made ourselves the allies of the reactionary junta in its attempt to crush the Constitutionalists." Free elections were not held until a year later at which time the conservative candidate for president, Joaquin Balaguer, was a surprise victor over the liberal Juan Bosch.

Because of his deep concern over U.S. neglect of South America, Lippmann devoted a series of columns to overall problems affecting Latin America. The Alliance for Progress, initiated by Kennedy, was a fine start, but concentration on victory in Vietnam diverted attention and appropriations away from the Western Hemisphere. Interest had to be renewed before more Communist-inspired revolutions erupted. Lippmann called for bold action, including a Marshall-type plan to raise living standards in Latin America; engineering projects to link South American countries to one another; and a hemispheric common market to stimulate economic growth in the entire region. This ten-year program could not be achieved with only half hearted efforts or by alloting a little money now and then to prevent Castroite takeovers in Central America. "Our simple-minded anti-Communism" was not the answer, he averred; either the United States must commit itself to reforms in Central and South America through massive aid or Latin society would ultimately disintegrate into a "kind of proletarian anarchy."

Why try to make South Vietnam a democracy when all of Latin America was in jeopardy? Admonishing L.B.J. and the Secretary of State, Dean Rusk, Lippmann lectured: "I wish President Johnson would put his mind, and would put Secretary Rusk's mind, on the portents of revolutionary change right here in our midst, within our own western society. They will find plenty of work to do."

Not only did Lyndon Johnson resent Lippmann's criticism of his Latin American policy (or absence of one), but he felt the press was unfair in its coverage of the Dominican Republic affair. Intervention prevented another Castro in our backyard, so he argued, and all the fuss about supporting rightists was nonsense. L.B.J. complained to aides, "When you duck, dodge, hesitate, and shimmy, every man and his dog gives you a kick." Had he not acted, the President reasoned, the same journalists who were throwing brickbats would have castigated him even more for failing to head off a Communist *coup d'etat*.

It was true also that Lippmann himself had seldom taken a great interest in social welfare of the Latin American people. In fact he was taken to task by others for his overemphasis on the importance of an Atlantic Community to the exclusion of assistance to free nations in Asia or other parts of the world. His opposition to any involvement in Asia leading to a land war was almost an obsession. Lippmann saw disaster lurking in the vast expanses of the Asian mainland and L.B.J.'s refusal to disengage from the Vietnam war impelled him to increase the tempo of his criticism until it led to a bitter feud between the two.

During a television interview in 1965, a continuation of his annual network appearances, Lippmann talked much about the situation in Vietnam. "The most we could hope for, is that there will be a sufficient political truce in the civil war, for a period of time—some years—so that they can adjust themselves to each other." By designating the fighting a civil war he was labeling it an internal dispute. Hence it was an affair that had to be settled ultimately by the Vietnamese people themselves and not by the United States. "What we do is to see that it doesn't become a Chinese military outpost, which is quite a different thing from saying that it will be eventually within the Chinese sphere of influence." To prevent any misunderstanding, he underscored the point, "I don't know of any man living who thinks that 35 years from now, when the Chinese are one half of the whole human race, they aren't going to be the dominant power in Southeast Asia."

By continuing "diplomatic explorations," using the good offices of Russia or even Japan, a means of terminating the conflict would be found. Admittedly American withdrawal had to be gradual to protect those who might be liquidated by the Vietcong, but it was to be a pullout all the same. "You can't expect to get out gloriously from a mistake," he added. Once U.S. forces were removed the next step, in his judgement, was a *détente* with Red China. For too long normal diplomatic contact with China had been avoided. They would "go through the same evolution that every revolutionary society goes through." This meant Communist China would undergo a "softening process," similar to that which had taken place in the Soviet Union, and within twenty years it would act like other major powers. In other words, he believed China would become reasonable and rational in its international relations. Lippmann concluded the television broadcast with a congeries of reasons why American should extricate itself from Vietnam:

"We are not the policemen of mankind. We are not able to run the world, and we shouldn't pretend that we can. Let us tend to our own business which is great enough as it is.

"It's very great. We have neglected our own affairs. Our education is inadequate, our cities are badly built, our social arrangements are unsatisfactory. We can't wait another generation.

"Unless we can surmount this crisis, and work and get along on the path of settlement in Europe, all of these plans of the Great Society here at home, all the plans for the rebuilding of backward countries in other continents will all be put on the shelf because war interrupts everything like that."

L.B.J. did not think his friends should criticize him publicly. Certainly he had not reckoned on Lippmann's staunch opposition to his foreign policy. To regain the columnist's support, which was considered essential for retention of the intellectual community's loyalty, Johnson requested his assistance in drafting a speech. The President's address, to be given at Johns Hopkins University, was intended to be a major policy statement on Vietnam. Collaborating with President Johnson and his aides for an entire day, Lippmann helped prepare the text. While so engaged he made a determined effort to persuade L.B.J. of the need to seek a negotiated peace. At day's end he felt confident that Johnson was convinced of the soundness of his advice. Verbal assurances made to him by L.B.J. indicated the forthcoming address would announce American willingness to start peace talks.

In the speech, delivered on April 7, 1965, Lyndon Johnson echoed many of Lippmann's sentiments. The President said straightforwardly, "We must deal with the world as it is, if it is ever to be as we think." Indicating, seemingly, a desire to de-escalate the level of warfare, Johnson asserted, "We will use our power with restraint and all the wisdom we can command." Again, using conciliatory language, he called for a solution to the conflict without recourse to "bombs and bullets." Economic aid was offered to both sides with the appeal that each seek "peaceful association with others." Negotiations rather than the pursuit of an "endless course of battle" was suggested. But no sooner had L.B.J. held out the olive branch, than he drew a sword in defense of U.S. intervention. "We are there because there are also great stakes in the balance." This put the American intrusion in Asia on the basis of preserving the balance of power in favor of the non-Communist nations. His concluding words were a defiant mixture of friendly overture and firm warning: "We do not want to bury anyone . . . but we do not intend to be buried."

Despite the bellicosity of some portions of this speech, Lippmann recognized many of his own ideas. For the moment, he was persuaded that L.B.J. was sincere in his intention to initiate measures leading to an end of American involvement. This optimism was shortlived. When Dean Rusk spoke to the American Foreign Service Association on June 23, 1965, he announced brusquely and without reservations that North Vietnamese leaders had turned their backs on the President's peace offer. Not only that, they had deliberately increased the intensity of their military attacks. The Secretary of State took the occasion also to denounce Peking and Hanoi for their truculent attitude. Clearly the "root of the trouble" as he saw it was the continuance of a "cruel and sustained attack by North Vietnam upon the people of South Vietnam." Despite his reiteration of the U.S. offer to provide funds for economic development in the region of the Mekong Delta, Secretary Rusk acted for all intent and purposes as if he were withdrawing from the record any peace overture President Johnson may have made at Baltimore. Resuming a hawkish stance, he laid down stiff terms for ending hostilities. Included were an "end to aggression"; the "removal of foreign military forces"; and "effective guarantees for the independence and freedom of the people of South Vietnam." Prerequisites such as these presumed military victory—not diplomatic compromise.

Had President Johnson used the foreign policy statement made at Johns Hopkins as a political placebo? From the tone of his press conference on July 28, 1965, it would appear his so-called peace proposal was a gesture to pacify the "doves" rather than an invitation to start *bona fide* negotiations. "Three times in my lifetime, in two world wars and in Korea, Americans have gone to far lands to fight for freedom," Johnson told newsmen at one of his irregularly scheduled press conferences. "We have learned at a terrible and brustal cost that retreat does not bring safety and weakness does not bring peace." Red China and her client North Vietnam were to blame for the war. Their goal, L.B.J. insisted, was to "defeat American power and to extend the Asiatic dominion of Communism." The American position seemed to him both clear and honorable:

"We did not choose to be guardians at the gate, but there is no one else.

"Nor would surrender in Vietnam bring peace, because we learned from Hitler at Munich that success only feeds the appetite of aggression. The battle would be renewed in one country and then another country, bringing with it perhaps even larger and crueler conflict, as we have learned from the lessons of history."

From 1965 to 1968 domestic dissension grew as anti-war protesters increased the tempo of their demonstrations. Eventually Dr. Martin Luther King, Jr. became alarmed over the administration's failure to fund anti-poverty projects aimed at providing equal opportunities for Negroes. Before his untimely death at the hand of an assassin, he spoke out vehemently against continuation of the war in Vietnam.

Draft card burnings increased in number while outbursts on college campuses grew in intensity. When rioting in cities began, with ghettoes aflame, popular support for the war began to wane. It became obvious to many that the grievances of slum dwellers, black and white, should have priority over military assistance to South Vietnam. Cost of American participation had risen to an astronomical figure of thirty billion dollars annually and that drain on the U.S. treasury all but ended domestic welfare programs.

Congress had staunchly supported the President's Vietnam policy. But events at home and abroad convinced a few the war was a mistake. Taking the lead was Senator J. William Fulbright, Chairman of the Foreign Relations Committee, who publicly reversed his stand. Other Senators, such as Wayne Morse of Oregon, Frank Church of Idaho, Ernest Gruening of Alaska, and George McGovern of South Dakota, all denounced the war. These so-called doves, frequently citing Lippmann's articles for support, based their opposition primarily on moral grounds. Minnesota's Eugene McCarthy also advanced the notion that U.S. intervention interfered with the process of self-determination in Vietnam. Finally, even Senator Robert F. Kennedy, whose brother had committed some 17,000 military personnel to Southeast Asia, also took a stand against continuing the struggle.

Seeking to coalesce the anti-war sentiment, Lippmann kept a flow of criticism directed at Lyndon Johnson. Although eschewing the violence and techniques used by hippies and other clamorous demonstrators, he did tend to dignify their actions by his own refusal to publicly condemn their excesses. Undemocratic means used by such groups as the Students for a Democratic Society received no censure from him despite their obvious violation of the traditions of civility. Unrestrained ranting of radical groups made rational debate well nigh impossible. Yet Lippmann refrained from criticizing their crude tactics. He made no comment about draft card burners or those who paraded with Viet Cong flags. His desire to see the war terminated was so strong it took precedence over everything else. Harsh words were used instead to castigate the President:

"He does not understand that when the issues are life and death, victory and defeat, everything else becomes pale and irrelevant and unimportant. Some of the measures for the Great Society are still on the White House list of desirable legislation.

"But with a half million men fighting in Asia nobody cares, or can care, about what life is like in a Detroit slum."

With incisive and sometimes unflattering language, Lippmann kept up his journalistic attacks on L.B.J. for making "one of the most serious miscalculations in our history." Labeling the President a most "complicated human being," he described the Texan as a man with "two spirits wrestling within him." Defining this quality, he wrote, "One is that of the peacemaker and reformer and herald of a better world. The other is that of the primitive frontiersman who wants to nail the coonskin to the wall, who wants to be the biggest, the best, the first, a worshipper of what William James called the bitch-goddess, success."

L.B.J. was definitely not the turn-the-other-cheek type of person and seldom took a public slap in the face without responding in kind. Stories began to circulate in the capital, some true and some no doubt apocryphal, about his extreme displeasure over the contents of Lippmann's articles. The President went out of his way to remind visitors of the columnist's past errors in judgment. These included references to some of his isolationist-type articles of the 1930's, an assessment in 1933 that Adolf Hitler could be trusted, and the endorsement of Alf Landon in 1936. On one occasion Johnson was reputed to have exclaimed in anger, "God is not dead, he appears twice a week in the *Washington Post*." Outbursts such as these began what Herblock, the famous cartoonist, called the "W. on W.L."—meaning the administration's "War on Walter Lippmann."

Others aroused the President's ire, but in many ways Johnson regarded Lippmann as the chief culprit. When Senator Fulbright conducted public hearings on the administration's conduct of foreign affairs, members of the academic community by and large spoke out against the war. Had Lippmann remained his "friend," rationalized L.B.J., this defection might not have occurred. He now began to use the disparaging term "once great" when referring to the columnist. The tale made the rounds in Washington, D. C. that President Johnson told the dovish Frank Church of Idaho, after the Senator showed him a particular Lippmann article, "Well, Frank, the next time you need money to build a dam in your state, you better go to Mr. Lippmann." Interestingly enough, Church's re-election in 1968 was generally attributed to his interest in reclamation projects rather than foreign policy issues.

Part of L.B.J.'s predicament was frustration. "Guns and butter" did not mix; the thirty billion dollars per year that was poured out for military expenditures in Vietnam relegated the war on poverty at home to mere tokenism. Congressmen began to re-examine their positions; projects in their districts were halted. Some politicians worked both sides of the street. Richard Nixon, after visiting Saigon, defended the war in general but criticized its handling. Nelson Rockefeller had often voiced approval of administration policy in Vietnam, but he, too, qualified his support when dissent rose to clamoring heights. A typical dodge employed by more than one Congressman was to call for an "honorable peace" through negotiation. Just how this was to be brought about, none dared to predict. Likewise, little advice was forthcoming to specify in detail what constituted an acceptable settlement. Without knowing exactly how to extricate himself from an unpopular war, with domestic protests and rioting creating havoc, and with deep division developing within his own party, the President floundered. He pleaded for public support, but his credibility bank was broke because of too many pronouncements about impending victory. Military setbacks belied his optimistic promises and soon L.B.J. stood virtually alone. This made him strike out at his critics even more viciously.

Did militant opposition of the doves, for whatever reasons advanced, encourage the North Vietnamese? L.B.J. thought so because any display of disunity at home actually emboldened the Viet Cong. The enemy was being misled into thinking the U.S. will to fight would weaken if they continued the struggle a while longer. Lippmann contended democratic debate was essential and whatever advantage the adversary gained from it had to be discounted. On no account should free speech be curtailed. James Reston, a fellow columnist and friend, took issue with this. Writing for the *New York Times*, Reston reflected hawkish views. He had long defended administration policy. In the 1966 Elihu Root Lectures, given before the Council on Foreign Relations in New York City (and published in book form as *The Artillery of the Press*), Reston asserted: "Lippmann argues that it is a fallacy to consider that a divided public opinion in the United States will have any effect on the enemy. I do not agree. The essence of the problem is that there is a great deal to be said for both the dangers and the necessity of criticism."

By 1967 Walter Lippmann decided to go into semi-retirement. Meeting deadlines for fifty years and now, at 77, the strain of daily writing was too much. His home in the Georgetown section of the District of Columbia was sold to Senator Eugene McCarthy for a reputed price of $70,000. New York City was once again to be Lippmann's place of residence. Future plans included proposed trips abroad and a reduced writing schedule. This included occasional essays for syndication and irregular articles for *Newsweek*. Because of his keen interest in the new Public Broadcasting Network, he indicated his intent to make appearances on this educational medium. So it was on May 28 that millions of his regular readers saw the brief announcement: "I am going to stop the regular column. But as I do not mean to retire and lapse into silence I have been experimenting with new forms—with longer articles which cover a wider range of subject matter."

There was considerable gossip in the capital that Lippmann's exit was meant to be a symbolic rebuke to President Johnson. Perhaps a sort of shaking the dust from the shoes sort of thing. When asked if this were the case, Lippmann replied: "I wouldn't give him that satisfaction. I stuck it out here through the McCarthy era." L.B.J. did not let that remark pass unanswered. At a White House dinner for correspondents, to which Lippmann was not invited, he made a sarcastic remark about the departure of a "political commentator of yesteryear." In the same ill-tempered vein, Lippmann responded bitterly, "I feel he misled me. He was saying different things to me than to other people." The depth of this resentment was revealed by his parting shot at Johnson when he called the President an "absolute monarch" who "wishes to be the sole source of information about his administration and has frightened his subordinates from talking to journalists."

If L.B.J. thought Lippmann's pen was to remain inactive, he made a big mistake. After a brief trip abroad longer essays were printed where his column formerly appeared. The very first of these reflective pieces dwelt on the theme of how "pygmy nations," in both the Middle and Far East, were defying superpowers. Promptly renewing his criticism of the President, he wrote: "It is a naive illusion to think that 1967 is 1939, that Southeast Asia is Western Europe, that Mao Tse tung is Hitler and that Lyndon Johnson is Churchill." The war, he argued, was "not producing a firm and free international order but the largest quagmire in which this country has ever foundered." To those who claimed he was advocating a return to isolation and insularity, he retorted, "If this be isolationism, so be it."

Many backers of the war, including former President Eisenhower, complained about the increasingly violent methods used by the antiwar protesters. When Dean Rusk, Vice President Hubert Humphrey, and even the President were harassed by ugly demonstrations, some columnists condemned the lawless nature of this dissent. Lippmann, who might at last have been expected to speak out against the practice of shouting down speakers, called this criticism a form of "cheating." It was unfair, he insisted, to regard those opposing the fighting as "an assorted mixture of hippies, peaceniks, draft-card burners, pacifists, agents and supporters of Hanoi, Peking, and Moscow, black-power Negroes and what not." Instead of denouncing the outrageous behavior of these groups, he came close to condoning it. Lippmann insisted "free debate" was not possible when the "government turns upon its weakest opponents; it is destroying the process by which a free people ascertain what is true and agree upon what is right." He might well have considered the fact that no debate was possible unless each side used rational arguments and democratic means. Under his calm exterior, perhaps Lippmann too harbored strong inner emotions. When locked in combat over an issue so important to him, he tended to excuse the atrocious behavior of his extremist allies.

During a conversation with six college students on the Public Broadcasting Laboratory, November 19, 1967, Lippmann declared "if Lyndon Johnson is re-elected, I don't know what would happen." The man he wanted to see elected President was Governor Nelson Rockefeller. A "crucial question" he conceded, was "whether the Republicans, who are still distraught by their ideological caper in 1964, can pull themselves together and seize an historic opportunity which is theirs for the asking."

Writing for *Newsweek*, Lippmann sought an alternative for the Democrats by urging Senator Robert Kennedy of New York to make a bid for the presidential nomination. If Kennedy assumed 1972 was soon enough to seek this office, he contended, the Senator "had better wonder what will be the condition of the party after four more years of distrust, division, and dissent." The magnitude of his alarm over the war, and its adverse repercussions at home, manifested itself in every article he wrote. After the Tet offensive, when the Vietcong invaded Saigon and proved that no part of South Vietnam was beyond their reach, Lippmann's *Newsweek* column featured a one-word caption for a title. It was: "Defeat." When Senator Eugene McCarthy decided to enter the New Hampshire primary in opposition to President Johnson, Lippmann commended him for coming forward as the "defender of the American faith" (a statement that quickly showed up in campaign literature). Even though McCarthy was not his first choice, he wrote, "What he stands for is the avowal that the American system of party government shall not be held to be a fraud and a deception, that it is a valid way by which the mass of our people can redress their grievances, can express their will, and can participate in the government of the nation."

Senator McCarthy's victory in the New Hampshire primary, followed quickly by Senator Kennedy's entrance into the presidential primary campaign, caused President Johnson to reconsider his own future. With dramatic suddenness L.B.J. announced a partial halt to the bombing of North Vietnam and his withdrawal from consideration as a candidate for 1968. Some time later the President told the Association of American Editorial Cartoonists they would certainly miss him as an object of caricature. "All of me—my button nose, my cute ears," he taunted them, would not longer provide subject matter for the delight of cartoonists. With a sardonic smile, the President added: "I suppose I could have had it worse. After all, I could have been up against a columnist with your talent. Thank goodness Walter Lippmann never learned to draw."

The presidential campaign of 1968 offered only a "dismal choice," stated Lippmann, after listening to Richard Nixon, Hubert Humphrey, and George Wallace. Quoting Erasmus, he described the state of national affairs as "irremediable confusion of everything." Obviously "the Democratic party today is unable to offer the country the genuine prospect of a coherent government." After much thought he endorsed the G.O.P. nominee in these words, "It seems to me the better, though not the most beautiful course, to elect Nixon as President." A Republican victory in November, Lippmann explained, would mean a different approach: "It does not mean that all the good things that have been accomplished will be repealed and undone. But it does mean that the virtues and ideals which conservatives cherish— particularly discipline and authority and self-reliance—will for a time prevail over the liberal alternatives of permissiveness and largesse and environmental improvement."

During his career as a syndicated columnist, Lippmann had striven to remain detached and objective, trying to view presidents and politicians in phenomenological terms as if they were entities and not personalities. Only in the case of Lyndon Johnson did he "get personal" in his commentary. Distress over domestic turmoil, nearing the stage of anarchy at times, affected him very profoundly. The same might be said of Lyndon Baines Johnson. Driven to despair by events seemingly beyond his control, he lashed out at his tormentors with careless abandon. L.B.J. wanted to defend democracy abroad and almost destroyed it at home. If he had feet of clay it was only because all men bear the infirmities of human frailty. Perhaps in the future when both men have time to reflect and write their memoirs, personal animosities will diminish. At home on his vast ranch by the Perdinales

River, Johnson will one day realize that much of the criticism he reaped was not meant only for him—but was a part of the "splendid misery" that goes with the institution of the Presidency. Because they occupy the seat of power, all Presidents have been subjected to such vilification. One can assume that Lippmann too will ponder the intangible aspects of the Presidency. During his long career he watched many men take up residence in the White House. It may be that he will come to appreciate more the unique contribution each man bestowed to this high office by humanizing it and making it a living institution.

A President will always have his critics and newspaper columnists must of necessity criticize the President. Together the Fourth Estate and Chief Executive serve the public interest. Real democracy thrives when each is strong and active. If that be the case, both Lyndon Johnson and Walter Lippmann have discharged their duties honorably.

CHAPTER XII

APPRAISALS

George Santayana's description of his former Harvard pupil as both an "eidtor" and a "brave philosopher," was a perceptive and appropriate observation by a man of great wisdom. To make the news intelligible, Lippmann did indeed go far beyond the job of merely reporting the facts. Concerned with the many implications connected with events, he explained his approach: "The modern world . . . [has been] so complicated and so hard to understand, it has become necessary to explain it and to interpret it." Because his own political philosophy provided him with a conceptual framework to comprehend what was going on in the world, Lippmann was an editorial writer rendering judgments and evaluations on the basis of criteria he had established for himself. In this sense, his commentary was definitely subjective and reflected his personal opinion. Because of his stance as a disinterested observer, there was also an objective quality to Lippmann's commentary. Reason and reflection, combined with knowledge and incisive writing, produced a newspaper column of unusual excellence.

Despite the voluminous nature of his journalistic output, the quality of content and style remained high. Those who read the T & T column, constituting some 2,500 separate articles from 1931 to 1968, expected to be enlightened. They were not disappointed. Independence of mind and a serious approach to journalistic writing made him required reading for the literate public. When asked about his reaction, knowing important government officials read his column regularly, Lippmann replied: "I do not think about that. It would be ruinous, like an actor always worried about applause." His intent, and it was an ideal he did not always follow, was *not* to insist "now this is what you ought to do." Instead, he professed, I try to say, "This is what has been developing and that is what it means."

There have always been two groups among major columnists of the newspaper world; gossip mongers or peddlers of partisan platitudes in one category, perhaps the largest, and the mature, intelligent political commentators. Lippmann usually headed the list of those classified in the second category. Some would even rate him a *sui generis*, that is one in a class by himself. Certainly at the time of his retirement his only close rivals were such syndicated columnists

163

as Arthur Krock, James Reston, and Joseph Kraft. The hallmark of
Lippmann's writing has been integrity. This was substantiated in a
poll conducted among 273 correspondents of the capital city, in 1962,
which rated him "highest" in terms of "fairness and reliability."
William L. Rivers, who made the survey and published its results in
Columbia Journalism Review, indicated that "no other columnist
was even close." James Reston, himself a Pulitzer prize winner, called
his colleage the "greatest journalist of the present age . . . not because he was always right, but because he gave us a model of what
newspaper criticism should be."

Another survey in 1964, described in the *Saturday Review*, consisted of a symposium of outstanding literary men, historians, and
scholars from many different fields who compiled a list of the twentieth century's most important works. Two of Lippmann's books were
included in a special classification that, according to a general consensus "most significantly altered the direction of our society." Those
cited were *A Preface to Morals* (1929) and *The Good Society* (1937).
Lippmann himself was a member of this distinguished panel and his
two choices were John Maynard Keynes' *The General Theory of
Employment* (which placed first) and *Pacem in Terris* by Pope John
XXIII.

Editors of *The American Scholar* asked a select group of academicians, writers, and noted thinkers to respond to this question: "To
what book published in the past ten years do you find yourself going
back—or thinking back—most often?" One expert, Professor Hans J.
Morgenthau of the University of Chicago, well known for his contributions in the fields of political science and international relations,
replied:

"I chose Walter Lippmann's *The Public Philosophy* as the book
of which I think most often and to which I go back most frequently.
My reasons are as follows: This book presents the most cogent criticism of modern political philosophy. It does so . . . from the vantage
point of the tradition of Western political thought.

"That is to say, it confronts modern political thought in the form of
Marxism, Fascism, and modern démocracy with the eternal verities
that have developed by the Western tradition from Plato through
Locke."

Such testimonials are not isolated cases relative to the lasting influence of Lippmann's books. Adolf Berle, an economist of no little
stature and a former member of F.D.R.'s famed Brain Trust, also
made use of ideas contained in *The Public Philosophy*. In his analysis

of modern industrialism and its impact on society, Berle had this to say concerning "checks" on corporate power:

"To explain this it becomes necessary to import a political conception—the public consensus—familiar to the political scientists and brilliantly explained a few years ago by Mr. Walter Lippmann [in *The Public Philosophy*].

"So, it seems, the ultimate protection of individuals lies not in the play of economic forces in free markets, but in a set of value judgments so widely accepted and deeply held in the United States that public opinion can energize political action when needed to prevent power from violating those values."

A leading Marxist scholar, Herbert Aptheker, disagreed strongly on the merits of the same book. He regarded *The Public Philosophy* an attempt on Lippmann's part to formulate a "reactionary ideology" which "form[ed] a rationalization for an increasing arbitrary and secretive manner in which public affairs in general are being administered in our country." Aptheker also criticized Lippmann for his views on foreign policy by dismissing him as a "rigorous realist serving the Economic Royalists." This was a Communist-type euphemism for the more familiar propaganda phrase—"lackey of the capitalists."

Throughout the years, many scholars in varied fields have employed theoretical constructs and interpretive devices developed by Lippmann. A few examples will demonstrate this usage. Charles Hirschfeld, an historian, utilized the concept that a public figure could be "at once conservative, liberal [and] progressive." Deftly applying it to the life of Brooks Adams, he could explain the actions of an individual heretofore difficult to categorize neatly as being either liberal or conservative. The authors used a variation of the same mode of interpretation in their biographical study, *Henry A. Wallace of Iowa: The Agrarian Years, 1910-1940*. This controversial person was at once a liberal and a conservative; and held views that were both idealistic and realistic when applied to agriculture.

In still another instance, Daniel Boorstin, a political scientist from the University of Chicago, expanded on the pioneering theory set forth originally by Lippmann in *Public Opinion* (1922). Having been used to explain distortion in newspaper reporting, Boorstin utilized such ideas as "pseudo-environment" and "pseudo-fact" to elaborate on the image making power of modern television. Image making and means of rallying public opinion for the support of government policy was also the subject of Theodore Sorensen's *Decision-Making in the White House: The Olive Branch or the Arrows*. A close confidant of the late President Kennedy, and influenced by Lippmann's *Public Opinion,* Sorensen wrote: "Public opinion is often erratic, inconsistent, arbitrary, and unreasonable—with a 'compulsion to make mistakes,' as Walter Lippmann put it. It rarely considers the needs of the next generation or the history of the last. It is frequently hampered by myths and misinformation, by stereotypes and shibboleths, and by an innate resistance to innovation."

If there was an area where Lippmann's views tended to run contrary to those generally held by the public at large, it was in the field of international relations. Because Americans were notoriously susceptible to arguments favoring a foreign policy based on morality, idealistic objectives, and defense of democracy elsewhere, they seldom heard elected officials speak of national self interest, spheres of influence, or preservation of the balance of power. *U.S. Foreign Policy: Shield of the Republic* (1943) and *U.S. War Aims* (1944) were outstanding examples of Lippmann's attempt to reorient American thought away from its soaring idealism toward a policy of international realism. Dr. James B. Conant, then President of Harvard University and later to be High Commissioner of Germany, took note of just this point. He wrote Lippmann, "I particularly like the general point of view . . . that national interest should be determined by past experiences of a nation and not by the blueprints for the future." Conant added the pertinent observation:

"It seems to me that among the many sources of ills of the present, one can identify an overemphasis among our intellectuals and leaders on the conceptual type of thinking characteristic of political science and the more philosophic aspects of law.

"There is a corresponding lack of appreciation of the significance of history and a detailed knowledge of the past of this country. . . . Your book is a healthy corrective to this point of view."

From Emporia, Kansas came a letter from William Allen White. "If your publisher would like to have me do so," he volunteered: "I would be glad to send out ten or a dozen with a letter commending it to statesmen like Hoover and Willkie and McNary and Jim Wadsworth, Republicans in government who are teetering on the edge of international commitments. Your book should persuade them." Unknown to the Kansas editor, Wendell Willkie had long been in contact with Walter Lippmann. As the Republican nominee for the presidency, he had sought Lippmann's assistance in drafting a foreign policy statement. The four points they worked out together for general G.O.P. endorsement stressed: (1) support of the war effort; (2)

"peace with victory"; (3) "reasonable international responsibilities [which] may be demanded in a modern world" and (4) "safeguarding and encouragement of individual enterprise." Since Willkie was trying to outmaneuver the isolationists in his own party, Lippmann encouraged him in this endeavor and told the titular head of the Republican party, "I hope you will keep me informed as to what progress you make."

John Foster Dulles, Governor Thomas Dewey's foreign policy adviser, contacted Lippmann in order to let him know that he was working for G.O.P. approval of a platform plank approving U.S. participation in the proposed United Nations Organization. This man, who was to be Eisenhower's Secretary of State in the future, expressed his appreciation for those arguments in *U.S. War Aims* aimed at isolationists. Nothing was said about the warning it contained about undue idealism or over reliance on abstract principles. Lippmann answered Dulles rather nonchalantly, not knowing about the latter's moralistic outlook, and made mention of the fact that Sumner Welles had given his book an adverse review. He therefore revealed his intention to take up the "cudgels" against the "Wilsonians" who, with their hostile attitude, give "me a good deal of incentive to go on with the matter." Lippmann did not know that Dulles was also a Wilsonian; and little did either of them know they would be future adversaries over foreign policy issues.

Strangely enough, the old New Deal curmudgeon Harold Ickes let Lippmann know of his favorable reaction to the message contained in *U.S. Foreign Policy.* Usually finding fault with everything, on this occasion he thought Cordell Hull would benefit from reading it. With his characteristically blunt language, he claimed the State Department "might have had fruitful results diplomatically, if some of us had shown less respect for the supposed esoteric character of an organization that, after all, is only a world political club dressed in spats."

At State Department request, Quincy Wright prepared an analysis of *U.S. Foreign Policy* for Cordell Hull which was by and large critical in tone. "Lippmann's history is also incomplete," Wright claimed, "in that it over emphasizes military, geographical and political factors to the neglect of economic, social and legal factors." Wright said of Lippmann, "He tends to think of world politics exclusively in terms of rivalry for power and geographical position." Although an expert on international law, he misinterpreted that portion of the book dealing with world order and Woodrow Wilson. "Lippmann accepts the

Wilsonian conception in his final chapter," Wright informed Hull. "He repudiates his earlier attack on Wilson's recognition that the world order must rest primarily on consent . . . and he repudiates his earlier insistence that subordination of the sovereignty of national states to the world order is impracticable in our time."

Harvard historian William Chamberlain, was equally critical of Lippmann's ideas on international relations. Writing in *America's Second Crusade*, he took issue with the contention that coexistence with the Soviet Union was possible. Its proponents were guilty of "bad reasoning, supported by bad history." Then he leveled this broadside:

"Lippmann occasionally recognized that Communism was a disturbing element in international relations. In his *U.S. War Aims . . .*, he suggests wistfully that it would be nice if the Soviet regime would begin to carry out the democratic promises of its constitution.

"As he had never spent any appreciable amount of time in Russia, he could perhaps not be expected to understand the extreme unlikelihood, or rather impossibility, of such a development."

Michael Straight was a friendlier critic. As editor of the *New Republic*, he was far more liberal than his father, the original founder of the magazine. Reviewing *Isolation and Alliances* (1952), Straight said of Lippmann that he was a "master of diplomacy but a postulant in democratic politics." The key point was that the mass public demanded "simple laws by which transgressors can be judged, and simple rules by which they can be punished." Straight suggested that classical diplomacy might be obsolete or at least unworkable in a democracy. "The voters," he argued, "are determined to shape policy" and they "cannot follow the intricate web of Lippmann's world of alliance and secret diplomacy." With some justification, he concluded: "Just as Lippmann maintains that Wilson's universalism is archaic for the present, so his own prescription of alliances directed by the foreign offices may be archaic for the military and economic pressures that confront the Atlantic nations bound only with NATO's twine."

Since Lippmann has challenged many tenets of philosophical liberalism, it followed that the validity of his own ideas would be contested. Louis Hartz, the historian, believed Lippmann's analysis of liberalism, set forth in *The Good Society*, was more European than American in spirit. Since Hartz considered the liberal philosophy, as it evolved in the United States, to be a fusion of "submerged Lockianism" with "handy pragmatism," he naturally viewed Lippmann's approach as useless ruminations "amid the abstractions of Europe."

Lippmann did study the writings of Englishmen such as John Locke and Thomas Hobbes (whose social contract theories contributed to the development of constitutionalism), nevertheless he placed equal importance on the historical development of political ideas in America. What Lippmann did was to place newer ideas in perspective by contrasting them to the thought of past centuries. To do this he made use of works produced by European thinkers.

Another academician who entered the lists against Lippmann was Heinz Eulau of Antioch College (presently at Stanford University). With disdain, he described *Essays in the Public Philosophy* as a "strange potpourri of natural law theology, Burkian Whiggery, and Hobbesian authoritarianism." Claiming the work represented the "end of a long and lonely intellectual road" for one who had gone from Socialism to Progressivism, and then from Wilsonian idealism to cultural conservatism, he made the allegation that it seemed to indicate an "inner conflict." Without the benefit of a psychiatrist's couch, he attributed this gravitation towards conservatism to Lippmann's "alienation and apartness" because of his rejection of Judaic creeds and Zionistic expectations. Lippmann was then depicted as a migratory mentality vainly seeking truth.

"I deplore Lippmann's revival of the ancient and obscure theory of essences and natural law," asserted pragmatist Morton White of Harvard University. This disciple of John Dewey regarded tradition and time-tested verities as mere rationalizations for the "weak man" who "needs support." Challenging Lippmann's traditionalism, he wrote:

"Finally we must ask ourselves about the man who does believe that there are self-evident principles of morality. Can he be persuaded that there are essences which, when unpacked, yield moral principles? . . .

"The point is, then, that all this philosophical machinery is not so much an effective instrument of rational persuasion as a kind of self-encouragement, useful for philosophical whistling in the dark."

Still another dissenter was Fred Gladstone Bratten, a Professor of History and Literature of Religion. Taking exception to Lippmann's assertion about secularization being destructive of modern morality and that it contradicted the normal range of spirituality inherent in Western thought, he felt that Lippmann and Dewey, in terms of their respective philosophies, were both a part of the liberal movement to formulate a "Naturalistic Humanism." Each, he argued, advocated a "religion of the future." Lippmann's "high religion" represented the

best of Western wisdom and Dewey's "ideal ends of society" constituted the ethical consensus of contemporary society. Their systems
were evolutionary; devoid of creeds and cosmologies; and concerned
themselves primarily with the development of mature personalities.
Mutual philosophical kinship lay in the fact that both men denied
principles of morality based on supernatural guides for human
behavior.

An unusually strong attack on Lippmann was made by William J.
Newman in *The Futilitarian Society*; when the columnist analyzed
contemporary events, it was evident "He still has a distrust of democracy and the public and a consequent need for a firm point of reference from which to understand the ever-increasing dizzy changes of
modern society." Following this complaint, Newman averred: "The
Eastern seaboard intellectual of the days of Wilson and Theodore
Roosevelt is displayed in both the contorted, fastidious, and painful
prose of Lippmann, and in his deep despair that not one in a crude
society will listen to the sensible few. Lippmann is our last aristocrat,
detached, aloof, and just able to bear the sights he must look upon."

Writing for the *American Mercury* in 1945, Professor Fred Rodell
of Yale University's Law School took exception to the well-publicized
"Lippmann legend." The columnist possessed the ability "to state the
disputed as though it were the obvious and to intone the obvious as
though it were profound." When asked by the authors if his opinion
of Lippmann had changed, Rodell replied: "The only 'mold' that
I think he has always fit into is that of a conventionally literate eastern American pseudo-liberal whose whole training and approach, both
political and economic (as well as, if you insist, philosophical) is
rather narrowly bounded by the Allegheny Mountains to the west and
the so-called Western European nations to the east."

Journalists also have expressed divergent views on the merits of
Lippmann's writings. Rather unkindly, A. J. Liebling tabbed him
"perhaps the greatest on-the-one-hand-this writer in the world today"
in his study *The Press*. Morrie Ryskind of the *Los Angeles Times*
was equally unflattering in labeling Lippmann a "pitchman from
Olympus." *Time* magazine once called him the "high priest of liberal
Democratic pundits." Max Lerner, a political scientist and columnist,
described his writings as being approximations of "liberalism of the
right." E. Stanton Evans, in *The Liberal Establishment*, was sure
Lippmann was in truth the Eastern Establishment's "verberlizer."
The most devastating detractors, however, were Seymour Freidin
(formerly an executive editor of the *New York Herald Tribune*) and

George Bailey of the *Reporter* magazine. These two debunkers sought to dethrone Lippmann as dean of the journalists by their scathing indictment in a work called *The Experts* (a better title would have been *The Pseudo-Experts*). They sought to demolish his reputation as a columnist by asserting: "His declamations and omniscience are wrapped around a simple, rather lucid writing style. It is easily understandable, most decisive—and usually wrong." By stressing his comparatively few errors in judgment they endeavored to prove him totally unreliable. Amid their own pungent prose and vast generalizations one criticism of merit did emerge. They noted Lippmann's innate dislike of war and his proclivity to counsel concessions for which nothing substantial was asked in return. "His unilateralism," as they described it, tended to make him too much of an apostle of appeasement. Although Lippmann supported military intervention in both world wars, hence was no appeaser per se, he did loathe the use of force. He was too much a man of reason to consider war the best means of settling international disputes. Lippmann always urged rational restraint and negotiation as basic behavior for all nations—especially major powers.

Public debate on Vietnam became rancorous even among columnists. Howard K. Smith let go a fulminating blast at his colleague when he wrote: "The remarkable thing about Lippmann's wrong guesses . . . [are] their dogged consistence down to the latest day." He then rehearsed how Lippmann opposed the Truman Doctrine, military aid to Greece, the Korean War, and during the missile crisis proposed U.S. "concessions to Russia that Khrushchev had not even dared demand" (referring to the columnist's suggestion that Russian rockets be withdrawn from Cuba in exchange for U.S. dismantling of its bases in Turkey). Relative to Lippmann's arguments for U.S. withdrawal from South Vietnam, he considered them a "world of dreams fashioned to fit a thesis; not a thesis to fit the world." Smith lectured his professional associate for a reversion to isolationism: "Had we heeded . . . [Lippmann's] advice . . . any one of three generations of tyrants might have had an easier time—Hitler, then Stalin, and now Mao and Ho. This urbane and humane man would not want that, but that is where his logic leads."

Kenneth Crawford of *Newsweek* has agreed with Howard K. Smith.

"Lippmann," Crawford declared, "is against what he calls an 'unlimited' commitment in Vietnam because he thinks the U.S. can't win without destroying the country, is making a land war with China 'well-nigh inevitable' and can't prevent similar wars elsewhere.

"All of which is reminiscent of his warning that Truman in Greece was projecting 'a vague global policy' and 'an ideological crusade that has no limits.' As it turned out, what Truman started in Greece saved Europe."

While Smith and Crawford were recalling Lippmann's opposition to Truman's foreign policy to bolster their case that his judgment was faulty, George F. Kennan came to his defense. As one who had helped formulate the policy of containment, he averred: "Mr. Lippmann . . . mistook me for the author of precisely those features of the Truman Doctrine which I had most vigorously opposed—an assumption to which, I must say, I led squarely with my chin in the careless and indiscriminate language of the X-article ["The Sources of Soviet Conduct" published in the July, 1947 issue of *Foreign Affairs*]." Kennan blamed himself for not making it clear he did not condone a policy for global containment of Communism. "So egregious were these errors I must confess to responsibility for the greatest and most unfortunate of the misunderstandings to which they led." Writing thus in 1967, he denied advising American commitments all over the world and concluded, "This was the . . . [erroneous impression] created in the mind of Mr. Walter Lippmann."

Perhaps the most outspoken denunciation on this point has come from Allen Drury, whose fictional character Walter Dobius, a Washington columnist resembling Lippmann in the novel *Capable of Honor*, is depicted as "destroying the fragile bonds of world order" by his "powerful carping." Written in a vein of jealous mockery, the book lampoons Lippmann's right to be so influential, so patronizing as to presume that he can tell "everybody how to do everything." This "above-and-beyond-us" attitude Drury satirically attributes to a sad case of "*ego gigantea Washingtonia.*"

Despite occasional clashes and criticisms, by and large Lippmann's associates admire him. News commentator Joseph C. Harsch once remarked, in relating a facetious story, that "new arrivals come to Washington with private letters of accreditation from their governments to Walter Lippmann." This was not a literal fact, but symbolized the deference paid to Lippmann by foreign officials. Why had he gained such a notable reputation? Harsch gave these reasons: "A consistent non-involvement in causes and a disciplined attitude of objectivity towards issues explain both the seeming erratic record and also the respect accorded his views even among those whose causes suffer from his disapproval." Despite his brilliant mind and acute powers of observation, Harsch conceded that Lippmann had "not

always been right in all his judgments, as he himself recognize[d]."
His redeeming factor was that he "always attempted to be judicious."
In trying to think of some historical figure with which to compare
Lippmann, he used the great French thinker, Francois de Voltaire.
The brilliant Frenchman, like Lippmann, was "first a philosopher and
second a journalist."

Philosopher George Santayana once remarked that even God could
not change the past. Although Walter Lippmann's constant concern
was with the future, he believed the past yielded meaning for the
present. For this reason his longer works explored major themes in
American history and provided philosophic foundations for contemporary life. This supplemented his newspaper articles which constituted reasoned commentaries on current events. For over five decades
this philosopher-journalist engaged in a continual dialogue with the
public over national and international affairs. Never a reed in the
wind, what he wrote was based on keen perception and careful reflection. Right or wrong, wise or unwise, Lippmann provided mature fare
for millions of readers. Not many of his newspaper articles will be
remembered, but through books Lippmann's ideas will continue to
influence future generations. They would do well to consult him.

"The movement of events," this philosopher-journalist once stated,
was "always greater than the movement of our minds." Young people
especially had to learn from the past if they were to live happily in
the present. Again, with his focus on the future, Walter Lippmann
offered restless youth this wise counsel:

"What older people may be able to offer is not the translation of
modern knowledge, but the transmission of that which is above knowledge, that is to say human wisdom . . .

"This is an art which cuts across all specialties. It is possessed by
those who have an imaginative feeling for what really matters . . .
To be wise is to have a certain familiarity with the deposit of human
values that persist in any environment."

REFERENCES

Citations and references are by chapter in the approximate order of their use. Some paperback editions have been cited.

INTRODUCTION

Elmer L. Kayser, "History and Contemporaneity," *The American Historical Review*, January, 1962, 564. John K. Jessup, "Two Most Eminent and Strikingly Different Columnists," *Life*, May 7, 1965, 40.

CHAPTER I

Morton White, *Social Thought in America*, 1957, ii ff. Henry Steele Commager, *The American Mind*, 1950, 405-407. Arthur M. Schlesinger, Jr., *The Age of Roosevelt*, 1957, Vol. I, 130-134. Louis Filler, *Crusaders for American Liberalism*, 1961, 241. Van Wyck Brooks, *The Confident Years: 1885-1915*, 1953, 279. David E. Weingast, *Walter Lippmann: A Study in Personal Journalism*, 1949, 20-22. Charles Forcey, *The Crossroads of Liberalism: Croly, Weyl, Lippmann, and the Progressive Era, 1900-1925*, 1961, 94-95. H. V. Kaltenborn to authors, Oct. 28, 1963. Clarence Randall to authors, Oct. 25, 1963. Walter Lippmann, "Harvard," *The Red and Blue*, June, 1908, 50-52, in Lippmann Collection at Yale University, (hereinafter designated as LC-Yale).

Walter Lippmann, *A Preface to Morals*, 1929, 331 (hereinafter Walter Lippmann is designated as WL). Anne Freemantle, *This Band of Prophets: The Story of the Gentle Fabians*, 1956, 50. Richard Hofstadter, *The American Political Tradition*, 1959, 260. Graham Wallas, *The Great Society*, 1961, preface. Allan Nevins to authors, January 31, 1963. Upton Sinclair to authors, January 31, 1964. Harry Laidler to authors Feb. 10, 1964. Granville Hicks, *John Reed*, 1936, 24 ff. Harry Fleischman, *Norman Thomas: A Biography*, 1964, 90. "Annual Statement of the Intercollegiate Socialist Society," Sept., 1911, Taminent Institute Library (New York City). David A. Shannon, *The Socialist Party of America*, 1955, 56 ff. John Herling, "Harvard's Class of 1910 Rode Comet's Tail to Fame," *Minneapolis Star*, June 15, 1960. WL to Randolph Bourne, Dec. 13, 1909, Papers of Randolph Bourne at Columbia University. WL to Lincoln Steffens, March 18 and May 18, 1910, Papers of Lincoln Steffens (Columbia University).

Lincoln Steffens, *Autobiography of Lincoln Steffens*, 1959, 592-597. Ella Winters and Granville Hicks, eds., *The Letters of Lincoln Steffens*, 1938, 631. Henry E. May, *The End of Our Own Times*, 1959, 302-329. Henry Eulow, "Mover and Shaker," *Antioch Review*, Fall, 1951. Mabel Dodge, *Intimate Memories*, Vol. III, 1936, 432. Alfred Kazin, *On Native Grounds*, 1956, 112-113. Norman Thomas to authors, March 30, 1964. Morris Hillquit, *Leaves From a Busy Life*, 1934, 72. WL to Lincoln Steffens, April 17, 1911, Steffens Papers. WL, "Schnectady the Unripe:

A Study in Antagonism," *New York Call,* June 8, 1912. Morris Hillquit, *Socialism Summed Up,* 1913, 85. WL to Carl D. Thompson, Oct. 29, 1913, Files of the Socialist Party of America at Duke University. WL to G. August Gerber, campaign manager of the Socialist Party, November 3, 1914, Taminent Institute Library. WL to Upton Sinclair, May 6, 1914, Papers of Upton Sinclair at Indiana University. Theodore Draper, *The Roots of American Communism,* 1963, 49, 404. Hillquit, *Leaves From a Busy Life,* 72.

CHAPTER II

WL, "A National Diagnosis," *Everybody's Magazine,* Feb. 1913. WL, "The Greatest Question," *Everybody's Magazine,* April, 1914. WL, "The Changing Focus in Politics," *Forum, March,* 1913. WL, "An Open Mind: William James," *Everybody's Magazine,* Dec., 1910. WL, "For Theorists," *Forum,* April, 1913. WL, "Women's Movement," *Forum,* August, 1914. Graham Wallas, *Human Nature in Politics,* 1908, 50. James Mackaye, *Americanized Socialism,* 1918, 6, 51, 70. WL, "All the Mackayes," *The International,* 1911, as cited by Edwin Grover, editor of the Mackaye Collection at Dartmouth College, *Annals of an Era: Percy Mackaye and the Mackaye Family,* 1932, 301. WL, "The Most Dangerous Man in the World," *Everybody's Magazine,* July, 1912.

WL, "For Theorists," *Forum,* April, 1913. Lewis Mumford to authors, October 10, 1964. F. M. Colby, review of *A Preface to Politics* in *North American Review,* April, 1914. WL, *A Preface to Politics,* 2d ed., 1914, vii-viii, 8-12, 30-103, 236-318, *et passim.* Stow Persons, *American Minds,* 1958, 393. WL, *Drift and Mastery,* 1914, 1-177, *et passim.*

CHAPTER III

Herbert Croly, *Willard Straight,* 1924, 472-474. Eric F. Goldman, *Rendezvous With Destiny, A History of Modern American Reform,* 1953, 231. Willard Straight to Theodore Roosevelt, May 26, 1914, Papers of Willard Straight at Cornell University. Alvin Johnson, *Pioneer's Progress,* 1960, 234-243. "A New Journal of Ideas," *The Outlook,* Nov. 18, 1914. WL, "Notes for a Biography," *New Republic,* July 16, 1930 (hereinafter *New Republic* is designated *NR*); WL, "A Tribute to Theodore Roosevelt," n.d., LC-Yale. Elting E. Morison, ed., *The Letters of Theodore Roosevelt,* Vol. VIII, 872. Theodore Roosevelt, "Two Noteworthy Books on Democracy," *The Outlook,* Nov. 11, 1914. John Chamberlain, *Farewell to Reform,* 1932, 201. Alvin Johnson to authors, Nov. 11, 1963. George Soule to authors, August 17, 1963. Allan Nevins to authors, August 9, 1963. Edmund Wilson to authors, Feb. 2, 1964. Willard Straight to Dorothy Straight, Feb. 10, 1918, Straight Papers. Willard Straight to Herbert Croly, March 1 and 5, 1915, Straight Papers. Walter E. Weyl, *The New Democracy,* 1964, vii-xix.

WL, *The Stakes of Diplomacy,* 2d ed., 1917, 1-82, 106-189, 221-222, *et passim.* Robert E. Quirk, *An Affair of Honor,* 74, 113. WL, "Notes for a Biography," *NR,* July 16, 1930. "The Spoken Message," *NR,* Dec. 5, 1914.

WL to Willard Straight, April 6, 1916, Straight Papers. Willard Straight to Theodore Roosevelt, June 9, 1917, Straight Papers. Felix Frankfurter to authors, August 26, 1963. Editorials in *NR* for Jan. 16 and Feb. 20, 1915. Ray Stannard Baker, "Memorandum of Conversation with Walter Lippmann," n.d., Papers of Ray Stannard Baker, Library of Congress. Signed articles by WL in *NR* from 1914 to 1917: "Integrated America," "Life Is Cheap," "The Campaign Against Sweating," "The N.A.M. Speaks," "A Clue," "Mr. Wells at War," "The Hope of Democracy," "Footnote," "The White Passion," "Books and Things," "The Lost Theme," "Insiders and Outsiders," "Miss Lowell and Things," "Trotter and Freud," "Freud and the Layman," "Uneasy America."

CHAPTER IV

Daniel Aaron, *Men of Good Hope*, 1961. See House MS Diary, July 26, 1917, cited in Christopher Lasch, *The New Radicalism in America*, 1965, 220-221. Johnson, *Pioneer's Progress*, 244. *NR*, March 27, May 22, June 26, and Sept. 4, 1915. Willard Straight to Herbert Croly, March 16, 1916, Straight Papers. WL, "At the Chicago Convention," *NR*, June 17, 1916 and "The Puzzle of Hughes," *NR*, Sept. 30, 1916. Robert F. Wesser, *Charles Evans Hughes: Politics and Reform in New York*, 1967, 340-347. "The Case for Mr. Wilson," *NR*, Oct. 14, 1916. Ray Stannard Baker to WL, Oct. 25, 1928 and August 31, 1932, Baker Papers. WL to Ray Stannard Baker, Sept. 14, 1932, Baker Papers. Ray Stannard Baker, *Woodrow Wilson: Life and Letters*, Vol. VI, 29. Josephus Daniels, *The Wilson Era*, Vol. I, 329. WL, "Notes for a Biography," *NR*, July 16, 1930. WL to Edward M. House, March 10 and April 12, 1917, Papers of Edward M. House at Yale University. Harold Laski, *The American Democracy*, 1948, 651; Willard Straight to Herbert Croly, March 1, 1915 and March 16, 1916, Straight Papers.

Johnson, *Pioneer's Progress*, 240-248. WL, "The Defense of the Atlantic World," *NR*, Feb. 17, 1917. Marquis Childs and James Reston, eds., *Walter Lippmann and His Times*, 1959, 32. Frederick Palmer, *Newton Baker: America at War*, 1931, 207. James Truslow Adams, "Walter Lippmann," *Saturday Review of Literature*, Jan. 7, 1933. *NR*, June 9, 1917. WL, "The World Conflict in Its Relation to American Diplomacy," *Annals of the American Academy of Political and Social Sciences*, July, 1917. Catherine Drinker Bowen, *Yankee from Olympus: Justice Holmes and His Family*, 1944, 386. WL to Henry S. Canby, April 11, 1917, Papers of Henry S. Canby at Yale University. Woodrow Wilson to Newton Baker, Aug. 22 and Dec. 14, 1917, copy in LC-Yale. WL to Julian Street, May 17, 1918, Papers of Julian Street at Princeton University. WL to Edward M. House, March 10 and Oct. 17, 1917, House Papers. William Allen White to WL, Nov. 20, 1917, in Walter Johnson, ed., *Selected Letters of William Allen White*, 1947, 184. Baker, *Woodrow Wilson: Life and Letters*, Vol. VIII, 275. Charles Seymour, ed., *The Intimate Papers of Colonel House*, Vol. III, 169-171. Edward M. House to WL, July 7, 1918, House Papers.

Joseph Dorfman, "Two Unpublished Papers of Thorstein Veblen on the Nature of Peace," *Political Science Quarterly*, June, 1932. Lawrence E. Gelfand, *The Inquiry: American Preparations for Peace, 1917-1919*, 1963, 47-51. Seymour, *Intimate Papers of Colonel House*, Vol. III, 37. Arno J. Mayer, *Political Origins of the New Diplomacy*, 1957, 4-5. George Kennan, *Soviet-American Relations, 1917-1920: Russia Leaves the War*, 1956, *passim*. Charles Seymour, *American Diplomacy During the World War*, 1942, 271. WL to Ray Stannard Baker, Jan. 2, 1920, Baker Papers. Ray Stannard Baker, *Woodrow Wilson and World Settlement*, 1922, Vol. III, 23-41. Ray Stannard Baker and William E. Dodd, eds., *The Public Papers of Woodrow Wilson*, 1927, Vol. II, 155-162. Newton D. Baker to General John Pershing, July 2, 1918, copy in LC-Yale. Robert Lansing to WL, July 3, 1918, copy in LC-Yale. Heber Blankenhorn, *Adventures in Propaganda*, 1919, 15, 25-56, 122, 161. "Secret Weekly Intelligence Summary," War Department, Reports No. 229, 242, and 249 (Oct. 16, 31, and Nov. 8, 1918), Papers of Woodrow Wilson in Library of Congress. WL to Edward M. House, June 26 and Feb. 19, 1918, House Papers. Steffens, *Autobiography*, 774-776. WL, "Legendary John Reed," *NR*, Dec. 26, 1914. Richard O'Connor and Dale L. Walker, *The Lost Revolutionary, A Biography of John Reed*, 1967, 150-152.

"Memorandum for the Secretary of War," circa August, 1917, copy in LC-Yale. Memorandum from WL to Edward M. House, "Origin of the Term 'Freedom of the Seas'," May 21, 1918, House Papers. WL to Edward M. House, Sept. 24, 1918, House Papers. *Foreign Relations, 1918 Supplement*, 1933, Vol I, 405-413. "Official American Commentary on the Fourteen Points" in Seymour, *Intimate Papers of Colonel House*, Vol. IV, 189-200. Baker and Dodd, *Public Papers of Woodrow Wilson*, Vol. VIII, 155-162. Herbert Hoover, *The Ordeal of Woodrow Wilson*, 1958, 44. S. E. Mezes to WL, Nov. 16, 1918, LC-Yale. Seymour, *Intimate Papers of Colonel House*, Vol. III, 171. James T. Shotwell, *At the Paris Peace Conference*, 1937, 4. Ray Stannard Baker, *American Chronicle*, 1945, 39. WL to Dorothy Straight, December 28, 1918, Straight Papers. WL, "Notes for a Biography," *NR*, July 16, 1930. WL to Edward M. House, March 18 and July 19, 1919, House Papers.

WL, *The Political Scene: An Essay on the Victory of 1918*, 1919, ix, 1-16, 41-42, *et passim*. WL, "Notes for a Biography," 252. Walter Weyl, *Tired Radicals and Other Papers*, 1921, 9. Thomas A. Bailey, *Wilson and the Peacemakers*, 1947, 21, 87, 373, *et passim*. R. F. Harrod, *The Life of John Maynard Keynes*, 1951, 290. Joseph C. Grew to WL, n.d., LC-Yale. WL, "The Peace Conference," *Yale Review*, July, 1919. Signed articles by WL in *NR* from May 31, 1919 to Jan. 21, 1920. WL, "The Basic Problem of Democracy," *Atlantic Monthly*, Nov. 1919.

CHAPTER V

Henry May, *The Discontent of the Intellectuals: A Problem of the Twenties*, 1963, 48-49. George E. Mowry, *The Twenties*, 1963, *passim*. Mark DeWolf, ed., *Holmes-Laski Letters*, 1953, Vol. I, 231. WL and Charles Merz, "A Test of the News," *NR*, August 4, 1920, Supplement, Part 2. WL, *Liberty and the News*, 1920, 1-51, 100-101, *et passim*. W. J.

Ghent, review of *Liberty and the News* by WL, *The Review,* May 29, 1920. WL, "Barriers to Information," *Century Magazine,* Nov., 1921. WL, "The Making of a Common Will," *Century Magazine,* Jan. 1922. WL, "The Nature of the News," *Century Magazine,* Feb. 1922. WL, "The Beginning of an Organized Intelligence," *Century Magazine,* March, 1922. C. Wright Mills, *Images of Men,* 1960, 2, 11. WL, *Public Opinion,* 1922, 13-27, 172-74, *et passim.* E. Digby Baltzell, *The Protestant Establishment,* 1964. Allan Nevins, *American Press Opinion,* 1928, 454. Allan Nevins, "Walter Lippmann," *New York Herald Tribune,* Sept. 11, 1932. James W. Barrett, *Joseph Pulizer and His World,* 1941, 131, 365-384. George Juergens, *Joseph Pulitzer and the New York World,* 1966, *passim.* James W. Barrett, *The World, the Flesh, and Messrs. Pulitzer,* 1931, 73. Dale Kramer, *Heywood Broun,* 1949, 169, 179-180.

WL, "Smith and Miller, As Liberal Observer Views Their Rival Claims for Voter's Support," *New York World* (NYW) Nov. 2, 1922. WL, "A Great Governor," NYW, April 13, 1924. WL, "Shall the Democratic Party Die," NYW, July 5, 1924. WL, "A Day of Judgment," NYW, July 6, 1924. WL, "Nominate Al Smith," NYW, Sept. 19, 1924. "Governor Alfred E. Smith Explains Programs of Reform Balked by G.O.P." Pamphlet in Norman E. Mack Papers in Buffalo Historical Society. "Scrapbook," in George Van Namee Collection in Library of the Monterey-Fresno Diocesan Chancery and Academy of California Church History. Memoranda of "How Railroads Saved a Critical Situation in the Great War for the Allies," and "An Agricultural Credit System," n.d., "Decent Treatment of the Public Corporation and Regulation of Monopolies," Jan. 30, 1911, in Papers of William G. McAdoo of University of California Library, Los Angeles. Burton J. Hendrick, "William G. McAdoo and the Subway," *McClure's Magazine,* March, 1911. WL, "An Early Estimate of Mr. McAdoo," June, 1920, in *Men of Destiny,* 1927, 115-119. WL to Edward M. House, July 10, 1924, LC-Yale, WL to Carter Glass, August 20, 1924, Papers of Carter Glass, Alderman Library, University of Virginia. WL "Al Smith, Man of Destiny," Dec. 1925, in *Men of Destiny,* 1-10. WL, "Liberalism Today," *New York World,* July 21, 1924. Edward L. and Frederick H. Schapsmeier, "Disharmony in the Harding Cabinet: Hoover-Wallace Conflict," *Ohio History,* Summer, 1966. WL, "Calvin Coolidge: Puritanism DeLuxe," May, 1926 and "The Greatness of Mr. Mellon," Dec. 1926, in *Men of Destiny,* 13-16, 195. Garrett, *Joseph Pulitzer and His World,* 399-400. James A. Farley to authors, July 21, 1965. Ernest K. Lindley to authors, July 28, 1965.

CHAPTER VI

Morton White, *Social Thought In America,* 1957, 11-31. Eric Goldman, *Rendezvous With Destiny,* 1956, 72-73. David Noble, *The Paradox of Progressive Thought,* 1948, 17. Schlesinger, Jr., *Age of Roosevelt,* Vol. I, 131-152. Wiliam James, *A Pluralistic Universe,* 1909, 329. Graham Wallas, *Human Nature in Politics,* 1909, 18. Graham Wallas, *The Great Society,* 1916, ix. Russell Kirk, *The Conservative Mind,* 1953, 363, Clinton Rossiter, *Conservatism in America*, 1955, 166-167. George Santayana, *Winds of Doctrine and Platonism and the Spiritual Life*, 1957, 2-35. Frederick J. Hoffman, *The Twenties*, 1962, 425. Francis Graham Wilson, *The American Political Mind*, 1949, 409. Paul E. More to Stuart P. Sherman, August 5, 1915, in Papers of Stuart P. Sherman at University of Illinois. H. L. Mencken to George Sterling, July 20, 1920, Correspondence of H. L. Mencken at Huntington Library, San Marino, California.

WL, "H. L. Mencken: A Review of His Notes on Democracy" (Dec. 1926), in *Men of Destiny*, 61-63. WL, "Sinclair Lewis," (June, 1927), in *Men of Destiny*, 71-91. WL, "Mr. Bryan's List," *New York World*, July 3, 1924. WL, "Bryan and the Dogma of Majority Rule," (March, 1926), in *Men of Destiny*, 45-58. Wiliam Jennings Bryan, "Vigilance," unsigned essay in William Jennings Bryan Collection at Occidental College, Los Angeles. William Jennings Bryan, "Who Shall Control?" closing statement in the State of Tennessee vs. John Thomas Scopes, June, 1925, in *The Memoirs of William Jennings Bryan*, 1925, 526. WL, *American Inquisitors: A Commentary on Dayton and Chicago*, 1928, 1-24, 98-120, et passim. Constance McLaughlin Green, *The Rise of Urban America*, 1967, 138, 145. WL, *The Phantom Public*, 1927, 39-174, *et passim*.

Carl Binger to authors, Nov. 27, 1963. Horace Kallen to authors, Nov. 11, 1963. Daniel Cory to authors, Sept. 8, 1963. Harry Laidler to authors, Feb. 10, 1964. Allan Nevins to authors, Aug. 9, 1963. John Mason Brown, *Through These Men*, 1956, 211. Richard Butler, *The Mind of Santayana*, 1955, 1-62. Richard Butler, *The Life and World of George Santayana*, 1960, 184-187. Corliss Lamont, ed., *Dialogue on George Santayana*, 1959, 32-33. Daniel Cory, *Santayana: The Later Years*, 1963, 43-44. Alfred North Whitehead, *Science and the Modern World*, 1926, 250, 264. Paul Arthur Schilpp, *The Philosophy of George Santayana*, 1940, 26 ff. George Santayana, "Disinterested Interest in Life," in Logan Pearsall Smith, *Little Essays*, 1920, 97-99. George Santayana, *Three Philosophical Poets*, 1922, 49-70. George Santayana, *The Life of Reason or Phases of Human Progress*, 1962, Vol. I, 15-33 and III, 173-186. George Santayana, *Character and Opinion in the United States*, 1920, 11 ff. George Santayana, *The Middle Span*, 1954, 157 ff. George Santayana, "Alternatives to Liberalism," *Saturday Review of Literature*, June 23, 1934. Benjamin Stolberg, "Walter Lippmann: Connoisseur of Public Life," *The Nation*, Dec. 7, 1927. WL, *A Preface to Morals*, 1929, 1-19, 68-69, 137-329, et passim.

Mary L. Coolidge, "Today's Philosophy and Tomorrow's," *The Journal of Philosophy*, Nov. 7, 1940. George Santayana, "Enduring the Truth," *Saturday Review of Literature*, Dec. 7, 1929. WL, "A Footnote to Santayana," *Saturday Review of Literature* Dec. 7, 1929. George Santayana to Henry S. Canby, Jan. 16, 1930, Papers of Henry S. Canby at Yale University. Allan Nevins, "Walter Lippmann," *New York Herald-Tribune*, Sept. 1, 1932. WL, "Farewell," *New York World*, Feb. 27, 1931. WL, "The Scholar in a Troubled World," *Columbia University Quarterly*, Sept. 1932. Cabell Phillips, ed., *Dateline Washington*,

1949, 176. Bernard A. Weisberger, *The American Newspaperman,* 1961, 178.

CHAPTER VII

Weisberger, *The American Newspaperman,* 178-179. Howe, ed., *Holmes-Laski Letters,* 1438. Walter Johnson, *Selected Letters of William Allen White,* 1947, 323. WL, *Notes on the Crises,* 1931, 28 ff. Allan Nevins, ed., *Interpretations, 1931-32 by Walter Lippmann,* 1932, 73-336, *et passim.* WL, "Poverty and Plenty," address to the National Conference of Social Workers, May 20, 1932, LC-Yale, John Chamberlain, *The Enterprising Americans,* 1963, 223-242. WL, *A New Social Order,* 1933, 1-28. Allan Nevins, ed., *Interpretations, 1933-35 by Walter Lippmann,* 1936, 11-350, *et passim.* WL, "Self Sufficiency: Some Random Reflections," *International Conciliation,* April, 1934, 95-103. WL, "The Van Zeeland Report," *International Conciliation,* March 1938, 110- 113. WL, *The Method of Freedom,* 1934, ix, 1-12, *et passim.*

WL, *The New Imperative,* 1935, 1-35, *et passim.* Harrod, *The Life of John Maynard Keynes,* 445-446, 505. Robert Sherwood, *Roosevelt and Hopkins,* 1948, 835. Henry Steele Commager, *The American Mind,* 1950, 221. Charles I. Schottland, ed., *The Welfare State,* 1967, *passim.* WL, *An Inquiry Into the Principles of the Good Society,* 1937, ix-x, 4-12, 19-374, *et passim.* See also Preface of WL, *The Good Society,* 3d ed., 1943, x. Lewis Mumford to authors, Oct. 20, 1963, George Soule to authors, Aug. 17, 1963. Stuart Chase to authors, Oct. 14, 1963. Ernest Conins, "Red Revolt Led by Economists," *Los Angeles Times,* March 8, 1964. David E. Weingast, "Walter Lippmann: A Content Analysis," *Public Opinion Quarterly,* Summer, 1950. "Walter Lippmann on Leadership," CBS Reports, July 7, 1960, script in LC-Yale. WL, "Peace Without Honor," *New York World,* July 10, 1924. WL, "Roosevelt and Smith," *New York World,* Oct. 3, 1928. WL, "The Inaugural Lecture on Government," *New York World,* Jan. 3, 1931. WL, to Edward M. House, April 27, 1932, House Papers. Harlan B. Phillips, ed., *Felix Frankfurter Reminiscences,* 239. WL, "The Candidacy of Franklin D. Roosevelt," Today and Tomorrow column, Jan. 8, 1932, LC-Yale (hereinafter Today and Tomorrow is designated as T & T).

Rexford G. Tugwell, "Notes from a New Deal Diary," Jan. 16, 1933, Franklin D. Roosevelt Library at Hyde Park, New York. WL, "The End of the Period," T & T, July 18, 1935, LC-Yale. WL, "Basic Recovery," T & T, Dec. 3, 1935, LC-Yale. WL, "The Paramount Issues," T & T, Dec. 26, 1936, LC-Yale. Alfred B. Rollins, Jr., *Roosevelt and Howe,* 1962), 223. Stephen Early to WL, Oct. 18, 1933, President's Personal File—Franklin D. Roosevelt Library (hereinafter President's Personal File—Franklin D. Roosevelt Library shall be designated as PPF-FDRL). WL to Stephen Early, Jan. 30, 1934, PPF-FDRL. Early to WL, Feb. 2, 1934, PPF-FDRL. Josephine Chase, research assistant to Lippmann, to Early, Sept. 14, 1934, PPF-FDRL. WL to Franklin D. Roosevelt (hereinafter Franklin D. Roosevelt is designated as FDR), Dec. 7, 1934 and FDR to WL, Dec. 14, 1934, PPF-FDRL. WL to FDR, March 8, 1935 and

FDR to WL, March 20, 1935, PPF-FDRL. Telegram, Marvin McIntyre to WL, June 4 and Sept. 13, 1935, PPF-FDRL. "Memo for *Mac*," handwritten by FDR, Sept. 10, 1935, PPF-FDRL. FDR to Norman Hapgood, July 10, 1935, PPF-FDRL. WL, "Government Philosophy in a Sick World," *Westchester Medical Bulletin,* June, 1936. "General Resumé of Sept. 8, 1936," summary of newspaper comment prepared by Ballard Dunn for Alfred M. Landon, Papers of Alfred M. Landon in Kansas Historical Society. "Landon Given Lippmann O.K." and "Walter Lippmann Declares for Landon," summaries prepared by Dunn for Landon, Landon Papers. O. Glenn Saxon to Carl Ratt, Secretary to Governor Landon, Sept. 16, 1936, Landon Papers. Eugene Meyer to Alfred M. Landon, Sept. 16, 1936, Landon Papers. Joseph M. Martin, Jr. to authors, July 31, 1963. Walter Johnson, *1600 Pennsylvania Avenue,* 1963, 90 ff. Alfred M. Landon to authors, June 12, 1963. William Allen White to Alfred M. Landon, Nov. 5, 1936, Landon Papers. Donald R. McCoy, *Landon of Kansas,* 1966, 296-297, 326-327. FDR to Norman Hapgood, Feb. 24, 1936, PPF-FDRL. Schlesinger, Jr., *Age of Roosevelt,* Vol. III, 585. WL to FDR, Dec. 17, 1936, PPF-FDRL. WL, "To a Show-down," May 20, "Chickens Come Home to Roost," June 23 and "New Leviathan," June 26, 1937, T & T Mss., LC-Yale. Arthur A. North, *The Supreme Court,* 1966, 61-64. David C. Doyle, *Ordeal of the Presidency,* 1960, 372. As quoted in Louis L. Snyder, *Masterpieces of War Reporting,* 1962, 423.

CHAPTER VIII

Selig Adler, *The Isolationist Impulse,* 1966, 52-54, 219-249. Norman A. Graebner, *Ideals and Diplomacy,* 1964, 487-498. Manfred Jonas, *Isolationism in America,* 1966, 70-135. William L. Langer and S. Everett Gleason, *The Challenge to Isolation,* 1964, 1-51. Jonathan Daniels, *The Time Between the Wars,* 1966, 311-315. L. Ethan Ellis, *Frank B. Kellogg and American Foreign Relations,* 1961, 3-22. WL, "Why I Shall Vote for Davis," NR, Oct. 29, 1924. Irving Stone, *They Also Ran,* 1964, 383, WL, "Poincare In and Out," *New York World,* March 27, 1924. WL, "Famine, Plenty-and-Peace," *New York World,* March 30, 1924. WL, "Republican Foreign Policy," *New York World,* Aug. 28, 1924. Frank B. Kellogg to WL, July 21, 1928, in Papers of Frank B. Kellogg at Minnesota Historical Society.

WL, "Diplomatic Fiasco," *New York World,* Jan. 18, 1928. WL, "Briand," T & T, March 8, 1932, LC-Yale, WL, "Mr. MacDonald in Washington." *The Nation and Athenaeum,* (Nov. 2, 1929). WL, "America and European Unity," T & T, Jan. 22, 1932, LC-Yale. WL, "France and the Maintenance of Treaties," T & T, Feb. 19, 1932, LC-Yale. Herbert C. Hoover, *Memoirs,* 1953, 342-347. Adler, *The Isolationist Impulse,* 196. Elting E. Morison, *Turmoil and Tradition,* 1964, 274, 291, 317. Nevins, ed., "Introduction," *Interpretations, 1931-1932,* viii. Nevins, ed., *Interpretations, 1931-32,* 202-208, 360-361. Frederick Lewis Allen, *The Big Change,* 1961, 140 ff. WL, "The Shattered Dream," T & T, July 11, 1935, LC-Yale. Ralph Henry Gabriel, *The Course of Democratic Thought,* 1956; 451. Dorothy Thompson, *Let the Record Speak,* 1939; 277-280. WL,

"The Generation That Was Duped," T & T, June 16, 1940, LC-Yale. WL to Dorothy Thompson, July 22, 1946, Thompson Papers at Syracuse University Library.

William Allen White, *Autobiography of William Allen White*, 1946, 640-641. Joseph and Steward Alsop, *The Reporter's Trade*, 1958; 8. J. T. Talter, *Public Men In and Out of Office*, 1946; 261. Lord Casey to authors, Feb. 14, 1964. William L. Langer and S. Everett Gleason, *The Undeclared War: 1940-1941*, 1953; 180. T. R. Fehrenbach, *F.D.R.'s Undeclared War, 1939 to 1941*, 1967; 136, 177. WL, "Where Is America to Be Defended?" T & T, July 16, 1940, LC-Yale, Robert Murphy, "Diplomat Among Warriors," *Saturday Evening Post*, Feb. 22, 1962. Clinton Rossiter and James Lare, eds., *The Essential Lippmann, A Political Philosophy for Liberal Democracy*, 1963; 534-538. Upton Sinclair to WL, Dec. 10, 1941, Sinclair Papers at Indiana University.

Ellsworth Barnard, *Wendell Willkie*, 1966; 189, 215, 291. Memorandum for the President written by Edwin M. Watson requesting an appointment for WL, July 12, 1939, PPF-FDRL. Rossiter and Lare, eds., *The Essential Lippmann*, 143-145, 162-168, 185-187, 470-472, 490-492. WL, "Teheran," T & T, Dec. 7, 1943, LC-Yale. WL, "To Certain Idealists," T & T, Oct. 2, 1943, LC-Yale. FDR to WL, November 8, 1943, PPF-FDRL. Russell Lord, ed., *The Century of the Common Man*, 1943, 41-52. *United Mine Workers Journal*, April 15, 1943. Leland M. Goodrich and Marie J. Caroll, eds., *Documents on American Foreign Relations, July 1943-1944*, 1945, Vol. VI, 25-35. WL, *U.S. Foreign Policy*, 1943, 7-81, 100-135, 146-175, *et passim*. Copy of manuscript of *U.S. Foreign Policy*, LC-Yale, WL, *U.S. War Aims*, 1944, 3, 65, 88-194, 208-209, *et passim*. WL, "On Deflating Our Pretensions," T & T, August 31, 1943, LC-Yale. "Walter Lippmann on Leadership," *CBS Reports*, July 7, 1960, p. 16, copy of script in LC-Yale. WL, "The Cairo Declaration," Dec. 2, 1943, "The President's Return," Dec. 21, 1943, "On Power Politics," Dec. 18, 1943, "Mr. Hull on Foreign Policy," Sept. 14, 1943, "Preface to the Allied Meeting," Jan. 23, 1945, "The World and the Big Three," Feb. 20, 1945, "Before San Francisco," March 13, 1945, "The Inner Working," Oct. 20, 1945, "The Crimean Conference," Feb. 15, 1945, T & T, LC-Yale. Eleanor Roosevelt to WL, April 11, 1955, LC-Yale.

CHAPTER IX

Cabell Phillips, *The Truman Presidency*, 1966, 1-47. G. F. Hudson, *The Hard and Bitter Peace*, 1967, 8-65. Barton J. Berstein and Allen J. Matusow, *The Truman Administration*, 1966, 158-289. William D. Leahy, *I Was There*, 1950, 351. "Byrnes, 1945-1946," Newspaper Scrapbook in James F. Byrnes Papers at Clemson University, Clemson, South Carolina. James F. Byrnes, *Speaking Frankly*, 1947, 240 ff. George Curry, *James F. Byrnes*, Vol. XIV of *The American Secretaries of State and Their Diplomacy*, eds., Robert H. Ferrell and Samuel Flagg Bemis, 1965, 194-295, 300-302, 311. Harry S. Truman, *Memoirs*, 1956, Vol. II, 546-553. Memorandum, Henry A. Wallace to Truman, July 23, 1946, Papers of Alfred Schindler in Truman Library, Independence, Missouri (hereinafter Harry S. Truman Library designated as HSTL), Karl M. Schmidt, *Henry A. Wallace,* 1960, 124-152. Curtis MacDougall, *Gideon's Army,* 1965, Vol. III, 853-884. *Public Papers of the Presidents of the United States, Harry S. Truman . . . January 1 to December 31, 1947,* 1963, 176-180. Robert H. Ferrell, *George C. Marshall as Secretary of State, 1947-1949,* Vol. XV of *The American Secretaries of State and Their Diplomacy,* 99-134. Dexter Perkins, *The Diplomacy of a New Age,* 1967, 13-70. Joseph M. Jones, *The Fifteen Weeks,* 1955, 228-229.

Radio Script, "Walter Lippmann on Leadership," *CBS Reports,* July 7, 1960, LC-Yale. WL, T & T, April 14 and Oct., 1945, May 27, Nov. 4 and 6, Dec. 22, 1947, April 1, 1948, Jan. 20 and April 28, 1949, LC-Yale. "Walter Lippmann; Outstanding American," *United Nations World,* May, 1947. WL, *The Cold War: A Study in U.S. Foreign Policy,* 1947, 4-39, 47-62, *et passim.* WL, "We Are Overextended," T & T, March 30, 1948, LC-Yale. WL to Dorothy Thompson, Sept. 9, 1948, Sept. 1, 1950, and March 15, 1953, Papers of Dorothy Thompson at Syracuse University. WL, "Commentary on American Far Eastern Policy," Institute of Pacific Relations, Lucknow, India, Oct. 3-15, 1950, 3-4. Peter Calvorcoressi, ed., *Survey of International Affairs,* 1952, 42 ff. Gar Alperovitz, *Atomic Diplomacy,* 1967, 194-242. Harry S. Truman, Press Conferences No. 63 (May 9, 1946) and No. 98 (Feb. 20, 1947), Papers of Harry S. Truman, HSTL. Charles G. Ross to Harry S. Truman, Feb. 13, 1950, HSTL. "Walter Lippmann," Papers of John M. Redding, HSTL. Dean Acheson to authors, August 2, 1963. Acheson, address at the University of California, Berkeley, in *State Department Bulletin,* March 16, 1950. Acheson, extemporaneous remarks at press conference, in *State Department Bulletin,* Feb. 8, 1950. Norman A. Graebner, *An Uncertain Tradition,* 1961, 269. Edward L. and Frederick H. Schapsmeier, "Walter Lippmann: Critic of American Foreign Policy," *The Midwest Quarterly,* Winter, 1966. George Kennan to authors, August 28, 1963. Walter Millis, ed., *The Forrestal Diaries,* 1951, 127-128, *et passim.* George E. Kennan, *Memoirs, 1925-1950,* 1967, 358-367.

WL, "The Rivalry of Nations," in Edward Weeks, ed., *Jubilee: One Hundred Years of the Atlantic,* 1957, 734-740. John W. Spanier, *The Truman-MacArthur Controversy and the Korean War,* 1965, 15-40. Mathew B. Ridgway, *The Korean War,* 1967, 245. WL, T & T, Jan. 2, Feb. 14, June 29, July 3, 11, and 20, Oct. 2 and 3, 1950, Jan. 15 and May 21, 1951, Oct. 14, 1952, LC-Yale. WL, *Isolation and Alliances: An American Speaks to the British,* 1952, 1-56, *et passim.* Herbert J. Muller, *Adlai Stevenson, A Study in Values,* 17, 313. Daniel Bell, *Passion and Politics in America,* 1956, 58. Richard H. Rovere, *Senator Joe McCarthy,* 1960, 134-145. Roy Cohn, *McCarthy,* 1968, 212. WL, "Nightmare in Washington," May 3, 1954, T & T, LC-Yale. Sidney Lens, *The Futile Crusade, Anti-Communism As American Credo,* 1964, 57-78. Daniel Bell, *The End of Ideology,* 1962, 112. WL, "Morale and Disciplines," Dec. 2, 1952 and "The Eisenhower Mission," Jan. 5, 1954, T & T, LC-Yale. Emmett John Hughes, *The Ordeal of Power,* 1963, 63. George H. Mayer, *The Republican Party,* 1964, 495. WL, T & T, May 21 and June 2, 1953, Jan. 20, 1955, Jan. 5, 1956, Dec. 31, 1959, LC-Yale. WL, "Is a Constitutional Amendment to Provide for Cases of Presidential Disability Needed?" *The Congressional Digest,* January, 1958. Address of John Foster Dulles, *Department of State Bulletin,* January 25, 1954. James Sheply, "How Dulles Averted War," *Life,* Jan. 16, 1956. Kenneth W. Thompson, "Towards a Theory of International Politics," *American Political Science Review,* Sept. 1955. T & T, Jan 12 and July 6, 1950, LC-Yale. WL to Dorothy Thompson, Sept. 1, 1950 and March 15, 1953, Papers of Dorothy Thompson at Syracuse University. George Kennan to WL, April 27, 1956, LC-Yale. Eleanor Lansing Dulles to authors, April 24, 1964. WL, *America in the World Today,* 1957, 14 ff. WL, *The Communist World and Ours,* 1959, 41-56. WL, "Interview with Nikita Khrushchev," Oct. 24, 1958, MSS, LC-Yale. Dwight D. Eisenhower, *Mandate for Change,* 1963, 233. James C. Hagerty to authors, August 1, 1963. Sherman Adams to authors, Jan. 21, 1964. Kenneth W. Thompson, "Towards a Theory of International Politics," *American Political Review,* Sept. 1955. WL, "The Country Is Waiting For Another Innovator," T & T, June 20, 1960, LC-Yale.

CHAPTER X

Adrienne Koch, *Philosophy for a Time of Crisis,* 1960, 22. Marshall W. Fishwick, "Diagnosing the American Dream," *Saturday Review,* Dec. 21, 1963. WL, "Classical Studies Urged," *Supreme Council Bulletin,* Jan. 15, 1941. WL, "Man's Image of Man," *Proceedings of the American Catholic Philosophical Association,* Dec. 29, 1941, reprint in LC-Yale. WL, "Education Without Culture,"*Commonweal,* Jan. 17, 1941. WL, "The Shortage of Education," *Atlantic Monthly,* May, 1954. WL and Allan Nevins, eds., *A Modern Reader: Essays on Present-day Life and Culture,* 1946, *passim.* WL, "The Shortage in Education," *American Essays,* ed. Charles B. Shaw, 1961, 189-190. Peter Vierick, *Conservatism,* 1956, 107. Alan P. Grimes, *American Political Thought,* 1960, 478-510. Clinton Rossiter, *Conservatism in America,* 1962, x, 9. Samuel Lubell, *Revolt of the Moderates,* 1956, 249. Russell Kirk, *Prospects for Conservatism,* 1956, 31 ff. Arthur Larsen, *A Republican Looks at His Party,* 1956, 2, 10. Clarence Manion, *The Conservative American,* 1964, 77 ff. Hughes, *The Ordeal of Power,* 63, *et passim.* A. K. McComb, ed., *Selected Letters of Bernard Berenson,* 1964, 284-85. Peter Vierick, *Conservatism Revisited,* 1962, 32.

George H. Mayer, *The Republican Party,* 1964, 495-520. WL, "Democracy in Trouble," T & T, Jan. 5, 1956, LC-Yale. WL, *Essays in the Public Philosophy,* 1956, *passim.* WL, "The Administration and Senator McCarthy," T & T, March 12, 1953, LC-Yale. *Washington Post,* Nov. 26, 1964; Daniel Bell, *The End of Ideology,* 1962, 121. WL, "Pope John," "Prayer Case," and "Old Philosophy Up to Date" in T & T, April 21 and June 20, 1963, LC-Yale. WL, "Commencement Address at the New School for Social Research," June 9, 1959, MSS in LC-Yale. Reinhold Niebuhr in *Lippmann and His Times.* 170.

WL, *The Confrontation,* 1959, 2. WL, "The National Purpose," television program produced by the Westinghouse Company, June 14, 1960, Script in LC-Yale. WL, "Some Political Notions," T & T, Dec. 31, 1959, LC-Yale. WL, "Rockefeller and His Party," T & T, Dec. 29, 1959, LC-

Yale. Appleton (Wisconsin) *Post-Crescent,* Sept. 26, 1965. *Rochester Democrat and Chronicle,* Oct. 5, 1956. WL, "Introduction," to reissue of Woodrow Wilson, *Congressional Government,* 1956, 16-17. WL, "The Country Is Waiting for Another Innovator," *Life,* June 20, 1960. WL, "The Changing of the Guard," *Newsweek,* May 13, 1963, 25. James Mac-Gregor Burns, *John Kennedy: A Political Profile,* 1960, 202. Pierre Salinger to authors, August 18, 1967. Pierre Salinger, *With Kennedy,* 1966, 120. James Reston to authors, Feb. 5, 1964. John F. Kennedy, *Profiles in Courage,* 1963, 2-3. John F. Kennedy, *The Strategy of Peace,* 1961, 241. Robert F. Kennedy to authors, Sept. 22, 1967.

"Address of President Kennedy in Philadelphia, July 4, 1962, text from White House Press Secretary. John W. Gardner, ed., *To Turn the Tide,* 1962, XXVIII-XIX, 183. *Newsweek,* Dec. 24, 1962. James Tracy Crown, *Kennedy in Power,* 1961, 85. "The Columnists JFK Reads Every Morning," *Newsweek,* Dec. 18, 1961, 65. Hugh Sidey, *John F. Kennedy,* 1964, 167. Fletcher Knebel, "Kennedy vs. the Press," *Look,* August 28, 1962. "The Presidency," *Time,* Jan. 15, 1965. Theodore Sorensen, *Kennedy,* 1966, 122, 273, 285. Letters to authors: Theodore G. Sorensen (August 5, 1963), Christian A. Herter (Jan. 14, 1964), Robert Murphy (March 11, 1964), Theodore H. White (Feb. 24, 1964), Abraham Ribicoff (May 5, 1964), Walter W. Rostow (Feb. 18, 1964), Paul H. Nitze (Dec. 26, 1963), and Arthur J. Waterman, Jr. (Jan. 14, 1964). Theodore G. Sorensen, *Decision-Making in the White House.* WL, *The Communist World and Ours,* 1958; *Western Unity and the Common Market.*

WL, "The Unraveling Alliances," *Newsweek,* March 18, 1963. WL, T & T, Jan. 1961-Nov. 1963. WL, "The Block in Path of Republicans," T & T, *Los Angeles Times,* Feb. 19, 1962. WL, "Election Result Shows Voters of the Center Dominate Left, Right," T & T, *Los Angeles Times,* Nov. 11, 1962. "Walter Lippmann on Kennedy," *Newsweek,* Jan. 21, 1963. "Walter Lippmann-1964," CBS Reports, April 8, 1964, text of script, Columbia Broadcasting System. WL, "Segregation Problem," T & T, *Los Angeles Times,* Sept. 1, 1963. WL, "Worldwide Calm After President's Death Teaches a Powerful Lesson," T & T, *Los Angeles Times,* Dec. 1, 1963. WL, Address at meeting of the American Association of Museums, *Museum News,* June 15, 1948.

CHAPTER XI

Barry Goldwater, *Where I Stand,* 1964, 16. Theodore H. White, *The Making of the President,* 1965, 241, 285. WL, T & T, *Los Angeles Times,* June 10, Oct. 6, and Dec. 29, 1963. Arthur M. Schlesinger, Jr., *A Thousand Days,* 1965, 914-925. Theodore Sorensen, *Kennedy,* 1965, 849-853. Allan Nevins, ed., *The Burden of Glory,* 1964, 189-231. WL, T & T, *Washington Post,* Dec. 19, 1963. WL, T & T, *Los Angeles Times,* June 18, 1962. WL, "Rockefeller and the GOP," *Newsweek,* April 1, 1963. WL, "America Must Grow," *Saturday Evening Post,* Nov. 5, 1960, 94. WL, T & T, *Los Angeles Times,* Jan. 24 and March 7, 1963. WL, "CBS Reports," May 1, 1963. WL, T & T, *Los Angeles Times,* Jan. 12, 1964. WL, T & T, *Sacramento Bee,* August 29, 1963. WL, "The Goldwater Movement,"

Newsweek, August 5, 1963. WL, T & T, *Los Angeles Times,* Jan. 8, 1964. WL, "The Republican Agony," *Newsweek,* June 22, 1964. WL, T & T, *Los Angeles Times,* January 15, 1964.

Zygmund Dobbs, *Keynes at Harvard,* revised ed., 1962, 6. WL, *The Communist World and Ours,* 1958, 54-56. WL, *Western Unity and the Common Market,* 1962, 32-41, *et passim.* Sidey, *John F. Kennedy,* 167. WL, T & T, *Los Angeles Times,* Feb. 7, 1963. Louis J. Halle, *The Cold War As History,* 1967, 343-387. Barry Goldwater, *The Conscience of a Conservative,* 1960, 71 ff. Barry Goldwater, *Why Not Victory?,* 1961, *passim.* WL, T & T, *Los Angeles Times,* April 26, July 12, July 19, 1964. Paul Seabury, *The Rise and Decline of the Cold War,* 1967, 71. "Goldwater Wins Texas' 56 Delegates," *Los Angeles Times,* June 17, 1964. Gene Grove, *Inside the John Birch Society,* 1961, 114. John A. Stormer, *None Dare Call It Treason,* 1964, 145, 209-212. Herbert Aptheker, *American Foreign Policy and the Cold War,* 1962, 14, 266-267.

WL, T & T, Sept. 16, Oct. 11, 14, 18, 1964. WL, articles in *Newsweek,* Oct. 26, Nov. 9 and 23, 1964. Edmund Stillman and William Pfaff, *Power and Impotence,* 1967, 88. *America Tomorrow, Creating the Great Society,* Preface by Walter Lippmann, 1964, 41. "The Great Society," *Saturday Evening Post,* Oct. 31, 1964. David Lawrence, "A Century of Thought on the Great Society," *Los Angeles Times,* Dec. 13, 1964. WL, T & T, *Milwaukee Sentinel,* Nov. 19, 1965. "President Johnson's Inaugural Address," Jan. 20, 1965, in *Los Angeles Times,* Jan. 21, 1965. Bill Moyers to authors, Sept. 13, 1965. WL, *Newsweek,* January 19, 1965. WL, T & T, *Los Angeles Times,* Feb. 7 and 28, 1965. WL, T & T, *Columbus Dispatch,* Sept. 17, 1965. WL, T & T, *Los Angeles Times,* Feb. 7 and March 7, 1965. WL, "CBS Reports-1965," transcript of broadcast, Columbia Broadcasting System. "The Oval Office *vs.* the Attic." *Life,* May 19, 1967. Walter Jenkins to authors, Jan. 28, 1964. Text of President Johnson's address at Johns Hopkins University, April 7, 1965, in Manfred Jones, ed., *American Foreign Relations in the Twentieth Century,* 1967, 173-178. Rowland Evans and Robert Novak, *Lyndon B. Johnson: The Exercise of Power,* 1966, 433.

McGeorge Bundy to authors, July 13, 1965. Dean Rusk, *Vietnam: Four Steps to Peace,* June 23, 1965, Department of State pamphlet. "South Vietnam: Reality and Myth," in *Foreign Affairs Outline,* Bureau of Public Affairs, Department of State. Lyndon B. Johnson, *We Will Stand in Vietnam,* text of President's statement at his press conference July 28, 1965, Department of State pamphlet; J. William Fulbright, *The Arrogance of Power,* 1967, *passim.* James Reston, *The Artillery of the Press,* 1967. WL, "Temptation of Lyndon Johnson," *Newsweek,* Feb. 27, 1967. WL, T & T, *Daily Pantagraph* (Bloomington, Illinois), Dec. 30, 1966, Feb. 27 and May 25, 1967, hereinafter *Daily Pantagraph* is designated as *Pantagraph.* Alfred Steinberg, *Sam Johnson's Boy,* 1968, 740. WL, "Latin Poverty," *Milwaukee Sentinel,* Dec. 17, 1965. WL, "Dominican Affair, *Los Angeles Times,* May 23, 1965.

Pantagraph, May 28, 1967. *Newsweek,* Jan. 9 and June 5, 1967. *Pantagraph,* July 23, 24, 25, 1967; *Newsweek,* Oct. 9, 1967. Drew Pearson and Jack Anderson, *The Case Against Congress,* 1968, 22, *Pantagraph,* August

20, 21, 22 and Oct. 1, 2, 3, 1967 and Jan. 7, 1968. *Newsweek,* Oct. 23, 1967 and Jan. 3, 1966. *Pantagraph,* Dec. 8, 9, 10, 1967. *New Republic,* Dec. 2 and 9. *Pantagraph,* Dec. 17, 18, 19, 1967. *Newsweek,* Dec. 18, 1967. *Pantagraph,* Nov. 22, 1967 and May 19, 1968. *Newsweek,* Jan. 1, 1968 and March 11, 1968. "Washington is Full of Arguments," *Milwaukee Journal,* May 14, 1967.

CHAPTER XII

George Santayana, "Enduring Truth," *Saturday Review of Literature,* Dec. 7, 1929. WL, "A Columnist Is an Editorial Writer," *The Quill,* March, 1951. WL, "Modern Thucydides," *The Key Reporter,* Winter, 1944-45. WL, "On Editorial Writing," *Bulletin of the American Society of Newspaper Editors,* Jan. 1, 1956. Joseph C. Harsch, manuscript of article for the *New York Herald Tribune,* dated 2/29/61, LC-Yale. "The Columnists JFK Reads Every Morning," *Newsweek,* Dec. 18, 1961. WL, "The Scholar in a Troubled World," *Columbia University Quarterly,* Sept. 1932. *Los Angeles Times,* May 8, 1962. William L. Rivers, "The Correspondents After 25 Years," *Columbia Journalism Review,* Spring, 1962. Kenneth Stewart, *Makers of Modern Journalism,* 1952, 459. Curtis P. MacDougal, *Interpretive Reporting,* 1948, 34. James Reston as quoted in *Newsweek,* June 5, 1967. M. Stanton Evans, *The Liberal Establishment,* 1965, 92.

Rochelle Girson, "Mutations in the Body Politic," *Saturday Review,* August 29, 1964. *American Scholar,* Summer, 1965. Charles de Gaulle to WL, May 16, 1956, LC-Yale. Adolph A. Berle, Jr., *Power Without Property,* 1959, 22. Charles Hirschfield, "Brooks Adams and American Journalism," *American Historical Review,* Jan. 1964. Daniel Boorstin, *The Image: A Guide to Pseudo-Events in America,* 1964, *passim.* Arthur M. Schlesinger, Jr., "The Historians and History," *Foreign Affairs,* April, 1963. Karl E. Meyer, "The Washington Press Establishment," *Esquire,* April, 1964. Douglas Cater, *The Fourth Branch of Government,* 1959, 98. Clinton Rossiter, *Parties and Politics in America,* 1964, 50. Bernard C. Cohen, *The Press and Foreign Policy,* 1963, 143. John Mason Brown, *Through These Men,* 1956, 215. Andrew Berding to authors, March 11, 1964. William J. Newman, *The Futilitarian Society,* 1961, 257, 285.

Answar Hussain Syed, *Walter Lippmann's Philosophy of International Politics,* 1963, 7-11. John Lukacs, *A History of the Cold War,* 1962, 67. Paul Seabury, *The Rise and Decline of the Cold War,* 1967, 5. Eric F. Goldman, *The Crucial Decade—and After, America 1945-1960,* 1960, 60. Louis J. Halle, *The Cold War as History,* 1967, 136. Senator J. William Fulbright to authors, August 21, 1963. Christian A. Herter to authors, Jan. 14, 1964; McGeorge Bundy to authors, July 13, 1965. Pierre Salinger to authors, August 18, 1967. Robert F. Kennedy to authors, Sept. 22, 1967. Andrew Berding to authors, March 11, 1964. Paul H. Nitze to authors, Dec. 26, 1963. U.S. Senate, *Hearings Before the Committee on Foreign Relations,* 87th Congress, 1st Sess., May 9, 1961. Herb McGushin, Deputy Director of the Office of Public Information, to authors, Feb. 3, 1964. Iverach McDonald, "The Logic of Allied Unity," in Childs and

Reston, eds., *Walter Lippmann and His Times*, 140. Harold Macmillan to authors, Jan. 22, 1964. Richard Mayne to authors, Jan. 19, 1964. Wilfred Knapp, *A History of War and Peace, 1939-1965*, 1967, 301, 436. George P. Hunt, "Editor's Notes," *Life*, March 20, 1964. David Paslavsky, "A Few Questions to Walter Lippmann," (Moscow) *New Times*, Feb. 8, 1956, reprint in LC-Yale.

William Allen White to WL, May 20, 1943, LC-Yale. Warren Austin to WL, May 12, 1943, LC-Yale. Dean Acheson to WL, May 10, 1943, LC-Yale. James B. Conant to WL, May 5, 1943, LC-Yale. Henry L. Stimson to WL, June 1, 1943, LC-Yale. Harold H. Burton to WL, May 31, 1943, LC-Yale. John Foster Dulles to WL, July 5, 1944, LC-Yale. WL to John Foster Dulles, July 10, 1944, LC-Yale. Field Marshall Sir John Dill to WL, August 18, 1944. Lord Halifax to WL, May 12, 1943, LC-Yale. Lord Beaverbrook to WL, June 8, 1943, LC-Yale. Harold Ickes to WL, May 15, 1943, LC-Yale. Letter and memorandum, Wendell Willkie to WL, April 11, 1942, LC-Yale. WL to Wendell Willkie, April 14, 1942, LC-Yale. Hull Papers, Library of Congress.

William Henry Chamberlain, *America's Second Crusade*, 1950, 248-249. Michael Straight, "The Atlantic Community," *NR*, Oct. 20, 1952. Louis Hartz, *The Liberal Tradition in America*, 1955, 272-283. Heinz Eulau, "From Public Opinion to Public Philosophy," *American Journal of Economics and Sociology*, July, 1956. White, *Social Thought in America*, xii, 275. Fred G. Bratten, *The Legacy of the Liberal Spirit*, 1943, 281-282. Fred Rodell, "Walter Lippmann," *American Mercury*, March, 1945. Fred Rodell to authors, Feb. 4, 1964. A. J. Liebling, *The Press*, 1964, 236. Kennan, *Memoirs, 1925-1950*, 354-367. George Kennan to authors, August 28, 1963. Kenneth Crawford, "Yet Another Debate," *Newsweek*, Feb. 28, 1966.

WL, T & T, *Washington Post*, March 11 and April 1, 1948, as quoted in summary of Lippmann's articles on the election, Papers of John M. Redding, HSTL. WL, "The Democrats in 1968," *Newsweek*, Jan. 1, Sept. 23 and Oct. 7, 1968. Howard K. Smith, "False Paths of Lippmann," *Pantagraph*, May 14, 1967 and "War Dissenters Depart from Reason and Fairness," *Pantagraph*, Oct. 29, 1967. WL, Notes for a talk given on the eve of his seventieth birthday, Sept. 22, 1959, LC-Yale. Carl Binger to authors, Nov. 27, 1963. Alvin Johnson to authors, Nov. 11, 1963. Daniel Cory to authors, Sept. 8, 1963. WL, "The Ultimate Decency," *Newsweek*, August 17, 1964. Joseph C. Harsch, manuscript of article for *New York Herald Tribune*, dated Feb. 29, 1961, LC-Yale. WL, "What We Offer," *Harper's*, October, 1967.